D0867144

CHRISTOLOGY
and
SPIRITUALITY

CHRISTOLOGY
and
SPIRITUALITY

L Cunningham
Notre Dame, 1991

William M. Thompson

CROSSROAD • NEW YORK

All biblical citations are from *The New American Bible* with *The Revised New Testament*, copyright 1970 and 1986 by the Confraternity of Christian Doctrine, Washington, DC.

The publisher is grateful for permission to quote from the following: *Bérulle and the French School: Selected Writings*, Classics of Western Spirituality, edited by William M. Thompson, selections translated from the French by Lowell M. Glendon (New York: Paulist Press, 1989). Reprinted by permission of the publisher.

1991

The Crossroad Publishing Company
370 Lexington Avenue, New York, NY 10017

Copyright © 1991 by William M. Thompson

All rights reserved. No part of this book may be reproduced, stored in a retrieval system, or transmitted, in any form or by any means, electronic, mechanical, photocopying, recording, or otherwise, without the written permission of The Crossroad Publishing Company.

Printed in the United States of America
Typesetting output: TEXSource, Houston

Library of Congress Cataloging-in-Publication Data

Thompson, William M., 1943–
    Christology and spirituality / William M. Thompson.
        p.   cm.
    ISBN 0-8245-1098-4
    1. Jesus Christ—Person and offices. 2. Jesus Christ—History of doctrines. 3. Spirituality. I. Title.
    BT202.T472   1991
    232—dc20   91-7733
                                                                             CIP

FOR THE SULPICIAN FATHERS OF THE UNITED STATES
in celebration of their bicentennial
1791 – 1991

AND FOR THE SOCIETY OF SAINT SULPICE
in celebration of three hundred and fifty years of service
1641 – 1991

*Il n'y a non plus de différence entre l'Évangile
écrit et la vie des saints qu'entre une
musique notée et une musique chantée.*
— *Francis de Sales*

Contents

Preface

I hope that all who are especially interested in theology give thanks for their training in, and the discipline given to them by, the rigors of logic and philosophical analysis. Theology would really cease to be theology — good, coherent discourse (*logos*) about God (*theos*) — without these. To the extent that the turn to spirituality can become a sort of "quietism of the intellect" camouflaging good, solid thinking, this book would want no part of it.

But this book believes that quietism, of whatever kind, is really a derailment. Spirituality, of the Christian kind, and at its core, can be at least partially described as the vitalizing, through the Holy Spirit, of our human and grace-bestowed capacities, the intellectual included. That Spirit is the "breath" of all that we are, especially our minds and our hearts. A "pneumonia of the mind" is a critical sign that the Spirit's gifts are not yet fully appreciated. And so this book believes that theology has nothing to fear, and really everything to learn and gain, from a theology attuned to spirituality in the proper sense.

The book's belief is that Christian spirituality makes it possible for the theologian to breathe theologically. But the Spirit is the breath, if I might build on St. Basil's insights a little, of God who is Father/Mother and Word/Jesus. Their "converse" happens in and with the Spirit's breath — their bond — and in the Spirit spills over onto us, helping us to learn the arts of conversation practiced so well by our triune God. If we would learn these arts, we must go where the Spirit's conversation-bestowing breath is at work in this modern and "postmodern" world. There are surely many "conversations" at work with something of the Spirit's breath enlivening them. But the primary one has to be that of the dialogue of Jesus with us, in his earthly life, and now as risen in the community of the church.

Theological reason, then, is part of a larger, trinitarian conversation. The "breath" of this conversation — even of the meaningful pauses, which are more like outbursts of adoration — is what authentic Christian spirituality inhales. And it is what a theology seeks to inhale when it turns to this kind of spirituality. As it does so, it remains no longer a "theology in print," but becomes a "theology that is sung." Rather like the relationship between the gospel and the lives of the saints mentioned in the epigraph from St. Francis de Sales.

This book tries to inhale the Spirit into theology, and especially christology. But our inhaling is the other, and "smaller," side of a greater "exhaling." And that seems to be why theological *logos* is but the tip of a much greater *doxology*. For petition, thanks, praise, and adoration are what we ought to pray when we are vitalized simply out of the Spirit's sheer desire to give. And we should have a sense of sorrow for our refusal to do so. The great spiritual masters seemed to know these things, and so it seemed a normal move to "consult" these masters, probing how they practiced theology and christology (when they did so); probing how theology and christology might look, if practiced under their guidance; and in general probing what they might have to teach theologians yet today. The book's topic has implications for how spirituality "challenges" the way we do theology in general. But the special focus will be christology. For christology focuses on the center of our faith, Jesus the Christ. Through it we are inevitably brought to the trinitarian depths of the faith, and from it we are opened out to the mysteries of the church, world, and afterlife. It is a key, then, or a hinge, which might serve as something of a model for how Christian spirituality can vitalize the many other theological fields.

This book builds on the insights and many other forms of support of many, from the great tradition, from my present church communities, from the academy at large and at Duquesne University in particular. And the author is deeply thankful. Particularly blessed is one who can count on the simultaneously enthusiastic and sobering conversation and support of departmental and non-departmental colleagues — among whom I am glad to number Bishop Donald W. Wuerl — that I enjoy at Duquesne. Let me express gratitude, too, to Father Thomas Faucher for helping me to refine the book's title. The editors at Crossroad were helpful in this regard as well, and in most other matters relevant to this book's production. My special thanks to them, especially Justus George Lawler and John Eagleson. My students at Duquesne have been a continuing source of support and challenge: special thanks to them for helping an "earlier generation" of theologians to make a small contribution to the hopefully great contributions they will make to theology. And most special thanks to Patricia Marie, and to Carolyn Rose and Stephanie Marie. There are many kinds of breath, depending upon what we mix into it. Patricia, Carolyn, and Stephanie more than others helped keep mine strong and fresh!

CHAPTER ONE

Theology, Christology and Spirituality: Intersections

... they fancy that they are being carried away in rapture [*arrobamiento*].
I call it being carried away in foolishness [*abobamiento*]. ...
— Teresa of Avila, *The Interior Castle*

Arrobamiento and *Abobamiento*:
The Promise and Ambiguity of Spiritual "Waves"

We may well be witnessing something like a spiritual "wave" today, not only outside the "academy," but increasingly within. I realize that the adjective "spiritual" and its implicitly related noun, "spirituality," are vague, but let's leave them that way for a moment and simply try to gauge the proportions of the wave. Sandra Schneiders, in her thoughtful overview and commentary, lists three World Council of Churches consultations on spirituality (1984, 1986, 1987); further conferences dedicated to its study at Louvain, Villanova, and Oxford; ongoing spirituality seminars at the conventions of the Catholic Theological Society of America, American Academy of Religion, and College Theology Society; new doctoral programs in the specialization of spirituality and spiritual theology; and a large number of new, scholarly publications in the area.[1]

Clearly something is happening, which likely is a reverberation in the academy of a larger movement among the Christian people at large. Some would be inclined to view this as an example of a "postmodern" sensitivity in fact. Joseph Tetlow's figure of 37 million Americans buying books on spirituality in 1985 is an indication of this "larger" phenomenon.[2] And if we need further indications, let this 1989 comment from the Vatican's Doctrinal Congregation be representative of many other possible citations from among Catho-

1

lics, Protestants, and Orthodox: "Many Christians today have a keen desire to learn how to experience a deeper and authentic prayer life despite the not inconsiderable difficulties which modern culture places in the way of the need for silence, recollection and meditation."[3]

Yet, as spiritually "electric" as the atmosphere appears to be to many of us, still history's verdict is, as usual, ambiguous, cautioning us to be hesitant but expectant simultaneously. The citation above from that wise mystical woman, Teresa of Avila, about the ability to confuse rapture and foolishness ("boobishness" perhaps captures the meaning of *abobamiento*) is a good one to keep in mind while navigating the waves of spirituality.[4] The Vatican document above brings the same critical spirit to its reading of spirituality's history when it refers to the "fundamental deviations" of Pseudognosticism and Messalianism as paradigms of how spirituality can derail into boobishness. The first flees from the creaturely into a kind of angelism; the second seems to reduce the Divine to human feelings and affections. The theologian might call these escapism and emotionalism. Either way, not a promising way to do theology, and one can understand why the theologian would be rather hesitant to wed the rigors of the discipline too closely to those kinds of "spiritual" tendencies.[5]

This is the problematic side of "spiritual waves," so to speak. The side that causes the "thinker" to suppose, as Friedrich von Hügel put it, that spiritual types (he called them "personalities and schools of the interiorly experimental, emotional kind") are but "stop-gaps or compensations... in periods of transition or reaction, of uncertainty or decay." After all, so Hügel's representative and fictional thinker can say, look at how Neoplatonism followed the Roman empire's decay; or how Bernard[6] followed the end of the period of the *patres*. Think, too, of Pico and Paracelsus following the great scholastic period; or of German Romanticism after the Enlightenment; "so now again in our own day, more slightly, but not less really, in a revival of spiritual philosophy."[7]

And yet there is the other side of the matter: spirituality as neither gnostic-like angelism or Messalian-like emotionalism, but as the highest flowering of the human spirit. Not a small amount of Hügel's effort was devoted to championing just this view, at least if we're speaking of the "proper" kind of spirituality and the "proper," "inclusive-mixed-incarnational" kind of mysticism. He considered the incarnational mystics as "amongst the great benefactors of our race," for they are the ones in whom the "instinct of the Infinite" vitalizes all the dimensions of the human physical-spiritual organism.[8]

2

So, too, not unlike Hügel, Evelyn Underhill thought that "the great periods of mystical activity tend to correspond with the great periods of artistic, material, and intellectual civilization." The mystic, far from negating the human and creaturely, becomes "humanity's finest flower; the product at which each great creative period of the race had aimed." And thus Underhill suggested that the great mystical waves tend to come "immediately after" the creative "outbursts" of great periods. Mystical waves are the "heroic" ages of humanity. And so we get almost the reverse view from that of the hard-nosed rationalist created by Hügel and just noted above. Underhill's three great mystical waves — of the third, fourteenth, and seventeenth centuries, C.E. — are the crowning of the Classical, Medieval, and Renaissance periods.[9]

What is our verdict to be, then? Is the turn to spirituality blessing or woe, heroism or escapism, the intellect's flowering or withering? History's verdict (basing ourselves for now on a widely held Christian consensus) is one of cautioning us to make distinctions and to be careful. Underhill's third century knew its spiritual giants (Clement and Origen, for example), but it had its gnostic underside too. The fourteenth century, likewise, saw Dante, Eckhart, Tauler, Suso, Ruusbroec, Angela of Foligno, and especially Catherine of Siena and the writer of *The Cloud of Unknowing*. But it also had the likes of the Flagellants, and its share of other radically apocalyptic/ millenarian-like groups. And the seventeenth century saw the great "principals" of the French School (Pierre de Bérulle, Madeleine de Saint-Joseph, Jean-Jacques Olier, John Eudes), as well as Francis de Sales, Jane de Chantal, Vincent de Paul, Marie of the Incarnation and the other Marie (Madame Acarie), Johann Arndt, Jeremy Taylor, George Herbert, Thomas Traherne, the Hesychast Renaissance, Thomas Goodwin of the *Heart of Christ in Heaven*, and others. But it had Molinos and Quietism, and Jansenism, among other extremities, as well.

In other words, the turn to spirituality can be, basing ourselves on a widely held Christian consensus, both *arrobamiento* and *abobamiento*.[10] All of us, but particularly theologians, need to be circumspect. I say "particularly theologians," for one of their main ministries is to keep the discerning mind alive for the sake of church and society. And how can that discerning eye stay alert, if it flees from the travails of history (angelism), or sinks into mental obscurantism (emotionalism), or allows itself to become simply blinded by various fanaticisms? As we proceed into this work, I would hope this little look at history will foster in us a second naivete, a critical spirit, as we go.

"Spirituality" Is...?

Throughout this book I am concerned with *Christian* spirituality, and not with spirituality in broader and analogous senses, as embracing traditions other than the Christian. I surely do think there are rich spiritual traditions beyond our own, and here and there, particularly in a later chapter in which I say something about the relationship between Christian estimates of Jesus' uniqueness and its implications for other religions, non-Christian spiritualities do emerge more centrally. But by and large, this is a book concerned with Christian spirituality and its possible relationships with Christian theology and christology.

The reader can consult the standard sources for the history of the notion of "spirituality." I will be using it in the Pauline-like sense of living one's entire life as fully as one can in tune with the Spirit of Christ through grace and faith (Rm 8:1–17). In this sense, it does not simply refer to the immaterial "spirit" as distinct from the body, but to the attempt to have the Spirit of Christ penetrate and permeate our entire existence, in all its dimensions. Paul, of course, uses the adjective "spiritual" (*pneumatikos*), in 1 Corinthians 2:15 for example, and from this usage is derived our now contemporary usage of the noun "spirituality." Spirituality becomes "Christian" when it is based upon attunement through faith to the Holy Spirit, and thus to Jesus and his Father, as well as to Jesus' church and its mission, to which the Spirit always leads. Christian spirituality, in other words, is trinitarian, christocentric-salvific, ecclesial, and humanly "inclusive" in the sense that nothing human is to be left untransformed by God. This especially includes evil and sin. And to be truly inclusive, we must think also of our relationship to the earth and universe as a whole. There is a legitimate ecological dimension in Christian spirituality. Finally, as the Trinity's transformation of humanity, spirituality is necessarily and strongly eschatological.

I am not entirely sure why, or even if, the word "spirituality" is emerging as the most popular term to describe the seriously committed Christian life entailed in attempting to allow the Spirit of Jesus to permeate the totality of one's existence. For myself, I recognize that other words might function in a roughly equivalent way, adding helpful nuances: "piety," "devotion," "godliness," and "holiness," to give a few of the more common ones, with extensive historical pedigrees too. For myself, besides the clear biblical, trinitarian, and christocentric aspects of "spirituality," etymologically the word suggests "life" and "dynamism" and "breathing." And that is what the spiritual life aims to be: coming to life in all one's dimensions. This last phrasing is rather anthropocentric, but we must keep in mind that Christian spir-

4

ituality is centered on the Spirit of Christ, who occupies the primacy and enlivens all else. As we will see, this gives a heavily doxological-adorational accent to Christian spirituality.[11] It's probably safe to say that the word "Spirit" is one of those primal symbols or metaphors that unlock multiple dimensions of our existence: time penetrated by eternity, the surface (knowable) resting on the depths of mystery (the spirit), the outer sacramentalizing the inner, the lifeless coming to life, and so on. Couple all this with its obvious biblical and traditional Christian pedigree, and one can see why the word "spirituality" — a word obviously "contaminated" by the "Spirit" — enjoys a certain prominence.

If we employ the above description, then it follows that theology and christology *can* be forms of Christian spirituality. I emphasize the word "can," for they only become such to the degree that they are practiced in attunement with the Spirit of Christ as understood above. Of course, theology/christology, even when so attuned, is never the whole of Christian spirituality. This latter embraces so much more. But the labors of the theologian, when so attuned, are genuine forms of Christian spirituality, it seems to me. This book, in fact, will be greatly occupied with exploring what happens to Christian theology in general and christology in particular when they do become forms of spirituality.

The lines between "spirituality" and "mysticism" blur somewhat, and it's entirely possible to use the two words in an equivalent way. My own preference is to suggest that we reserve the word "mystic" for the consciously, deeply, radically, "accomplished" living out of Christian spirituality.[12] In this latter case, the pneumatic permeation has become inclusive, embracing the basic dimensions of the mystic. This may not necessarily express itself in what are commonly called "extraordinary" phenomena like visions, ecstasies, and so on — although it commonly seems to — but the Spirit of Christ has fundamentally transformed the spiritual-somatic organism of the mystic. The latter has undergone the dark night of the senses and the spirit in some way.[13]

Following this understanding of the matter, theology and christology can become forms of mysticism too. That is, when the work of the theologian has become "fundamentally" and "radically" transformed by Jesus' Spirit, then we have a mysticism of theology. Here the theological activities of the theologian have undergone a dark, purifying night of the senses and spirit — a sort of "stigmata" of the theological mind and activity — by becoming basically and consciously transparent of the Spirit's grace. I am inclined to think that Catholicism's "doctors of the church" are examples of this.[14] Aroused by their example, and that of the great Christian mystics in general, this book hopes to be a study, at least in part, of a mysticism of christology, of what happens to christology when the work of the christologian has undergone the Christ-forming "stigmata."

Features of the "Turn to Spirituality" in Theology and Christology

Keeping in mind the broadly descriptive definition of Christian spirituality I have just offered, let me mention several basic implications this seems to entail for the practice of Christian theology in general, and christology in particular. First, I would suggest that the turn to Christian spirituality represents an intensive search for the origins of and font from which genuinely Christian renewal can come. On the most general level, this can be considered a "turn to Christian experience" as the ground for Christian living in all its dimensions. Karl Rahner perhaps captured much of what this means in his often-cited comment that, given the increasing breakdown of "cultural"[15] Christianity in the West, "the devout Christian of the future will either be a 'mystic,' one who has experienced something, or he will cease to be anything at all."[16]

Notice how Rahner thinks of the "mystic" as one who has "experienced" the reality of faith. It is the Christian "experiential" turn that Rahner has in mind. Abstracting for a moment from his view that it is the increasing breakdown of "folk Christianity" that means that Christian faith will have to be real and experiential in an intensified way these days, I only want to appropriate his idea of linking spirituality with experience. A turn to one is a turn to the other. If we were to think of biblical images, we might look to the story of Moses at Mount Horeb (Ex 3) or to Jesus at his baptism (Mk 1:11). Both of these can be considered examples of foundational experiences, shaping the length, breadth, height, and depth of the rest of one's existence. As Moses and Jesus live from these experiences, so today's Christian is seeking to live from the funding experiences of Christian faith.

A theology and christology seeking to be attuned to and permeated by this kind of spirituality could be viewed as wanting to become deeply "experiential," in the sense of attempting to rethink the faith in terms of Christian experience.[17] The term "experience" is widely used, and it can be ambiguous and misleading. Here it is not used in a narrowly empirical or even in a too narrowly "humanistic" sense, as if experience were only a matter of the senses or of mental states excluding religious experience as well as Christian experiences of grace and of God. It is Christian experience that we have in mind here, and the intent is not to "reduce" God to experience, but to indicate the mediation of the God of Jesus Christ through human experience.[18]

We can surely choose to use terms other than "Christian experience" to give expression to what we mean by the turn to spirituality. Given the spread of meanings attributed to the term "experience," some might prefer not to use the term "experience" at all. But the word seems particularly helpful for expressing the "reality" nature of the Christian faith as well as its "participationist" nature. "Experience" is something one undergoes; one must participate in it.[19] As we will see, it also suggests an element of discernment, discrimination, and testing. To become experienced is to go through a purifying process, which matures one and equips one for "learning" from further experiences. In this sense, there is a link between "experience" and "experiment." So, too, Christian faith is a kind of testing and refining, a maturing process that gifts one with greater insight and wisdom.

As we proceed, I would simply ask the reader to bear in mind the wider view of experience we are employing. It is "wide" in the sense that we are linking up with a view of human experience that tries to be open to the full range of possibilities of human existence. The senses, surely, are involved (humans are psychosomatic wholes), but so too is the rich "world" of mind and spirit, of transcendence. Human "action" as well as "thinking" are expressions of human experience as well. But our view of experience is "Christian," too, in the sense that we are speaking primarily of a turn to the fundamental sources of Christian existence: Trinity, Jesus, grace, and church. The reader should note, then, that Christian experience is a "shaped" experience. It has a certain "form." One might argue that all human experience is shaped or formed, but here I want to concentrate on the Christian case. It is shaped through the mediation of the founding sources of the Christian faith as transmitted in church tradition.

Because of this "shaped" or mediated form of Christian experience, a large number of thinkers want to stress the cultural-linguistic dimensions involved, and I want to as well. Surely in the Christian tradition our experience is shaped through tradition, and primarily through scripture. With many we can and should speak of the narrative quality of Christian experience, meaning by that the way in which the unfolding of events in Christian experience is connected to form a rough coherence or "plot." That is a rough description, and it leaves open the question of whether we should embrace all the cultural-linguistic dimensions of experience under narrative, or whether we should aim for a tighter use for the term. But for now it will serve — along with the adjectives "cultural" and "linguistic" — as a way of alerting us to the linguistically shaped, culturally mediated way in which experience reaches us. But it also serves to keep us in touch with the rich texture, the concrete fullness, of Christian experience. For narratives, however else we may describe them, are filled with the drama, the tension and struggle, the "lived" quality of human experience. And in this sense they exemplify what we might call "originary" genres, as distinct from forms of expression more removed from the concrete fullness of experience, more "second order" or "conceptual." Narrative also nicely brings out how one must participate in the form to undergo the experience of meaning and truth. And surely this is most appropriate for faith experience, a participative form of experience *par excellence*. We will be returning to this topic in succeeding chapters.[20]

This turn to spirituality as a turn to Christian experience and language is not simply a culturally "convenient" event in today's theology. To some extent, surely, the intensified turn to experience is a defensive sign, an indication that all is not well with established meanings and teachings. Hence the search for alternatives in experience. In the citation from Rahner above, which refers to the breakdown of folk Christianity, this need to search for alternatives is clearly underscored. But Rahner is well aware, and we want also to underscore, that a turn to Christian experience is required on grounds intrinsic to the Christian faith itself. For Christian faith is commitment and obedience to the real event of Jesus Christ, an event whose reality Christians claim is of universal significance for humanity as a whole, for in it we believe that the one God of all has spoken a definitive message for all. If you will, from the perspective of the Christian story, "God's pedagogy" seems to be to communicate with us through our human experience, by giving it a coherent form, especially and definitively the "form" of Jesus Christ.

Entailed in this turn to the experience and language of Christian spirituality is a turn to contemplation and prayer in general, for these are the common sources or avenues of openness to Christian experience. Through them that experience is personally appropriated. The attractiveness of the saints and mystics — what a Methodist document called "men and women of beautiful consistency and seraphic ardor, jewels of the Church"[21] — is of a piece with this attempt to find models and guides who can help us in this personal appropriation. Their lives, often expressed in wonderful narratives/autobiographies/journals, give expression, again in a more originary way, to the personal and lived quality of experience.

But one cannot turn to these great witnesses for long without recognizing how they have been shaped by the great tradition of the church, particularly its liturgy, and especially its scriptures. All of these, but especially the latter, will always remain the eminent and privileged sources of the encounter with the Jesus of past and present. And so a theology turning to spirituality will be a deeply ecclesial, and especially biblical theology, according these something of a primacy, seeking always to remain closely linked with them, never straying very far, even when moving into the "further reaches" of theological speculation. Readers familiar with the writings of John of the Cross will recall how he moves back and forth from poem to commentary, with the poetry, given its more originary character, occupying the primacy. The commentary is a rather more dry prose, a sort of guide to the world of the poetry.[22] But the poetry is like a musical score being played and not simply spoken about. So, too, for a spirituality-based theology, the more originary "texts" and "monuments" of the Christian tradition, especially the scriptures, are the "poetry" of our faith.

Readers will likely recall the "charismatic movement" that swept through a number of the churches not too long ago. If they do, they will remember the phenomenon of speaking in tongues as well. Well, whatever else one makes of this fascinating phenomenon, I tend to look at it in part as an "opening up" and "breaking down" experience. One is opened up to the rich world of the Spirit, and as we are, we end up stammering, excitedly overwhelmed, not unlike babies with their baby talk. But it is also a breaking down, of our narrow conceptualism, our nicely defined categories, our rather surface and almost positivistic form of religion. To the extent that this happened, we are at the beginnings of a new opening to the rich world of spiritual experience, and it is perhaps not without significance that the charismatic movement was caught up in a larger "wave" of spiritual interest, and hopefully genuine renewal. The academy, I am suggesting, may be undergoing an analogous opening up and breaking down in its turn to spirituality.

There seems to be a basic logic — a *logique du coeur* — entailed in the turn to spirituality as a turn to Christian experience and language-narrative. On the one hand, it means "reappropriation" in the sense that it is an attempt to recover the concrete fullness of Christian experience. For christology, as we will see, this inevitably means a reappropriation of the "full" reality of Jesus in his human, ecclesial, and especially his trinitarian dimensions. For Christian spirituality is a trinitarian, and ecclesial, as well as a christocentric reality. The fullness of the Christian spiritual narrative and experience keeps these dimensions interrelated, avoiding artificial separations. The Spirit, to which the theologian seeks attunement, is a Spirit leading us through the church community to a Jesus who is the gift of the Trinity to us.

Reappropriation seems to go hand in hand with another movement, which can be labeled in various ways: critique, correction, development, challenge. Perhaps the word "challenge" is wide enough to cover all these possibilities. Hans-Georg Gadamer has told us, in a fascinating discussion of the meaning of "experience" in herme-

9

neutics, that "the experienced person proves to be...someone who is radically undogmatic."[23] An experienced person, if you will, has become so, not only by living off the capital of "old" experiences, but by being open to "new" experiences. And in fact the prior experiences have enabled the person to be both open to and to learn from new experiences. Well, this is what seems to happen with the turn to spiritual experience too. We become open to the "new" to some extent.

For example, as we seek to reappropriate the christological heritage, we may discover dimensions left underemphasized or largely ignored by more recent trends in theology. The biblical movement in theology has largely meant a recovery of the larger concerns of the original Jesus in his trinitarian and ecclesial-soteriological aspects, and thus it has provided a balance to a more abstract Christ often presented in popular presentations of church doctrine. Here the challenge is really a recovery of something largely ignored. Sometimes the challenge comes in the form of a "development," a deepened understanding of our christological heritage, as we open ourselves to a deeper attentiveness to it. The Spirit-inspired sensitivity to our present experiences,[24] in and through which we appropriate the tradition, sometimes brings this kind of development about. Catholics would suggest that the Marian doctrines are examples of this. We might suggest that contemporary understandings of human historicity and development, and of the cultural-linguistic aspects of humanity, have brought about a growing appreciation of these dimensions of the reality of Jesus. Here we have what some might call a "Christian-friendly" postmodernism.

But the challenge can also take a more volatile form: an attempted correction or critique of the received christological heritage. Often this is a slow process, requiring much discernment, covering many years of dusk-like ambiguity and questioning. Something like a theological "dark night." The emerging field of women's studies in theology may be bringing about just such a critique of how misogynism has "infected" the various areas of theology. The struggle among differing kinds of "political" theologies — U.S.-democratic, liberationist, etc. — is perhaps also helping to correct aspects of political and social amnesia in our theologies and christologies. The encounter with modern forms of atheism, relativism, and radical philosophical systems (secular forms of postmodernism) is perhaps bringing a great challenge to what we mean by Christian truth and faith and witness, causing us to struggle through to our own views on these matters, but perhaps in a more pluralistic and "chastened" way.

My own suspicion, too, is that simply the reappropriation, through a renewal of Christian spirituality, of the trinitarian and ecclesial dimensions of christology will bring about an equally and perhaps even greater challenge to theologians, a challenge that might well be every bit as volatile as the challenges mentioned just above. A trinitarian christology, it seems to me, leads to a rather strong form of Chalcedonian incarnationalism and christocentrism. And an ecclesial sensitivity grants a very special guidance function, hermeneutically, to the church's liturgical and doctrinal traditions. Correspondingly, the role of obedience in the life of faith is enhanced.

At this point, the theologian will likely want some "controls," or at least some attentiveness to how we might go about sorting out "authentic" from "inauthentic" turns in Christian spirituality. This is why, as a second feature of the turn to Christian spirituality in christology, I would emphasize the "ascetical" dimension. Christian spirituality has always involved an ascesis, a discipline, through which the testing of spirits can develop and one can "mature" in a manner best enabling one to appropriate the challenges of the spiritual life. In fact, we can describe "asceticism" as a disciplined manner of staying attuned to the lessons of Christian experience and the Christian narrative.

Appropriate biblical images for this ascetical moment could be the desert experience of the Exodus, during which the Jewish people were tested, and Jesus' own desert experiences of testing (Mt 4:1–11), as well as much of the Savior's life as a whole. "For we do not have a high priest who is unable to sympathize with our weaknesses, but one who has similarly been tested in every way, yet without sin" (Hb 4:15). An especially important reason for the appropriateness of turning to the saints and mystics — the church's paradigmatic witnesses — is that they have undergone the testing of experience, like their Savior. Their own purgations and dark nights were the disciplining dimension, enabling them to become transparent of the Spirit of Jesus.

The turn to a life of deep spirituality is difficult and dangerous. We get lost. The realities of evil and sin "infect" our existence. Put in linguistic terms, there are many stories/narratives being told. Which is the authentically Christian story? And what is the discipline I need, to be able to read it? The gnostics find this project too costly and painful, and so they seek to flee it. The Messalians perhaps simplify it all too much, settling for a fuzzy sentimentalism that makes them the potential victim of whatever emotional current happens to be sweeping through. Ascesis is what keeps us open to *arrobamiento* and away from *abobamiento*, in its two forms of evil and sin.

It is not without interest that the word "experience" is related to the Greek (*peira*), which in turn is related to both "danger" and "testing." The word used by Hebrews 4:15, above, for Jesus' testing, for example, is the same *peira* that can mean "experience." The Latin *periculum* ("danger") brings out the note of danger in the word "experience," while our word "experiment" perhaps brings out the element of "testing" implied in the word. Thus, experience is a dangerous reality, fraught with "peril" (another related word). It is a "testing," a kind of "experiment" through which one is called to "prove" the authentic from the inauthentic. Asceticism is a disciplined way to do this, minimizing the "peril" and maximizing the benefits of experience.[25]

If we keep this ascetical dimension in mind, theologians should not think that the turn to spirituality aims for a particularly "soft" form of intellectual work, substituting fuzziness for the rigors of intellectual analysis. The theologian is not exempt from asceticism, but commits him/herself to it when seeking to bring theological work into a fruitful intersection with spirituality. In fact, we could rightly say that the discipline of sustained theological conversation, the humility of submitting one's labors to the judgment of one's colleagues, the labors of attempting to "master" the various theological methodologies, among other things that could be mentioned, are forms of theological ascesis, part of the spirituality involved in the spirituality of theology. For the mind, too, must allow itself to be disciplined and "formed," so that it can be in tune with the "form" of the Christian narrative itself. Of course, by undertaking to unite theology with spirituality, the theologian is recognizing that theology involves an asceticism of far more than only the disciplines of the intellectual life. There is the larger commitment to and discipline of attunement in faith to prayer and action based on a trinitarian, christocentric, and ecclesial way of life. But a vital dimension of this, especially for the theologian, is the discipline of linking all of these latter with the life of the intellect.

I have used the image of the "stigmata" a number of times, and perhaps here is a good place to reflect upon that usage a bit. This metaphorical use of the image brings to mind Jesus' own paradigmatic passion and death, his cruciform love for us. And in this regard, the ascesis of the theologian should be seen as "attempted" stigmata too, an attempt to conform one's entire life to Jesus' own cruciform love. The stigmata of the intellect indicate that learning is in the service of this cruciform love, and not of one's own pet theories. The image of the stigmata surfaces the dimension of *dolor*, of pain, of labor, of commitment. One also thinks of how the physical marks of the wounds are outward signs of something much deeper. And so, too, the labors of the theologian are signs of a deepening transformation of existence. It is not magic, but obedient love that is at work here.

But the stigmata are also an exceptional sign of the extraordinary grace of the Lord at work in history. The sign is a response to grace, and this lifts it out of the area of something that can be simply "mastered" like a technique. So, too, the particular ascesis of Christian spirituality is always in the service of this greater reality of a loving grace. Discipline serves this grace, not the reverse. Just enough "method" and "discipline" to keep the miracles of grace and love flowing and alive, rather than to smother them, is the nature of Christian asceticism. The passion was not willed for its own sake, but for the sake of love. Transposing this into intellectual and theological terms, we could say that "method" is in the service of "truth," and it never completely masters truth.[26]

The Doctrinal Congregation reminded us of these ideas in its statement on meditation when it said, "The love of God, the sole object of Christian contemplation, is a reality which cannot be 'mastered' by any method or technique."[27] But let me cite from St. John Eudes, a master of the French School of Spirituality, whose tradition of spirituality will be featured in the pages of this book:

> I ask you to notice carefully that the practice of practices, the secret of secrets, the devotion of devotions, is to have no attachment to any practice or special exercise of devotion, but have a great concern to surrender yourself, in all your exercises and actions, to the Holy Spirit of Jesus.[28]

This truth, so well known to the spiritual masters, surely has its validity in the areas of theology and christology. The theological "mind" and its "methods" are called, too, to this kind of surrender. This is especially appropriate for christology: the very methods of the discipline are not to be spared the following of the crucifixion of the One it seeks to know. Method and truth, form and content "blend" in theology and christology. At least this seems to be one of the lessons coming to christology from spirituality. And this book seeks to heed that lesson.

A third feature of the turn to Christian spirituality I would like to emphasize now is its crucially critical role in theology and christology. Hopefully this has begun to surface in the comments above. It is crucial, because once we think of spirituality as the fullness of concrete Christian experience and language, then we recognize that the very reality of theology itself depends upon its "spiritual" substance. If turning to spirituality is turning to the reality of Christian substance, then ignoring spirituality is like entering into theological illusion. It is critical, too, for it is the turn to Christian experience, narrative, and language that keeps theology and christology open to assimilating "new" experiences and narratives that it needs for its own self-correction and development. Perhaps this is why, as John Macquarrie put it, "It is not surprising that such great theologians as Augustine and Anselm slip naturally from speaking *about* God to speaking to him, and we experience no awkwardness in this transition."[29] That natural transition, which really comes from grasping that theology is called to be a form of spirituality, and indeed of mysticism in its proper sense, is something this book hopes to foster.

The Book As an "Experiment"

The chapters to follow will be an "experiment" in the sense we have given to this word above: a way of "testing" the contribution of the experience and language of Christian spirituality to the realms of theology and christology. These chapters are by no means exhaustive of what christology will look like when it is wedded with spirituality in a sustained manner. They are more suggestive and representative. I had to pick topics with which I am somewhat familiar. But I also tried to choose topics possessing an intrinsic significance for the field of christology.

Chapter 2 studies the contribution of contemplation to the role of conversation and narrative in christology's method. Theology is very "method-conscious" these days, given the challenges posed to theology by the modern and now "postmodern" spirit. Spiritual traditions of meditation and contemplation look to Jesus and the Trinity as the great exemplars of dialogue and narrative, and this chapter wants to explore how the "grafting" of the interest in a more dialogical and narrative style of christology onto meditative traditions will enrich modern method in christology, even while "toning down" in a refreshing way the sometimes exaggerated preoccupation with method. Contemplation is a conversation and narrative too, but one rooted in Jesus the storyteller and the trinitarian conversation.

The "theomeditative" style of theology and christology recommended by this chapter will set the tone for much that follows. For example, it suggests that we learn this style of theology by participating in the conversations echoing the trinitarian one, primarily that of the dialogue going on in the churches. The ecclesial dialogue is a hermeneutical bridge to the christological and trinitarian dialogue. The doxological tone of much that follows in this book surfaces in this chapter too. For the trinitarian conversation, as it spills out in Jesus, church, and world, fills us with petition, jubilation, gratitude, praise, and adoration. This "excess of love" in Trinity and Jesus is the richer matrix out of which theology comes.

Appropriately, then, chapter 3 turns to an actual "experiment" from the contemplative traditions, choosing as its focus the rich trinitarian christocentrism of the French School of Spirituality. This "school," reverberating still into our own times through such great representatives as Thérèse of Lisieux, Friedrich von Hügel, Hans Urs von Balthasar, Karl Rahner, and John Wesley and his disciples of

14

past and present, for example, has as its founding "principals" Pierre de Bérulle, Madeleine de Saint-Joseph, Charles de Condren, Jean-Jacques Olier, and St. John Eudes. We have concentrated on Cardinal Bérulle, the undisputed chief founder and very profound mystic as well as theologian, looking to the others when that seemed helpful and appropriate.[30]

The French School seemed an appropriate experimental study for a number of reasons: because of my own interests and attraction, but primarily because of its undisputed christological and trinitarian emphases. It quite explicitly was a search for an alternative to an abstract style of theology severed from its roots in experience and language, not unlike this book itself. Hopefully readers will find here a compelling example of the contemplative style of hermeneutics sketched in the second chapter. It is my hope, too, that this study will encourage others to continue exploring the hermeneutical and christological contributions of other great spirituals of past and present.

Chapter 4 attempts to situate our developing theomeditative approach to christology among the various kinds of christologies being developed today.[31] This seemed an appropriate time to do so: by now readers will have enough of a sense of what we're about to be able to do some situating, and they will be curious enough to want to do so. I have always been uncomfortable with the categories of "christologies from above" and "from below" — not to mention the analogous categories of the "Jesus of history" and the "Christ of faith" — and this chapter will explore my reasons for that somewhat more fully. We can be sympathetic to the often legitimate concerns implied by these categories. And indeed we have learned much from them and are fortunate enough to be able to "build upon" them. But it seems that it is time to search for categories that don't foster the dualisms the Incarnation Mystery in its inclusive sense was meant to overcome, without falling into a form of reductionism. History or faith, below or above — these ought not to be opposed to one another, if we judge by the standards of the Incarnation and the Trinity. Our own contemplative approach leads us to propose a more trinitarian and christocentric approach to experience — experience as shaped by the Christian narrative — rather than the more abstract or supposedly "neutral" notion of experience that seems to lie at the origins of the typological categories under consideration.

Adoration seems to surface repeatedly as an important theme in the French School, but also among those theologians most representative of the theomeditative style of theology and christology being explored here. Adoration is part of a continuum of prayer forms and attitudes, of course, but it seems the most intensive expression of God-centeredness we can imagine. Its very intensity makes it somewhat rare in its purer forms, perhaps, but also revealing, too, of the meditative posture we are exploring in these pages. It is one of those participative, originary, and narrative-like forms of expression that are our special concern. What fascinates me is that adoration seems to lead to a heightened sensitivity, not only to the God beyond us, but to the God with us, especially in Incarnation. Why is this?

We normally associate adoration with the divine "otherness." Yet think of Karl Barth, whose own work literally breathes in an adorational atmosphere, and yet notice his increasing christocentrism and incarnationalism, until one reaches the christological crescendo of *Church Dogmatics* 4. Bérulle, representative of the French School, moves from adoration to incarnational kenosis ("service" or "servitude") with an ease that amazes. It is the connection between these that our chapter 5 seeks to explore somewhat more fully, choosing as its guide the writings of Baron Friedrich von Hügel.[32] Hügel is well known as a leading Catholic philosopher of religion in the modern period. I chose him as my main guide here partly because he is well known as a philosopher who was deeply committed to serious philosophical and theological work, rather than fuzzy, sentimental grunting. At the same time, the adorational accent increasingly permeates his work as he struggles with the "modern" sensitivity, and it reaches a self-reflectivity that, despite its occasional nature, is still more pronounced than that found in many other authors.

Per adorationem ad Jesum — in a suggestive turn, Hügel helps us to grasp the link between adoration and Incarnation. God is the "sovereignly free Subject," and so we adore. But it is because God is such a sovereignly free *Subject* that a personal and intimate self-bestowal in Jesus can happen. Adoration points, not to God's "depersonalization," but to a "plenitude" of personality.[33] As "other," God is always adorable. But God becomes "adored" through becoming intimate for us, definitively in Jesus. We owe Hügel especially, but also all the other notable names mentioned in these chapters, a great debt for exploring this adorational posture that seems so crucial as a hermeneutical hinge to many of the great mysteries of christology and Trinity.

Chapters 6 and 7, on the saints/mystics[34] and the Blessed Virgin Mary, respectively, as christological sources, illustrate and extend the preceding chapters. The mystics can be said to be the adorers and contemplatives in an "eminent" sense, particularly the Virgin Mary, whose own intimacy with Jesus has to be unmatched. Here I am suggesting that the christologian and theologians in general can find in them examples of and guides to the style of theology being explored in this book. They have the advantage, too, of being good

16

examples of the more originary and narrative-like kind of theology that a theomeditative theology never wants to depart from.

There has been a steady interest in the mystics/saints in relatively recent times in the academy, which often has much to do with a reaction again against a theology uprooted from living experience and language. Think of William James and Rudolf Otto, for example, or the interest in Gregory Palamas among the Eastern Orthodox. On the Catholic side, one can think of Hügel's turn to the mystics, especially Catherine of Genoa, as a way of producing a theology "nearer... to the methods by which actual life, in its stress and poignancy, instructs us," as he tells us.[35] Hügel, along with Henri Bremond's *A Literary History of Religious Thought in France*,[36] presents us with vivid, narrative-like approaches to theology, Bremond often offering careful analyses of the originary linguistic genres used by the mystics.

My chapters here are within this same trajectory, but with a special christological and trinitarian accent, and with perhaps a bit more attention to the linguistic and narrative dimensions involved. Not surprisingly, one finds a rich treasury of christological and trinitarian insight in these mystics, given their adorational sensitivities. I do not claim that they are always great theologians — although at times sanctity and theology fuse in a blessed manner — but I do suggest that when theologians consult them they are pointed back toward a more adorational and narrative style of christology that is remarkable in both its ability to exemplify as well as challenge the discipline.

For we must remember Gadamer's counsel: it is the "experienced" ones who are radically "undogmatic" and so open to "new" experiences. The saints and mystics would seem to prove this true, but the Blessed Virgin Mary presents us with an especially strong challenge in this regard. It is hard to imagine anyone more "experienced" in the affairs of christology than her, and so I take up my own challenge in chapter 7 and try to explore how she leads us into some of the mysteries of Jesus. I especially dwell upon the controversial topic of the virginal conception and birth, viewing its uniqueness as a sign of the uniqueness of the divine filiation of Jesus himself. The first "uniqueness" points to the latter one, but Matthew and Luke fascinatingly in their narratives tell us that this mystery must be approached in an adorational posture. Think, in this regard, of Matthew's "magi" (Mt 2) and Luke's doxology-confessing heavenly host and angel (Lk 2). These are fascinating connections that are beginning to surface. The "connections" making up the narrative of Jesus' story, I think and hope.

We live in a world increasingly aware of its interconnections, on a global scale. To participate in the theological conversation today is to sense that, at least on the edges as a special challenge, is a forthcoming conversation with the venerable non-Christian religious traditions. This is not entirely new for Christian theology, — think of Judaism's continual challenge, the *patres* and Hellenism, Thomas Aquinas and Islam, the Jesuit missionaries and Hinduism and Buddhism — but perhaps our awareness of the entire scope of the globe gives it a new edge. Chapter 8 is a modest christological intersection with these relatively new partners in the Christian conversation. And, of course, we Christians need to learn that we are relatively new partners in their conversation too.

In any case, this book is trying to stay as close as possible to the originary, conversational style of christology that it espouses. And the intersection with the non-Christian traditions seemed to emerge now in the flow of that conversation. Hence our eighth chapter attempts to probe what Christians confess in the "uniqueness" of Jesus.[37] It tries to suggest a link between a meditative and adorational approach and the confession of Jesus' definitively personal revelation of God. The Jesus revelation seems to disclose a personalistic universe, which moves between religious monism on the one hand and extreme religious heterogeneity on the other. Monism seems to deny the uniquely personal in divine revelation; extreme heterogeneity seems to deny the real participation in God that a personal God seems to offer. It seems that in a personalistic universe, such as the Incarnation discloses, not all "religions" are or even need to be equally or similarly concerned about the same things, even the revelation of God. Does God create a "space" within which religions can pursue matters that are relatively distinct from one another, even from God's own personal self-communication?

Chapter 9 takes up the question of the relationship between contemplation and action within the context of christology. It is something of a self-critique, inasmuch as one of the dangers of a theomeditative style of theology, *improperly* viewed, is to lose contact with the realm of action, preferring to dwell in a sort of artificially induced world-amnesia. The gnostic tendency can always resurface. Properly understood, I suggest, the fullness of the contemplative experience and language should lead to a form of activity that wants to be open to self-reflective critique ("theory"), thus transforming "activity" into "action," or into "practice" in the sense of truly human and Spirit-transformed activity. Contemplation fosters a reflectivity toward our activity. But it also keeps our theory anchored to the concrete fullness of Christian experience, not letting it wander off into empty abstractions. For we must remember that the turn to spirituality is the turn to Christian experience, Christian ascesis, and to the conformity of our "story" to the story of Jesus.

This is where this book especially intersects with many of the concerns of more practical and social styles of theology and christology, trying to make connections with them, and exploring the benefits that come from a reflective weaving between the contemplative traditions and these more "advocacy-oriented" styles of theology. My aim is to learn from political, social, feminist, and ecological concerns in christology, but trying to do so in a way consistent with the meditative thrust of this book. In some cases this won't cause tension, but will be seen as something already well known to these fields. In other cases, I suspect that the primacy accorded the adorational and doxological in this book might lead to some "second thoughts."

In a certain sense this ninth chapter can be seen as a christological gloss on Jürgen Moltmann's comment that "only doxology releases the experience of salvation for a full experience of that salvation." For in doxological adoration we move beyond manipulation and narcissistic possessiveness. Our "triune God is not made [our] object," says Moltmann.[38] To the extent that we participate in this, we transcend the manipulative and the objectifying. We don't make ourselves objects either. Such is what trinitarian christocentrism is all about. This is the kind of theory and the kind of practice that a theomeditative style of christology is meant to foster. It seems particularly compelling to this author.

The Postlude retells the book's story again — like a meditation, hopefully at a deeper, more penetrating and suggestive level. The theme is the turn to Christian spirituality as the turn to the concrete fullness of Christian experience and language. That is a way of staying in touch with Christian reality, rather than eclipsing it. The experienced person is open to new experiences. Radically "undogmatic" in Gadamer's sense. Able to hear the Christian story, and not simply locked up in one's own. But this kind of "knowledge," says Karl Barth, comes from being gifted with the ability to "acknowledge." "Knowledge" springs from "acknowledge." The Word that is Jesus is the freely offered Word of the Father through the Spirit. It is a challenge, but a joyful one. And this returns us nicely to Karl Barth's wonderful phrase describing what we experience as a result of all of this: "sober exuberance."[39]

CHAPTER TWO

Conversation, Narrative, and Contemplation

Our times seem to be something of a battlefield in the area of theology's method or interpretation theory — frequently named "hermeneutics." Paul Ricoeur has spoken of the "conflict of interpretations," and this is an apt description, at least in current Western theology and christology. It seems that times of intense pluralism, information explosion, change, etc., bring with them a challenge to approaches to learning that are "in possession." And theology and christology are not exempt. In fact, they have been particularly scrutinized in our times, and other fields may have much to learn from them as they negotiate these difficult waters themselves.

Here I don't want to try to rehearse the many developments that have taken place. Suffice it to say that I, like many, have benefited from the struggles. Painful as it has been, contemporary Western christology has gained much from developments in philosophy, anthropology, history, the social sciences, literary criticism, "new" schools of systematic and philosophical theology, the current discussion about modernity and postmodernity (postliberalism/postcriticism), etc. My own strategy is increasingly one that tries to adhere to two principles. First, remember that theology's method was made for theology, not theology for method. It is theology's subject matter — revelation and its analysis — that should guide the theologian. Methods must be appropriate to it, not getting in its way. This imposes a certain humility upon methodical concerns, and indicates that the theologian can't remain in a kind of neutral space, but must be receptive and obedient to revelation and attracted, faithfully and humbly, to its pursuit, before method can be adequately articulated. I recognize that there is a back and forth intertwining between subject matter and method, but the primacy goes to the content.

Secondly, I find it helpful as well as intellectually proper to try to remain as receptive as possible to the many new developments, while at the same time preserving a critical perspective on it all. Openness and evaluation, receptivity and critique seem a not too preposterous goal. This is why I am attracted to what is becoming increasingly known as the "conversation model" in theology, seeing it as appropriate in the various regions of theology, christology — this book's major subject — included. Surely if I ask what I try to do when I engage in theology/christology, "conversation" is a plausible, generic answer. I find myself "conversing" with the theological/christological tradition, getting caught up in questions raised and partially answered by the back and forth movement of that historical heritage and my own current "formation" by the experiences-insights-questions of the time in which I live.

The conversation is possible, partly because I am a person of my own times. Current experience somehow becomes a part of me and leads me to formulate certain questions of christology and theology. "Conversation" seems an apt word here, for I ask questions, seek answers, and in some sense receive questions and answers "back" from both the currents of my own time and the theological heritage. Through the conversation, I sense that I am in the flow of a movement between all sorts of "voices": the theological heritage, as well as the voices, theological and not, that have helped form me into the person and questioning thinker that I am today.

Conversation and Narrative

Let me try to be a bit more precise and list a number of the major features of the conversation model that make it helpful in theology. First of all, it is helpful for the theologian and religious inquirer to remember that theology and christology are both a form of "*logos*," or "communication," and that conversation is a way to participate in that communication, that *logos*. Hence, "christ-o-*logy*" and "theo-*logy*." In fact, conversation is a mode of approaching a topic that is peculiarly appropriate to the free human inquirer. The "dialogue," another term for the conversation, is the genre Plato chose to explore philosophy, because he recognized that the philosophical quest was only possible through genuine openness to and freedom for truth and wisdom. Without such freedom to inquire, people become manipulated by power tricks. The dialogue is the "symbolic form" of the free human spirit.

Hans-Georg Gadamer, in his penetrating study of the Platonic dialogue/conversation, has grasped the connection between the dialogue and human freedom. By placing "language and concept back within the original movement of the conversation," says Gadamer, the "literary form of the dialogue...protects words from all dogmatic abuse."[1] I have learned much from Gadamer's study of the Platonic dialogues, and his adaptation of them in hermeneutics. But I mainly discovered the significance of the symbolic form of the dialogue from Eric Voegelin's demanding and compelling studies of Plato. Through the dialogue, suggests Voegelin, we have a "symbolic form" capable of "communicating, and expanding, the order of wisdom founded by [Socrates]." It corresponds to and symbolizes, if you will, the Platonic-Socratic understanding of the soul as a free ordering source of social order and wisdom. And Voegelin continues, in an important passage:

> The dialogue, however, can be conducted only if it does not degenerate into an exchange of rhetorical harangues without existential communication among the speakers. Decisive for this point are the scenes in *Protagoras* and *Gorgias* where Socrates threatens a walkout unless the sophistic partner stops his speechmaking and enters into the argument. The dialogue is the symbolic form of the order of wisdom, in opposition to the oration as the symbolic form of the disordered society. It restores the common order of the spirit that has been destroyed through the privatization of rhetoric.[2]

The point, I hope, is clear. Theology and christology are forms of *logos*, of inquiry and participative communication. To some extent, this is part of theology's legacy from the Classic tradition. As such, they presuppose that form of free inquiry characteristic of the human spirit and distinct from power plays and the manipulating of people that really blocks inquiry and substitutes biases and brute force in its place. Without this, it's hard to see how theology could lay any claim to being a genuine *logos*.

Secondly, the conversation or dialogue is appealing to an experiential approach to theology, for the dialogue corresponds to the basically interpretation-like character of our lived existence. Plato, and others, did not arbitrarily impose the dialogue form upon their characters and themselves. They found themselves engaged in a kind of conversation by the very nature of their experience itself. As Frederick Lawrence has nicely put it, "human living at its most primordial is always a process of making sense." At bottom, human life itself has a conversational structure, raising and arguing and answering questions, back and forth, in an ever refined manner. This is why Lawrence suggests that Gadamer "grounded his theory of human knowing/reading in a phenomenological thematization of the basic activity of life as human."[3] This is also why Eric Voegelin, building upon Plato, speaks of the "dialogue of the soul" coming into being when the soul " 'dialectically' investigates its own suspense 'between knowledge and ignorance.'" That suspense generates a sort of "erotic tension" that "breaks forth in its own dialogical exegesis."[4] Here is an area in which both the contemplative and the theological analyst can genuinely meet. For both want to be rooted in experience — amply understood — and attentive to its lessons. The dialogue corresponds to the rhythm of human experience itself.

Thirdly, the conversation or dialogue model coheres nicely with both the traditional nature of human and theological inquiry, as well as with the need for continual yet critical receptivity to the ongoing present and future. Gadamer is one of the most eloquent and noticed spokesperson's on behalf of the role of tradition. His critique of the Enlightenment's "prejudice against prejudice itself, which denies tradition its power," is often referred to.[5] Human knowing is tradition-bound, Gadamer has tried to remind us. In and through tradition's formative influence upon us, we are able to inquire in a meaningful manner. Gadamer has been criticized for ignoring tradition's harmful influence upon us, but he was aware of this, and was trying rather to indicate that even our ability to be critical of the past is partly made possible for us by tradition. Tradition, in fact, is the moving link between past and present, when it's understood in a truly historical manner. "The historical movement of human life," Gadamer tells us, is not a "closed horizon." "Thus the horizon of the past, out of which all human life lives and which exists in the form of tradition, is always in motion." We live "in this motion" and are enabled to ask the questions we do through it.

Tradition, in the Gadamerian sense, is a flowing, moving reality in some sense. The "handing on" movement that tradition is, itself a result of human time (temporality), unites past, present, and future. Gadamer speaks of tradition as a kind of "fusion," in which "old and new are always combining into something of living value, without either being explicitly foregrounded from the other." Real "understanding" for Gadamer is the "fusion" of the horizons of past and present, which can fuse because they are open rather than closed. "Rather, understanding is always the fusion of these horizons supposedly existing by themselves."[6]

Tradition is, in other words, a kind of conversation, a back and forth movement in which horizons of past and present fuse, moving toward the future. This is Voegelin's "dialogue of wisdom," referred to earlier. Now what I want to emphasize here is that the conversation model is sensitive to tradition. We all enter into the conversation in and through tradition. In fact, if I understand Gadamer correctly, it is because we have experientially tasted and been formed through the ongoing conversation of tradition that we find ourselves longing to and able to converse at all. We recognize that our ability to converse and dialogue is greatly facilitated by the horizon of the past from which we come and the questions it enables us to pose to our present. Saying that conversation is tradition-bound and tradition-enabled means, too, that conversation is a language-bound and story/narrative-bound activity too. We will return to this in time. All of this is important to the theologian, who recognizes that Christian revelation is a tradition-bound reality. This is supremely true of christology, which so stresses the historical origins of the faith in the historical event of Jesus, as well as its continuing effects in the ongoing tradition of the church "through the risen Christ."

We can say that conversation — or dialogue — is a very traditional act. In fact, we can even say that tradition has the form of a conversation — the back and forth of horizons and their fusion in various ways — and our ability to converse is facilitated, but also sometimes hurt, by our traditional formation. We're all aware of people who seem to possess a more developed ability to enter into dialogue: their preformation (Gadamer's "prejudices") is greatly the key to this.

Theologians may be able to appreciate Gadamer's notion of tradition if they think of it as embracing the "monuments" (*tradita*) of tradition, like texts, artifacts, various historical data, etc., within the supportive ground and environment of the historical "handing on" process (*traditio* now as the process of *tradere*). Scripture and the other monuments of the Christian tradition are aspects of the larger flow of tradition in which past and present horizons constantly fuse. The Christian tradition is itself a dialogue or conversation in which a living fusion or fidelity with the *tradita* is constantly attempted and in fact enabled through the ongoing flow of the open horizons of the traditioning process itself.[7]

A fourth feature of dialogue/conversation, at least one that tries to be in fidelity to Plato's view of it, is that it actually supports and builds up a continual "ascent" or openness to truth. Or in the case of theology, to the "subject matter" of theology, revelation. "To conduct a conversation means to allow oneself to be conducted by the subject matter to which the partners in the dialogue are oriented," says Gadamer.[8] The movement to-and-fro of question and answer, response and counterresponse, proffered insight and explored insight, and so on, is a way of "testing," of keeping open, of making sure that the climate of opinion of the day (the pejorative *doxa* of Plato's Sophists) does not suppress genuine understanding.

Plato's "dialectic" approach, which actually is the form all genuine conversation takes, "is not the art of arguing (which can make a strong case out of a weak one) but the art of thinking (which can strengthen objections by referring to the subject matter)." It is a continual ascesis, a discipline, through which one tries to transcend biases by continual openness to the truth. This is why Gadamer nicely points out how the conversation is an "art of strengthening,"[9] for through the breaking down of inferior positions one is building up ampler, more solid ones. This is why Gadamer and Voegelin, too, nicely see the intrinsic relationship between questioning and conversation. Questioning is a way of breaking through the *doxa*, the pressure of "received" opinions. An "interdict on the Question," Voegelin tells us, is the symptom of a self-contraction which makes the existentially open participation in the process of reality impossible."[10]

This art of strengthening, which genuine conversation is, allows for multiple strategies, and even in some sense fosters them. Openness to the subject matter helps us grasp that the proper object of our hermeneutical focus is not properly something "behind" speakers or texts, but the subject matter itself opened up for us through the conversation, with partners and texts.[11] This openness also imposes a modesty and humility on the dialogue partners. If the truth rather than biases, even those of emotional attachments to our friends, genuinely leads, then we should take the steps necessary to pursue it. As David Tracy put it in his study of conversation, "in the pursuit of truth, friendship must yield."[12] This will mean attentive humility in the one less tutored; a struggle against intellectual hubris in the one more tutored. It will surely mean obeying the rules of logic, so that genuine communication can ensue. It will generally mean a recognition of the greater weight of the wisdom of the past, a willingness to accord it a reverential respect and submission, until the dialectical process demands otherwise. This is surely one of Gadamer's great strengths, shared equally by Voegelin. Gadamer's famous lines bear repeating here:

> history does not belong to us; we belong to it. Long before we understand ourselves through the process of self-examination, we understand ourselves in a self-evident way in the family, society, and state in which we live. The focus of subjectivity is a distorting mirror. The self-awareness of the individual is only a flickering in the closed circuits of historical life. *That is why the prejudices of the individual, far more than his judgments, constitute the historical reality of his being.*[13]

And so do Voegelin's:

> The most important means of regaining contact with reality is the recourse to thinkers of the past who had not yet lost reality, or who were engaged in the effort of regaining it.[14]

This emphasis upon dialogue as an art of strengthening — the "dialectic" of Plato — seems to indicate that we can and must refine our conversing skills, if our conversations are to lead somewhere and not encounter roadblocks. There is an asceticism involved, which can aid us in the above features. Besides our initial level of "understanding" (what the German philosophers call *verstehen*) there is also a sharpening process (what they call *erklären*, "explaining"). The two seem to work together and mutually refine one another. In a sense, if we follow a Platonic dialogue, one seems to get better at both as one proceeds.

David Tracy and Paul Ricoeur, among contemporary thinkers, have particularly emphasized the place of "explanation" in modern hermeneutics. Modern methods of historical analysis, psychological and sociological analysis, and literary analysis, which studies the forms (images, symbols, metaphors, and genres) of thought, are particularly featured by them. They recommend, cautiously, a kind of grafting of these explanatory methods "onto" our hermeneutical efforts of understanding. Those methods might refine our insights and tighten our logic and supporting warrants, while the matrix of understanding can save our explaining from a simplistic deductivism, conceptualism, and positivism. Given the realities of error, illusion, pathologies of a personal and social kind, and other forms of evil (and sin, the theologian would add), methods of explanation seem particularly warranted. True, the word "explanation" carries a heavy rationalistic mortgage from which it must be severed, but fear of the word must not blind us to the need for disciplined argumentation.[15]

Contemporary theologians will surely see a number of features here that are quite congenial. The conversation model seems to be a return back to an "older" style of education/learning. One develops one's skills in an experiential manner. One learns from masters more "formed" than oneself, in a kind of "midwifery" or "apprenticeship," not unlike spiritual direction and other master-disciple relationships. One develops a great respect for the wisdom of the past, yet without lapsing into mere archaism. Here learning is collegial and "magisterial" in some sense. One develops a genuine relationship with a community of scholars. And a theologian would want to add: with the community of the church and its "formed" ones, the distinguished scholars, the saints and mystics, and surely the official magisterium. Knowledge here is mediated. This approach also makes room, I think, for the principle of authority and the response of obedience corresponding to it: recognizing those most "formed" as well as "submitting" to the maximal experiences of differentiation and their guardians.[16]

A fifth feature of the conversation, particularly noted by Friedländer, Gadamer, and Voegelin, is its "in-between" character. This deserves a certain amount of attention, because from this "in-between" feature of the dialogue a number of important consequences flow. Conversation in all its forms takes place in the space "in-between": our present as an intersection between the past remembered and the future to be expected, the tension-filled space of our knowing and not knowing, the space between the many "voices" playing within and outside oneself. This surely means that the kind of knowledge conversation yields is "participationist": "There is no vantage point outside existence from which its meaning can be viewed," says Voegelin. We can find "reality" knowable "only from the perspective of participation in it."[17]

This has led Voegelin, among many others, to argue that the model of truth most appropriate to the "truth" emerging from the dialogical experience of participation is not that based on the perception of objects — a kind of "objectifying" view of truth, corresponding to a consciousness intending objects — but rather a model of "luminosity." Within our participatory experience, dimensions of experience become luminous, focused, somewhat more differentiated. "The problem of reality experienced...becomes the problem of a flow of participatory reality in which reality becomes luminous to itself in the case of human consciousness."[18] Tracy refers to a "manifestation" model of truth, not entirely unlike Heidegger's own model. Back of all these, I think, is Plato's notion of "existential truth," the truth emerging from the person committed to and participating in the drama of existence.[19]

Just "how" reality becomes luminous to itself seems a very complex question, and there is room for the putting forth of ample candidates of explanation. I personally find Voegelin's impressive philosophy of experience-consciousness-symbolism-imagination-order adequately subtle and able to grapple at least basically with the problems raised, but others will be able to bring forth their own candidates of explanation. Human experience and consciousness, in and through imagination and language/symbolism, is reality in the process of becoming luminous. This luminosity brings clarity to human society itself and determines the kinds of "order" humans are able to achieve. Luminosity, clearly, covers a wide range, from compactness to differentiation, with all sorts of shades between, including serious failures to be sufficiently attuned to regions of experience and even "ideological repressions" of regions of experience. I mention Voegelin's view here only as one possible candidate. Clearly any full treatment of the theme of conversation has to move to the issue of the human consciousness(es) involved in such conversation, and helping to keep it flowing.[20]

From a theological perspective, the luminosity model of truth deserves highlighting at this point. It is a model that is most congenial to a belief in divine revelation, if we are to avoid reducing the Divine to an object among other objects within our finite world. Christian revelation, rather, might be viewed, in Jesus the Christ, as a freely bestowed and so gracious illumination occurring through experience, consciousness, and language. That is, through the "converse" with Jesus the Christ mediated through scripture and scripturally based tradition, the Divine Self becomes luminous for us. In this way, the conversation model helps us avoid "objectifying" or "thingifying" divine revelation (which does not mean to deny revelation's "reality").

This in-between, participationist mode of knowing and truth characteristic of the dialogue of existence also helps us weave a path between the extremes of "rationalistic universalism" on the one hand and relativism on the other. The first claims a special vantage point, a "foundation" outside the flow of the conversation, from which one can evaluate and judge the objects of thought. Hence its name of "foundationalism" in some circles. The latter capitulates to an inability to formulate any critical standards of truth, of adequacy to reality. Both seem based upon a model of truth as an "object" one can "intend" from a special vantage point. This is a thingifying approach to truth, more characteristic of a sense model of truth. Foundationalists believe such a view of truth is correct; relativists seem to presuppose it theoretically, but know that in fact it's not able to be achieved. The approach of the participationist-luminosity model is to question the starting point, and argue for the greater adequacy of the participationist approach.[21]

Theologians will perhaps note that this participationist model is also much more congenial to the role of "faith" in human knowing. This need not mean that participation in the dialogue of humanity demands "fully explicit" Christian faith. There is surely a wide range in which "faith" is differentiated, ranging from a fiducial trust in the potential meaningfulness of life's conversation on to the more elaborate articulations of faith positions of the varied religions. The point I want to underscore here is that the kind of committed and obedient posture characteristic of faith is precisely the kind of participation in reality that the conversational model of theology calls for.

Furthermore, as a result of this renewed appreciation for the "in-between, participatory" nature of the conversation, a certain hermeneutical priority ought to go, I think, to those experiences and "written texts" that manifest relatively more of the participatory drama of human and Christian existence in its action, meaning, and truth dimensions. In reference to written texts, the tendency to accord a priority to narrative, myth, poetry, dialogue, the drama, and other "originary" forms/genres of revelation, rather than the more abstract theological treatise, seems a sound one. At best the latter can highlight and clarify what is more compactly expressed in the former; it can never replace or fully paraphrase it. Ricoeur's attentiveness to the more originary genres of speech, such as myth, metaphor, and narrative, is a good example in the area of philosophy. Tracy's attentiveness to the same is a good example in theology. Voegelin's working with the "originating experiences of differentiation and symbolization" is another case in point. Think, too, of Balthasar's *Theo-Drama*, or of Barth's use of narrative, and of Karl Rahner's sensitivity to poetry and primal language. In Christology, the tendency to begin with and return to scripture seems sound in this respect. Theological treatises and magisterial doctrines have an essential but subordinate role to scripture in this regard. The sensitivity to the participatory, of which we are speaking, ought to reawaken the role of action (practice), service (mission), prayer, contemplation, the witness of the saints and mystics, liturgy, art, etc., in theology as well.[22] Contemplation, to which we will come more fully in a moment, is surely in some deep sense a "conversation" expressing much of the participatory drama of Christian existence deserving much more *theological* attention from the theologian. It is but representative of many other "forms" of that drama.

The current interest in narrative, within literary studies, philosophy, in the debate between modernity and postmodernity (the latter claiming a retrieval of narrative), and in theology particularly, seems to be a significant example of this attentiveness to the more originary forms/genres of language. Given the heavy use of narrative in the gospels, but throughout the scriptures and among the Christian founding figures, it is perhaps not surprising that narrative studies have become a focus for a renewed appreciation of the originary, participative, and language-bound and culture-bound nature of revelation. In a general sense, in fact, the word "narrative" could simply function as an abbreviated way of speaking of this participative, language-bound nature of experience. "Narrative-like," however, might be a better term for that, so that we might generally reserve the word "narrative" for more developed forms of story.

For our purposes here, we don't have to decide the many complex debates going on within narrative studies, nor are we competent to do so. In general I think the theologian convinced of our conversational model and its linking with the in-between and participative nature of existence cannot afford to ignore those narrative studies. At the very least narrative brings home the inseparability of form and content, the need to participate in the form to "experience" the content/ meaning. The lived, dramatic quality of life (what Voegelin calls the "event" dimension of story), with its "divine-human movements and countermovements," its elements of living activity, tension, struggle, reversal, etc., finds its irreplaceable expression in narrative. But this

29

event dimension of every story involves an attempt to convey "insights into the order of reality" (and Voegelin refers to this as the "narrative" dimension of story). "The story is the symbolic form the questioner has to adopt necessarily when he gives an account of his quest as the event of wresting, by the response of his human search to a divine movement, the truth of reality from a reality pregnant with truth yet unrevealed."[23]

The narrative conveys meaning in and through the drama of events, the actual unfolding of the events as they seem to come "to a point," or find some connectedness, if we follow Burrell and Hauerwas here.[24] Such, of course, is commonly called the "plot," and much current work focuses upon the many ways in which a plot can unfold, through character description, point of view emphasized in the story, settings, the important modes of expressing temporality, etc. Plots unfold commonly more temporally, historically, and existentially, rather than simply syllogistically. There are moments of syllogistic arguing within the plot, as there are moments of such "imposed order" in the lived drama of our lives, but they are moments within a larger drama transcending syllogistic and fully systematic logic. The drama never seems able to be reduced totally to words, and we will see that this is especially important for religious and Christian narratives. For divine meaning exceeds human form, surely.[25]

Conversation, we said, roots us back in this living, practical, narrative drama of human existence and indicates that we cannot really get away from it, nor should we want to do so. In a certain sense, conversation itself can be seen as a narrative, or at least as narrative-like, inasmuch as through its unfolding and tension and reversals, etc., insight and meaning emerge. The intrinsically historical and temporal nature of human existence is clearly expressed in the conversation, as well as its participatory and dramatic nature.[26] From our specific angle of interest, too, we might suggest that prayer and contemplation are surely forms of narrative in this sense, or at least narrative-like. To engage in them is to "participate" in the "originary" drama of divine revelation itself.

Perhaps the above features of this conversation/dialogue and language//narrative model will suffice, for now, as a sufficient legitimation for a theologian's attraction to it. The above is somewhat "rough," and the reader unacquainted with the literature may not know how to assess the relative merits of all the points indicated. A beginning in understanding can come from falling back upon a lived conversational and narrative skill, and testing the theoretical model against it. Model and skill should grow together in depth. I think all the points interlock, and one can enter into the issue from almost any of those entry points.

One issue that does remain "very rough" in the discussion is that of determining how we know we're really getting anywhere in our conversations, whether with ourselves (in our dialogical monologues[27]), with others in the face-to-face dialogue, or with texts. Or, should we express this same concern in narrative terms, how can we discriminate between differing narratives and plots? Are all stories equally crafted and of equal human and spiritual worth? Gadamer and Voegelin are hesitant to draw up concrete criteria, validly so, to be sure, for there are no magic recipes in this region. Openness to the subject matter is a result of much character formation and constant attunement to the subject matter, experience, and experience's ongoing refinement.

Still, the issue of developing some workable criteria that can aid us in distinguishing authentic from inauthentic "conversation" is important, particularly in times of intense pluralism, as our own. Plato, it seems, was faced with something similar in his own time, and his theory of "anamnesis" is a rough way of trying to be more self-consciously critical of what we do in our noetic inquiry. The discovery of truth is something like a "remembering," a "re-cognition," in the sense that it seems to be like the rendering articulate of what is the deepest but up to now "forgotten" meaning of our human existence. Thus, likewise, an appeal to a luminosity model of truth is like appealing to that kind of anamnesis: we "recognize" in the conversation, language, and narrative genuine possibilities of human (and Christian) meaning, truth, and self-realization or action. I mention this here, because there seems to be a broad agreement among thinkers in the hermeneutical tradition appealed to here that the basic criteria of the conversation must be "luminosity" and "recognition" in the sense that we have used these terms.

These criteria are rather "rough," I know. But that seems appropriate in these regions of the human spirit in which the mystery of existence is becoming luminous. They leave room for any number of other criteria to come forward and, through the dialogical art of strengthening, to suggest the merits of their case. Voegelin's philosophy of experience, consciousness, and symbolization is very helpful to many of us in this area, helping us to discern genuine differentiations from regressions of consciousness and illuminating symbols from the perverted use of the same. In fact, it is based on Voegelin's own profound retrieval of Plato's anamnesis symbol, which he interprets as a self-reflective working out by a kind of "reflective distance" within the "in-between" of existence, of what seems involved in the experience of luminosity and its opposite, "forgetting" the deepest truth of existence.[28]

Contemplation

Let me now pass from these general observations on the conversation model and narrative to some more specifically religious and especially "Christian" observations. If we return for a moment to our word "christology," the observations we've pursued above were chiefly concerned with the "logos" dimension in "christology." Because christology claims to be some legitimate form of "logos," I am suggesting that it be seen, at its best, as a form of conversation or dialogue, possessing a narrative or narrative-like character, between the theologian-christological inquirer and the christological heritage. It is a "communication," a "discourse," a "dialogue" (*logos*) in a real sense. And one could argue that the very existence of Christian theology as a truly noetic "science" has been greatly facilitated by the fusion between Greek philosophy's exploration of "logos" and Christian revelation.[29]

The observations to follow will be chiefly concerned with the *"christos"* dimension in the word "christology." As a form of would-be conversation, christology is truly a dialogue. But it's not just any kind of dialogue, but one about the "subject matter" of Christian revelation, especially that of the full reality of Jesus Christ. As such, there is a revelatory dimension to this conversation that needs a bit more surfacing.

First, chiefly using the "hindsight" of Christian revelation and history, we can say that there is a "dim" but real religious dimension to the experience of dialogue/conversation. It is dim, because it is not always explicitly the focus of attention, but also because it is the "hidden" ground and foundation of the entire conversation itself, in all its phases. As the ground or "environment," it is like the "space" within which the conversation occurs. Thus, it's not an object which we can notice "here" rather than "there." Using the word "space" is rather dangerous, too, for it can tend toward "thingifying" the divine ground of the dialogue. Thus, it is meant metaphorically, surely. This religious ground of the dialogue is the "attractive pull" of the horizon of Mystery that sets in motion and supports the questioning unrest giving rise to the dialogue of humanity. The erotic tension between ignorance and knowledge arises from this divine ground. From the human side, the dialogue is a "questioning in confusion." From the divine side, it is an "attraction" catalyzing the "desire to know." Voegelin puts it nicely: Humanity's dialogue is one in which "God is the partner."[30]

Noting this divine, transcendental dimension of the human dialogue and narrative is particularly important, since it enables us to grasp, at least somewhat, why it is that past and present, humans of then and now, and different humans of quite differing perspectives even now — why all of these can achieve Gadamer's "fusion of horizons" in the conversation. If you will, our common "participation" in the divine ground is the ultimate enabling factor for the conversation of the ages. Voegelin, I think, has put this powerfully, if I might yet again return to him:

> the dialogue of the soul is not locked up as an event in one person who, after it has happened, informs the rest of mankind of its results as a new doctrine. Though the dialogue occurs in one man's soul, it is not "one man's idea about reality," but an event in the Metaxy [in-between] where man has "converse" with the divine ground of the process that is common to all.... Because of the divine presence in the dialogue..., the event has a social and historical dimension. The Socratic soul draws into its dialogue the companions and, beyond the immediate companions, all those who are eager to have these dialogues reported to them. The *Symposion* presents itself as the report of a report over intervals of years; and the reporting continues to this day.[31]

If we pursue this line of inquiry, building now self-consciously from an inner Christian perspective, I would suggest that human conversation at least dimly intimates that it possesses a "christological-trinitarian" structure. And it is this "structure" that has become more focused and recognized in the Christian tradition, under the impact of the Incarnation, and as a result of divine freedom and grace, which Christian revelation always is. If you will, the divine ground making possible human conversation, language, and narrative is itself a conversational reality, a dialogue, a language and narrative, if we follow the clues given us in Christian revelation. The divine ground (Father/Mother) is not mute, but a self-communicative reality (*Logos*/Word), not hoarding its self-communication, but intrinsically a participative, inclusivistic reality (Spirit). The "one" God of Christianity seems to be a "Subject" of and through "interpersonal relations." If we express this in the more traditional terms of love, coming down partly from at least one strand of Augustine and Richard of St. Victor, as well as from the Eastern theologians, we might say that the reality of the "Spirit" points to the fact that the dialogue between Father and Son is not locked up in itself, a kind of exclusive club. Rather is it inclusive: sharable love. The Father's and Son's "bond" (the Spirit) is our "bond" with them. The Spirit — the "Third" — points to the non-selfish nature of the Divine. Which is why we, too, can participate in the "great dialogue." This seems to be why we are attracted to this "great trinitarian narrative" too. As Dumitru Staniloae exactly puts it: "Only when there is a Third does the love of the Two become generous and capable of extending and diffusing itself."[32]

33

Clearly I wouldn't expect everyone to find this convincing. But in a book on christology this may have a particular force. For those of us working from the Christian tradition, and out of a deep faith experience in the Incarnation (inclusively understood), this approach may prove illuminating both to trinitarian-christological studies on the one hand, and to the meaning of conversation, language, and narrative on the other. Human conversation reflects, in some sense, the divine conversation; human narrative, the trinitarian narrative. And we Christians have "discovered" this fundamentally and first, in a clear way through the Incarnation: in Jesus' conversation with us. We have found ourselves "sharing" in the Word Incarnate, a Word bringing us into the Divine Mystery Itself. This "triple" experience expresses in our historical experience the trinitarian mystery: sharing (Spirit) with Jesus (Word) in the Divine Mystery (Father).

We can think, for example, of the synoptics, which present Jesus as the teller of God's stories (parables), the willing dialogue partner who speaks and listens, who invites all into the dialogue of the Father (Mt 5:43–48), although Jesus must go through his own struggles and trials to keep the dialogue flowing (Mt 4:1–11) and to remain open to the story his Father wants to tell. Mark seems to surface the suffering love this holy story demands, the tragic element involved. Matthew seems to show particularly well how this story of Jesus builds a new kind of community, the church, whose words are "wisdom" from God's own wisdom. Luke/Acts presents this story told by Jesus as one in the telling from humanity's beginning but reaching its crescendo with Jesus (Luke), and now unfolding throughout the human world itself (Acts). John and the Johannine tradition link the story of Jesus and church with the trinitarian story itself: God's own *Logos* is in the telling here, in the unique Son, and we are being guided into it through the Spirit/Paraclete. The letters of the New Testament, especially Paul's, call to mind the new "I-thou" relationship happening for us through Jesus with God. We are personally addressed now in a uniquely new and personal way by a newly personalized God.

But John reminds us of something very important: "There are also many other things that Jesus did, but if these were to be described individually, I do not think the whole world could contain the books that would be written" (21:25). No form seems able to "contain" Jesus the Word. The Word occurs in and through and with the words of our existence, but it exceeds them too. This "excess" is crucial, maintaining the tension between divine and human, eternal and temporal, God and humanity, but not collapsing one into the other. Mark, too, ends on a note of "bewilderment" (16:8), perhaps indicating what this divine "excess" does to the likes of us. Luke has Jesus depart in the ascension, and as a result our human words turn into doxology (24:52), and doxology, we recall, populates the New Testament letters as well. Doxology is jubilant stammering caused by divine excess. And Matthew, too, ends with this tension between divine authority, human homage, and even an element of questioning (28:17–20).[33]

Insights like these occasionally surface in the tradition in a rather explicit manner. I am myself rather fond, in this regard, of the prayers for "before and during conversation," given us by Jean-Jacques Olier. M. Olier clearly views all human conversation as a participation in the conversation that is the Trinity. "I adore," he prays, "the communication of spirit and openness of heart that the three divine persons have with one another, mutually clarifying everything and sharing all their secrets." And he points to Jesus as the source of this insight: "I adore the conversation of Jesus Christ Our Lord with his disciples," a conversation about the Word that Jesus is just as Jesus is the fruit of the Father's desire to converse. And he ends with an insight that clarifies the sameness yet difference between the trinitarian conversation and our own:

> My God, my All, who, conversing in heaven with your Son and your saints, dilate yourself in them without losing anything of yourself, remaining complete in yourself, bring it about that when I share you with others I will not lose anything, and that I will not dry myself up in nourishing my brothers.[34]

Father Olier's prayer that we not "dry up" in our conversations points to the great difference between the trinitarian conversation, and its closest approximation in the saints, on the one hand, and our own rather more ordinary "conversations" on the other. The saints "approach" the infinite richness of the trinitarian dialogue, but even their approach retains the finitude characteristic of the human. While our own more ordinary conversations, and our language in general, suffer not only from our finitude, but also from our sinfulness.

Inspired chiefly by these more explicit religious and Christian considerations, but not only by them, I would suggest now that we highlight rather more the "meditative-contemplative" component in conversation, language, and narrative. Here I am inspired by Voegelin's suggestion that we take "precautions of meditative practice," in these regions of the dialogue of humanity.[35] The use of the terms "meditative" and "contemplative" is meant broadly. The spiritual tradition uses these terms somewhat inconsistently, sometimes assigning a more analytic nature to meditation, and, sometimes, a more transanalytic and intuitive nature to contemplation. But both are used interchangeably too, and it is that use with which I will align myself here. Drawing upon these terms is meant to sensitize us to the divine, trinitarian ground of conversation and language, which can only be approached in a posture of prayerful-mystical receptivity, obedience, and attunement in faith, hope, and love. One does not "seize" or "capture" the divine ground: it must be gift in some true sense. If the divine conversation is the transcending of all egocentric exclusivity, so, too, our participation in that conversation is a kenosis, a movement beyond the self-centered ego, a surrender into Mystery and a loving refusal to violate the Divine Person's freedom to address us.

Meditation also sensitizes us to the participatory and, indeed, loving nature of Christian, theological conversation and language. It is not the cool and detached observer, but the loving participator who "meditates" and "contemplates." Both the words "meditation" and "contemplation" at their origins seem to indicate this. "Meditation" was a form of "murmuring," "ruminating" (like the cooing of doves), and "interiorizing" (see Jos 1:8, Ps 1:2, Lk 2:19 and 51, 1 Tm 4:15; cf. Lev 11:3). We might say, today, that it is an intensive form of "presence." "Contemplation," likewise, seems derived from the notion of the "temple" in which one attentively looked for clues as to the will of the gods or as to meaningful signs. The Greek word *theoria*, used for contemplation, also seems derived from *thea* ("vision"), indicating an experience of luminosity and the attentive absorption that brings.[36]

Because meditation brings out the participatory nature of Christian conversation, it is, as Voegelin indicates, a kind of "protective device" by which we remind ourselves that conversation takes place in the "in-between." The "knowledge" meditation yields us is "not given in the manner of an object of the external world but is knowable only from the perspective of participation in it," as Voegelin said.[37] Thus, meditation and contemplation are traditions that help us avoid thingifying (or hypostatizing) the insights that are really rather experiences of luminosity within the conversational encounter.

One can also speak of meditation as a form of "personal" knowing. Here again, it is not the model of truth characteristic of sense experience that is operative, but rather a more humane and moral model, which we have been calling "luminosity" or "manifestation." All conversation is such, of course, but a sensitivity to the divine, personal God intensifies this personal dimension of the conversation. Such personal, participatory knowing involves the entire range of personal preconditions: trust, faith, obedience, attunement, freedom, openness, etc. This is what John Macquarrie has in mind when he says that "the kind of thinking which is required in theology has as its heart an act of meditation."[38]

For the Christian, stressing the participatory and personal makeup of the knowing in dialogue and language helps us appreciate somewhat more fully the properly "christological" dimension or moment in our theological efforts too. Oftentimes I have discovered that the use of the terms "meditation" and "contemplation" stresses, in the minds of some, the "ineffable" and "mysterious" nature of the Divine Mystery. Here the role of Jesus in our Christian conversation seems to become problematic: Does he not make too effable what is ineffable, and should we not transcend him in our movement toward the Divine? It is surely true that the divine ground is Mystery in the strict sense and so also ineffable. And one of the blessings of meditation is its adoring recognition of this reality: its sense of not being able to manipulate the Divine, or thingify it and thereby control it. At the same time, the Divine Self has become profoundly personalized for us in Jesus, the ineffable has become personally effable. This is why we experience a strong tug to share in the great trinitarian conversation: it has invited us in Jesus most especially. Meditation need not mean a bypassing of Jesus into a nameless "mystery," but the mode of personal, participative knowing that comes from a God becoming "personal" for us above all in Jesus. Meditation helps us recognize and stay with the Mystery on the one hand, and the Mystery's becoming personally available for us in Jesus on the other.

There is a back and forth movement between silence and saying, the mystical "unknowing" and partial knowing — the traditional apophatic and kataphatic ways — that seems to make up the basic dynamic of the meditative dialogue. But this is not a movement in which God can be separated from Jesus, for God always remains the God of Jesus Christ.[39] Rather does it seem to be a movement between a Personal God who is both Unknowable Mystery and Knowable Self-Communication. There is the silence, which comes from waiting receptively for the disclosure of a personal Mystery who cannot be forced or controlled. There is also the "no-saying" to our desires to "grasp" the ungraspable, the purification of our knowing and speaking. Something of the "crucifixion" is shared in here. And much of this, analogously, holds true for our conversations with our human partners too? Are there not the moments of silence in our human conversations, either with living partners or with great texts? The waiting, the non-forcing, the purifying of the ego? But there is also the speaking, the affirming, the learning, the moments of disclosure and luminosity. And the latter must trail off into the former. The ineffable must be somewhat effable if we are to know even its ineffability. But still the unknowability, the Mystery of the Divine Self, remains the greater. Hügel puts this well: "...the Clear depends even more upon the Dim, than the Dim upon the Clear."[40] And again, I would suggest that there are analogues of this "kataphatic" moment in our human conversations too.

I would hold, now, that there is a "primacy" to the meditative-contemplative dimension within the conversation phenomenon. This primacy seems indicated by the very nature of the divine, christic-trinitarian conversation as the matrix and ground of our own human and theological conversation. It is difficult to accord a "parity" between the Divine Self and anything or anyone else. A "mutuality," yes, surely, especially when we believe that the Divine is truly personal; but a "parity," no. Recognizing the primacy of the Divine is what finally demands and even grounds the meditative-contemplative nature of all genuine dialogue. In this sense, this approach accords the primacy to the "objective" element in revelation. In a later chapter I will propose the adoration experience as an especially eminent — in fact, the most intensive — way in which this comes about.

As ground, the trinitarian conversation creates and grants the tug within us toward dialogue, the yearning for and dissatisfaction with any conversation "cut short," broken down, inadequate, unenriching (in M. Olier's words, a conversation that "dries us up" or "exhausts" us), and so on. From a Christian perspective, the dialogue of the Trinity graces us with the ability to transcend the failures, through sin or otherwise, in our dialogues, the ability not to manipulate the partner or the subject matter, as we participate in the "non-manipulable" Other who is God. It also gives us the courage to move ahead in the conversation, even when we are afraid of where it might lead and what it might reveal. For there is a faith that the Spirit whose reality is "invitation to dialogue" is leading us to the to-and-fro exchange of Father and Son.

Dialogue and language in general, then, are at their maximal best when they are contemplative. The sections covered in this chapter need to remain together. It would be an interesting thought experiment to cast a glance back throughout this chapter and ponder what happens when the interrelation between the various aspects — dialogue, language, narrative, and contemplation — gets askew. Would the elements of dialogue, language, and narrative, sketched in the first portion of this chapter, suffer from the absence or underrecognition of the meditative element? I think they would.

Meditative openness to the non-manipulable "More," the transcendental experience grounding dialogue and language at their depths, insures a genuine commitment to the freedom needed for truth and action for which the dialogue is the "symbolic form" or genre of expression. Without faith in the More, the freedom that exists would be only partial and easily liable to the limits we all too quickly want to impose upon it. The self-interpretive nature of human experience, the eros of the tension between knowing and unknowing, arbitrarily imposes a limit upon itself without the meditative experience of transcendence. Furthermore, the environment or ground of the continuity or the flow of tradition (which humanity's dialogue throughout the ages is) is "removed" without the More. Thus our links with other partners to the dialogue, except perhaps those we "choose" to converse with, is broken. And the dialogue becomes a sectarian monologue or discourse in the disguise of a dialogue. The in-between, participative nature of the dialogue, the fact that we know only from the perspective of our participation within the drama of humanity's dialogue, would also suffer. For the ground of our participation, what links us and even more invites us into sharing, is denied.

Here we can perhaps "see" how *logos*, discourse, dialogue dries up and hardens into harangue and monologue the more it is severed from its meditative origins and center.[41] But it's also true, as we've indicated already in an earlier chapter, that attentiveness to the meditative "center" brings with it its own particular strains. The transcendent More, by its very primacy, exercises a profound "pull" upon us. The deepest orientation of our being is toward it. And so it is fascinating and adoration-inspiring at once. From our side — not from that of the Divine Self — what is an appropriate pull and tug, and even "primary" interest, can become an "unbalanced" absorption, Teresa of Avila's *abobamiento* ("boobishness") rather than *arrobamiento* ("ecstasy"), as we've seen earlier. Either a quietistic passivity or a "messianic" self-inflation can be the result. Authentic openness to the More should lead into *logos*, genuine conversation, the open space of mutual enrichment and critique, a willingness to undergo the "art of strengthening" of the dialogue that "imitates" the unbiased dialogue of Jesus and the Trinity itself. It *should* lead in this direction. But at times we derail. For we are sinful and biased, are we not? And we fail to take the "meditative precautions" of which Voegelin speaks. We fail to attune ourselves to the "actual pull" of the More, and attune ourselves to a lesser tune in ourselves that we camouflage as the "More."[42]

The remainder of this book will be an attempt to engage in this kind of meditative dialogue, with a theological and, particularly here, christological slant. If these observations are even somewhat correct, then there is surely in christological conversation a particular fit between content and method, although I would want to argue that every conversation at least "dimly" intimates the christological and trinitarian foundations sketched above. Now, before bringing this chapter to a halt, let me briefly indicate some implications for the study of christology today. Some of these have already been touched upon; others, at least implied. But it will be helpful to speak on them more concentratedly here before moving on.

I am suggesting that all theology, and in this book christology particularly, shares in the features of meditative dialogue and language sketched above. Of course, not all theology has "conversed" equally well at all times, but at least we had a "potential conversation" in those cases. Perhaps the most important lesson to be drawn from the above observations is that we must struggle to keep meditation and dialogue (and language in general) together, so that we can speak of a "meditative dialogue" or "conversation" as the approach proper to theology. Dialogue tends to break down into manipulative discourse and harangue, I think, the more its meditative dimensions are "pushed" from center. Or we might express this somewhat differently. To the degree that dialogue maintains its meditative axis, Mystery and disclosure, unknowing and knowing, symbol and luminosity, form and content, "understanding" and "explanation," faith and reason, stay together too. But sever or rupture them, and both sides of these pairs suffer. And I would suggest that the pressures have been rather enormous in the modern West to do the rupturing.

A further lesson is that contemporary christology should not hesitate to "own" the trinitarian-christological nature of its own hermeneutics. Here most emphatically in christology the general "trinitarian horizon" of human conversation operates as a hermeneutical guide. The faith experience in the loving, personal God revealed as Jesus opens us out to and invites us into the inner dialogue of the Trinity. It is difficult to see how theologians can do justice to christology if they ignore the "center" of the Incarnational Mystery as one grounded in the trinitarian dialogue itself. If you will, the Incarnation is the "definitive" analogy in history of the Trinity. The Mystery is personalized Word that is sharable and sharing (or Spirit), and because of this the Incarnation has happened. A christology that tries to operate without this faith experience will forever stay on the level of the relatively superficial or surface, finding it impossible to stay attuned to Jesus' divine-human duality in unity through which the unique Son of God becomes word for us in history.

Working more self-consciously within the "horizon" of the Trinity, we can begin to see why various "forms" of christology seem to recur again and again. It is as if they are expressions of the varied dimensions of the trinitarian Mystery underlying the Incarnation event. "Father-christologies," which stress Jesus' obedience to the Father, or his role as the Father's emissary and representative, give expression to the mysterious divine ground that "sends" Jesus to us. "Son-christologies," which feature Jesus as the intimate and unique offspring of the Father, give expression to the divine ground's "personal nature," as a mysterious source that wants to be in dialogue and intimacy. They help us understand, then, the traditional view

---

40

that only the Logos becomes incarnate. "Spirit-christologies," which stress Jesus' sanctifying and redemptive role in history and his saving work on behalf of the kingdom, give expression to the "unselfish, inclusivistic" being of the Father-Son as a dialogue open to all. The Spirit penetrates us completely (Rm 8:16), so that the transcendent becomes immanent, the God "outside" of us becomes "inside."

Father-christologies tend to become non-trinitarian monotheisms and low christologies without the "balance" of Son-christologies. They also tend in the direction of deism and christologies that view Jesus as only a kind of model to be imitated without the Spirit-christologies. Son-christologies tend toward a "Jesus-monism" or fetishism, without the balance of the Father-christologies, which bring out the universality of the divine ground. Without a Spirit-christology, Son-christologies tend to render our own participation in Jesus impossible; he becomes so singular that he is removed from sharing in the human condition. Spirit-christologies, as we can guess, can tend to collapse christology into salvation. They stress our own participation in God, but sometimes at the expense of the uniqueness of Jesus as the disclosure of God's own uniquely personal presence for us. Actually extreme Spirit-christologies seem to de-personalize God, and so to depersonalize the rest of us. The lesson, meditatively to remain open to the full trinitarian reality in our christological work, seems clear enough. Of course, all that we have said presupposes the unity of the trinitarian "persons," who can be said to constitute, I suggested, an "interpersonal Subject." Each of the "hypostases" ("persons") works together, in all activities and missions. But what we have been stressing is that these hypostases work together in a manner appropriate to each.[43]

A third lesson arising from a conversational and narrative style in christology is the crucial role of the historical, traditional community. The conversational/narrative style arises from the many voices we listen to, of past and present, and gladly recognizes the formative influence of these voices.[44] The "prejudices" of our tradition — the great, flowing dialogue of humanity — are hermeneutical guides enabling us to understand and critique our own, "inner" conversations, and enabling us to participate in that larger dialogue in which we stand. In christology we recognize that "special" dialogue of God with human partners that has broken out with special clarity in the Jewish and Christian traditions. It is as if the dialogical experience etched into our being, at least as possibility, has guided us to a "recognition" of this dialogue leaving its foundational traces in the Hebrew and Christian scriptures. This also means that we appreciate the hermeneutical role of the Christian community, and its leadership (true community includes both diversity and unity, or collegiality and centralism [a "Petrine"/"papal" dimension], mirroring the Trinity's diversity in unity), together with the "privileged" or "eminent"[45] monuments of its tradition. Where does one learn something of that decentering and kenotic love of the God of Jesus if not in the experience of the ecclesial community, which calls us outside ourselves for one another, including the "one anothers" we choose not to recognize? A christology that borders on the idiosyncratic, and that acts as if one can ignore the ecclesial community and its eminent monuments, fails, *ipso facto*, to keep itself attuned to the kind of dialogical experience and formation necessary for christological study.

Fourthly, conversational christology will also grant something of a "hermeneutical eminence" to the more "originary" manifestations of the "great dialogue" of history, especially christology's own special history. By "originary," I mean experiences and genres that preserve more of the participative, dramatic, practical, "in-between," and "personal" nature of the conversational phenomenon. Or, to echo Voegelin, I mean experiences in which more of the "eros" and fuller drama of the dialogue surfaces. We return here, too, to the theme of narrative and the narrative-like. This does not denigrate the "doctrinal" genre, which surely has its guidance role in the Christian community of intensifying and protecting aspects of the fuller revelation reality. But it reminds us that doctrine cannot substitute for the fuller reality, and only makes sense when set against the fuller reality.

In the light of this, contemporary christology seems correct to begin with, stay with, and always return to the scriptures, especially the New Testament, as the fundamental, fuller source with which all later christology must be in faithful continuity. The narrative, epistolary, symbolic-metaphoric nature of the scriptures are the foundational way in which the participatory nature of the Incarnation continues to be "remembered" ("anamnetically") in history. We have to participate in the form/genre, if you will, to encounter the Mystery. These observations complement, from a hermeneutical perspective, the "theological" normativity of the scriptures.[46] Here I would strongly recommend that the writings of the *patres* (and the *matres*, sadly less abundant) be accorded an eminent status in christology too. For surely in their writings the drama of the irruption of luminosity, found in the Incarnation, surfaces, especially in the great conciliar debates (the basic contours of the Incarnation are still "settling" into place), and they nicely preserve the meditative dimension of the theological conversation. For them theology comes from spirituality, and even profound "mystical" experience, and always remains in its service. Their relative closeness to the scriptural period preserves much of the newness and "irrupting" character of the Incarnation too, which is irreplaceable for later ages.

Here I have in mind Yves Congar's understanding of the category of the "Fathers" (to which I think we should add that of the "Mothers," despite the difficulty of lack of *written* monuments) as a "dogmatic" and not simply "historical" notion. In them the church recognizes something unique and irreplaceable for her existence, against which all later "developments" can be tested. If you will, they do not exactly "birth" the church, but they do develop the fundamental outlines of the basic christological and trinitarian positions. And they do this in a rather "originary" manner, through the struggles, tensions, and even battles of the early conciliar period, and through, most especially, their meditative dialogue on the biblical heritage. Let me cite Congar here: the age of the fathers (and mothers)

> belonged to the Church's youth; it was the period not of birth, nor of the very first years, but the time when there first come to light the themes and images, convictions and deep reactions, first orientations and experiences, and rejections, too, which define the bases of a character, and will continue to have an influence throughout the rest of life.[47]

As Congar also notes in the same place, we speak of the fathers (and now, mothers) in the plural, and this is not without its theological significance. It is not as isolated individuals (even though they are often eminently persons of unique genius), but as members in and for the church community that they realize their mission. From our conversational perspective, this means that they were people of "dialogue" — of letters back and forth, of treatises for the community, of conciliar meetings, of shared prayer — in which the dialogical character of Christian existence was maintained, acted upon, and "structured" for later ages. In this way, they call to mind and follow the lead of the scriptures as a canonical dialogue of many voices, not the thin monologue of one. The "councils" and liturgy/sacraments were an exemplary expression of the fundamentally dialogical nature of the Christian life, and perhaps we can better appreciate why heresy was so deadly for the fathers and mothers, for it meant the rupture of the dialogue. Does this dialogical dimension of Christianity help us to understand why the church's basic liturgical/sacramental, canonical, and doctrinal (christological and trinitarian) features emerged in the period under focus?[48]

Surely, too, the later Christian spirituals and mystics deserve an analogous eminence in christology. By definition these are the "eminent" Christian witnesses who have lived out and explored the depths of Christian experience and language. And their authority stems from that depth of experience and language. We find among them, then, a rich treasury of participative christology, which at times is conjoined to an extremely penetrating theological analysis. Thus their predilection for narratives/autobiographies (Teresa of Avila, Thérèse of Lisieux, Augustine, the Olier of the *Mémoires*, Newman's *Apologia* and lesser known *Loss and Gain*, John Wesley's *Journal*, Jonathan Edwards's narratives, etc.). And when they do pen more "scientific" works, these are a mixed genre, with a constant return to prayer (Bérulle, Bonaventure, Augustine, Teresa of Avila's *Interior Castle*, John of the Cross, Gregory Palamas, Luther and Calvin, etc.). In this regard we can perhaps also appreciate anew the nature of prayer, meditation, and especially liturgy as privileged sources of theology and christology.[49] Surely all of these are participative expressions of the dialogue-like form of Christian existence opening us out onto and into the dialogue with Jesus and the Trinity.

Finally, let me end with a comment on the "doxological" nature of christology and theology as a whole. It seems appropriate to end with this, for all theological assertions would seem to flow from the "primal" doxological experience of the Trinity in its overflow into revelation and Incarnation (again, inclusively understood), to stay with this experience, and to "return" to it on ever more profound levels. The "plenitude" and "abundance" of the trinitarian dialogue revealed to us by Jesus and "given" to us by his Spirit thrust us into adoration, praise, thanksgiving, mutual intercession, petition, and even sorrow for our refusal to believe in the magnitude of it all. The range of meanings of the Greek *doxa* spans this continuum from adoration to sorrow[50] and indicates the legitimate kinds of experience in which theological discourse is rooted. "Doxa" or "glory" — let this latter serve as a cipher for the range of meanings — embraces our dimensions of contemplation, conversation, narrative, and language. The divine glory thrusts us into wondering meditation as it guides us into deeper and deeper regions of attractive mystery. Yet that glory also illuminates and discloses to us features of the mystery that enable us truly to enter into theological dialogue and narrative-like speech. Here *contemplatio, conversatio,* and *narratio* stay together. Not unlike Jesus, whose own God-man unity is the glorious and, for Christians, definitive intersection between contemplative mystery and historical luminosity.[51] And it seems appropriate to end this chapter with the comment that doxology clearly leads us to eschatology. For the divine excess filling us with adoring wonder also gifts us with a longing for the jubilation promised us in eternity.

CHAPTER THREE

The Christologian and "Participating" in Jesus' Mysteries

Guided by the hermeneutical observations of the last chapter, I will explore what the christologian stands to gain (or lose, or both) by a greater attentiveness to an "older" approach to the realities of Jesus' work and message. If a "contemplative" posture is what we are claiming for it, then an approach to Jesus that is more heavily stamped by such a posture than many or most of the contemporary approaches to Christ ought to illustrate these claims. This chapter, let me repeat, wants to move somewhere between the positions of simply rejecting our rich, contemplative christological heritage in the interests of a supposedly "modern" and "critical" perspective, and simply taking up that contemplative heritage anew, as if we've learned absolutely nothing in our own day, as if the Holy Spirit abdicated from the "throne of the world" in these our times.

In order to give some control to this discussion, I will confine myself chiefly to the writings of Pierre Cardinal de Bérulle and some of his principal disciples. Hopefully the cardinal can serve as a representative example of the riches awaiting the christological scholar among the contemplative traditions of Christian spirituality and theology. Bérulle (1575–1629), the founder of the French Oratory, is widely regarded as the founder of the "French School of Spirituality," a school seeking to relink theology and spiritual experience into a "science of the saints." Bérulle's time was one of abstractness in learned theology, corruption in ecclesial structures, and spiritual exhaustion, on the one side, and varied reactions to these soul sicknesses on the other.[1] Besides my own personal, hopefully providential *attrait* to him, the cardinal recommends himself to me because he sought to return to the springs of contemplative experience, yet without surrendering his theological talents and his practical commitments for

45

ecclesial reform. Contemporary christologians may sense, as I surely do when I read him, something of the richness that comes from a renewal of the "wedding vows" between spiritual experience and good, solid theological inquiry.

Preliminaries

Bérulle's "science of the saints" is, as I've hinted, an attempt to relate "Christian enlightenment" (the "science" dimension) to "piety" (the dimension having to do with "sanctity" or the "saints"). Bérulle really aims for theological ("scientific") penetration of Jesus' mysteries, but it is the kind of penetration coming from and staying with the rich springs of Christian faith experience-consciousness, ecclesial and even mystical (meaning by this latter a much more profoundly transformative kind of faith experience).[2] And so he tells us in the "Second Discourse" of his great work *Discourse on the State and Grandeurs of Jesus:* "Let us try to enter with reverence and love into his [Jesus'] clarity, rather than enter by clarity into his love." "Clarity" here can represent the theological and scientific dimension; "reverence and love," the contemplative and mystical experience-consciousness. The cardinal does not want to slight either of these dimensions, but it is clear that reverence and love is the foundational experiential basis. "Of course we desire to receive from [Jesus] both of these qualities and impressions as we direct our stirrings and affections toward an object and a mystery that is one of love and clarity at the same time."[3]

Bérulle speaks of the "chain of love" comprising the "principal mysteries of the Christian religion" — namely, Trinity, Incarnation, and eucharist — and by extension of the various "mysteries" and "states" of the Incarnation, which are the emanation within history of the trinitarian life of intercommunication, and in which we participate through the sacramental and grace-giving life of the church. It is these "mysteries" and "states" of the Incarnation, the Trinity's "highest" and "final" revelation for the French School, which will occupy our attention here. In a rather striking phrase that he frequently returns to, at least by allusion, the cardinal thinks of the Incarnation and its mysteries as a kind of event in which "love triumphs over God himself," at least in the sense that God's rich, inner life of trinitarian love opens up through the Incarnation into an outer life of shared love too. It is also "the highest of all the orders" of God.[4]

As the reader proceeds, he or she will note the use of the terms "mysteries" and "states." The two terms seem often to be spoken or written with the "same breath" by the great writers and spirituals of the French School, and yet there is often a subtle nuance to be noted. The "mysteries" of Jesus are multifaceted, embracing a mixture of the passing and the permanent, the historical in the purely contingent sense, and the element of enduring value and power expressed in the historical, or the outer and the inner/interior. It is the latter of these pairs that the term "state" often seems to signify. Perhaps it will be well to cite a portion of Bérulle's famed "Work of Piety 77" in which he sketches some of these subtleties:

> We must ponder the perpetuity of these mysteries in a certain way: for they are over in certain of their circumstances and they endure and are present and lasting in a certain other way. Their execution has passed, but their power [*vertu*] remains, it never ceases, nor does the love with which they have been accomplished. The spirit, then, the state, the power, the merit of the mystery, is always present. The spirit of God, by which this mystery has been brought about, the interior state of the exterior mystery, the efficacity and the power making this mystery alive and operative within us...is always alive, actual and present to Jesus....This means that we must look at the deeds and mysteries of Jesus...as alive and present, and even eternal, from which we will receive a present and eternal fruit.[5]

Here we can note right away that the French School dwells upon the deeper dimension of human history, the "human" and "spiritual" dimension, which in a Christian perspective has an eternal dimension to it, inasmuch as what is going forward in Christian history somehow contributes to our eternal destiny and possesses its eternal validity in and through God. All of this, of course, evokes the Pauline sense of the "mystery" active in Christ that Ephesians 1 celebrates.

But there is more to it than that too. We even find in the French School a deep appreciation for the specialness, the uniqueness, of each Christian called to participate in Jesus' mysteries. It is as if the sensitivity to interiority, a sensitivity with roots in the personal God of the scriptures but also a sensitivity perhaps aided by the new sense of the person developing around the time of the Renaissance, promotes this appreciation for uniqueness. And so, besides our general call to participate in Jesus' mysteries, we find a unique one: "Jesus...wishes that we have a unique share in [his] various states, according to the diversity of his will for us and our piety toward him." In line with this, for example, Jean-Jacques Olier (1608–57) tells us in his *Mémoires* (Jan. 17, 1643) that "Our Lord showed that two persons had already worked to honor him in his mysteries, i.e., Monsignor de Bérulle who honored his Incarnation and Père de Condren his Resurrection, and that he wished me to honor him in his Blessed Sacrament."[6]

The "number" of the mysteries of Jesus still needs some commentary. Bérulle himself meditatively moves back and forth between the various mysteries of the Incarnation, leaving us with the impression that it is an inexhaustible treasury incapable of adequate measure-

47

ment. Hence the use of the symbolism "mysteries" of Jesus, rather than simply "events" or "deeds" of Jesus. Also, part of the charm and power of the many lyrical "Oh's" and "O's" appearing here and there in the Bérullian "elevations" comes from this always surprising and inexhaustible richness of the Incarnation. In practice, however, there are a number of central mysteries to which the cardinal returns in his writings. M. Olier spoke of six principal mysteries: Incarnation (in its narrower meaning of Jesus' conception and birth — at times it can be widely used as embracing the "entire" Jesus Christ event), crucifixion, death, burial, resurrection, and ascension (inclusive of Pentecost).[7] These are surely central for the cardinal, but perhaps we should add Mary and infancy, the desert, eucharist, Mary Magdalene as well, with a certain relative importance given to further mysteries, such as the presentation, transfiguration, St. Joseph, and so on. Here we note, by the way, how the incarnational christology of the French School is an "inclusive" incarnationalism, embracing the entire historical-spiritual reality of Jesus, earthly and risen.

Clearly we are going to have to settle upon some "practical" mode of entry into this "gigantically" rich tradition of contemplating Jesus' mysteries, if this chapter is not to become a book unto itself. My own proposal will be to do this primarily "intensively" or "qualitatively," with only secondary attention to ranging through the various contemplations and elevations of the French School on Jesus' mysteries. By this I mean looking at what seems to be something of the "heart" or "center" of the Bérullian contemplations, which is then reflected and amplified in the various other elevations. This might enable us to preserve some depth in our presentation, without a complete sacrificing of breadth of detail.

Approaching the Mysteries

"Participating" in Jesus' mysteries is just that, "participating." It is not a neutral kind of taking hold of an object in order to dissect or manipulate it. Rather one adheres to and participates within the mysteries of Jesus already, and within this participational experience there are moments of luminosity. This "participationist" knowledge — a kind of "existential knowing" — again evokes Paul: "Have among yourselves the same attitude that is also yours in Christ Jesus... " (Phil 2:5). Depth of spiritual and even mystical experience is the foundation and ever-present source of christological awareness. As we noted above, Bérulle counsels us to "try to enter with reverence and love into [Jesus'] clarity, rather than enter by clarity into his love." "Reverence" and "love" indicate two dimensions of the divine reality operative in one's experience: the truly transcendent and adorable

One (= reverence) has entered into our existence and invited us to share in its rich plenitude (= love as revealed in Jesus the incarnate one).

Here clarity or knowledge is not suppressed but clothed within a larger reality and experience of reverence and love, linked to them and in their service. If you will, "understanding" flows from an obedient faith, stays with that faith, and returns to it. Thus Bérulle uses terms like "contemplation" and "elevation" throughout his writings to indicate and underscore this loving and reverential mode of awareness, source and stimulant of our more "reflex" kind of thinking. An "elevation" is a "lifting up" — "Lift up your hearts!," says the priest at the Preface of the Mass — and thus a symbolism for an experience of transcendence into the adorable Mystery.

One of the better examples, perhaps even the best example, of how Bérulle would have us approach the mysteries is found at the beginning of the "Second Discourse in the Form of an Elevation to God upon the Mystery of the Incarnation" in the *Grandeurs*. I will ask the reader's patience and present much of it here in the recent and beautiful Glendon translation. As the reader will see, it embraces the "reverence/clarity" theme addressed above.

Those who contemplate a rare and excellent object are pleasantly surprised by the astonishment and admiration they experience at the first sight of that object, even before they recognize in detail the particularities of the subject they are contemplating. Furthermore, this astonishment, which appears to cause a weakness in the soul, gives it strength and vigor. For the soul draws strength from its weakness, elevating itself to a greater light and to a higher and more perfect knowledge. This same thing happens to us when we first behold and think of the excellence, the rarity and uniqueness of our Lord Jesus Christ and of the sacred mystery of the Incarnation. Because we are deeply and tenderly touched by the grandeur of this rare object ... we believe we should lift ourselves to God and praise him in this unique work of his, waiting until later to reflect more on the state and grandeurs of Jesus and to penetrate the secrets and the depth of this most exalted mystery.

Thus we are like one who emerges from a deep, dark cave, finds himself on a high mountain and beholds the sun for the first time. He sees this sun as a serene, beautiful day breaks over our hemisphere, decorating and embellishing the universe and enlivening it with its light and rays. Touched by the sight of such a beautiful object, no doubt he would be surprised and delighted by this view. He would feel the need to honor God in this work of his, without taking the time to measure, by the rules and principles of astronomy, the size and dimensions of this great star. He would not stop to study and observe with curiosity the properties of its light, the power of its influence, the phases of its movements and the other perfections of this great heavenly body.

In the same way, we leave the obscurity of earthly things and we come to contemplate the true Sun of the world, the Sun of this sun that enlightens us, the Sun of justice who enlightens everyone coming into the world. We are taken aback in astonishment and infatuated with love and admiration at the first brightness, the first sight of this splendor. For at the beginning of this work and as we first begin thinking about so worthy a subject, we need to interrupt our discourse in order to approach God and contemplate the greatness of his only begotten Son and the state of this most holy mystery. Let us contemplate God made man and let us approach this sanctuary with a spirit of humility and devotion. Let us try to enter with reverence and love into his clarity, rather than enter by clarity into his love. Of course we desire to receive from him both of these qualities and impressions as we direct our stirrings and affections toward an object and a mystery that is one of love and clarity at the same time.[8]

It would be hard to match this text in both its lyrical force as well as its comprehensiveness of Bérullian themes relevant to approaching the mysteries of the Incarnation. M. Olier's famous formulation on how to "meditate" — to be used "only when the more individual attentions of the Spirit... are absent" — underscores Bérulle's contemplative-reverential posture. We are called "to look at Jesus, to unite ourselves to Jesus, and to act in Jesus," or, equivalently, "Let us place our Lord before our eyes," "Let us have our Lord in our hearts," and "Let us hold our Lord in our hands," Father Olier counsels us. His formulation brings out the "supraanalytical" and even "transformative" nature of the Bérullian elevation, leaving the role of clarity and analysis only dimly intimated. "The first is called adoration; the second, communion; the third, cooperation." Olier's view of "adoration" clearly evokes the Bérullian sense of love and reverence: "After our heart has expressed freely its love, praise and other duties, let us remain for a while in silence before him, with these same dispositions and religious sentiments in the depth of our soul." The soul's "depth" is a translation of Olier's technical term *fond*, the comprehensive ground of mystical consciousness that reason can illuminate but never exhaust.[9]

The Incarnation As a Mystery of Adoration and Service

Following the indications of Bérulle's writings, as well as those of his principal disciples (particularly M. Olier and Ven. Madeleine de Saint-Joseph, the first French prioress of Paris's Great Carmel), we gain the impression that the center of the Incarnation mystery is an irruption within history of adoration and service (or "servitude"). Alluding to the "hidden mystery" of Ephesians 3:9, the *Grandeurs'* very beginning describes the Incarnation as the mystery opening heaven, sanctifying earth, and adoring God. "This adoration is new," it continues. "For although heaven previously had adoring spirits and an adored God, it had not as yet an adoring God." And participationist that he is, the cardinal tells us that "the Church should be caught up in this mystery" as well as "transfixed with wonder and admiration," for it is a "résumé" of faith's mysteries.[10] Now, finally, Bérulle is telling us that Jesus reveals just how awesomely lovable God truly is. The Divine is so rich, such a plenitude, that it transcends anything like it on earth: it is to be thus adored, the prayer offered properly only to God, but only a God-Man can truly know, express, and so reveal this adorable plenitude. Somehow, before Jesus, the awesomeness of God's love had remained only incompletely known.

Adoration seems a constant motif of the Bérullian elevations, but two texts from the second and eleventh discourses of the *Grandeurs* respectively, contemplating the Incarnation as an adoration event, are particularly celebrated.

From all eternity there had been a God infinitely adorable, but still there had not been an infinite adorer. There had been a God infinitely worthy of being loved and served, but no man nor infinite servant able to render an infinite service and love. You are now, O Jesus, this adorer, this man, this servant, infinite in power, in being, in dignity, so that you can fully satisfy this need and render this divine homage.... And just as there is a God worthy of being adored, served and loved, so there is also in you, O Jesus my Lord, a God adoring, loving and serving him eternally.[11]

If you will, this text looks at salvation history, or revelation, as one of finding a way to express adequately just how lovingly adorable the trinitarian Mystery really is. The Incarnation is just that revelation, and the second celebrated text tries to probe the "how" of this revelation: what is it about the Incarnation in Jesus that makes it this supreme disclosure of adoration?

That text, from the *Grandeurs*' eleventh discourse, tells us that "Jesus...bears in himself a state which contemplates and adores his eternal state." As a state rather than just an activity, "it is solid, permanent, and independent of powers and actions, deeply imprinted in the depths of the created being." Jesus' entire being as incarnate is adoration. But note how the deepest ground of the Incarnation-as-adoration is trinitarian. Jesus' own incarnate adorational being reflects, or is an analogy of, the relation of the Son to the Father within the Trinity itself. This grounding of the Incarnation, and all its mysteries, in the life of the Trinity is typical of the trinitarian exemplarism of the French School. As another text puts it, "Because in the Trinity there is a God regarding God, referred to God, a God

51

who is a relation to God [that is, the Son],...it comes to pass [in the Incarnation]...that the Son both regards God as his Father and his God and simultaneously as man...is relational...a substantial and personal relation to God...whom he regards, loves, and adores."[12]

The cardinal allows himself to be swept up in the adorational movement. Or better: one senses the attractive beauty of adoration "pulling" the cardinal into its many depths, as one reads throughout the *Grandeurs*, and indeed throughout most of his writings. "The Church should be caught up in this mystery," he tells us; "advanced souls" should be "transfixed with wonder and admiration" as they admire the inner trinitarian life and its overspill into the Incarnation. As Bérulle moves further, now, he discovers "servitude" (or "service") as another key dimension of the incarnate Jesus. And like adoration, this kenosis and service has its ultimate analogue in the Trinity as well. Jesus' "own birth and eternal filiation" as Son of the Father who "honors his Father" finds its earthly analogy in the "new birth" which "again honors the eternal Father" through becoming "the serf and slave of the Father" who "offers himself" to the Father.[13]

In the *Grandeurs*' second discourse Bérulle "commits" himself to a state of "perpetual servitude" honoring the servitude of Jesus' humanity toward the divinity. This elevation to servitude, which cost the cardinal much in grief personally,[14] was his way of participating in this further dimension of the Incarnation. His own experience of servitude was an experiential hinge toward a growing appreciation and discovery of the depths of Jesus' own servitude itself. As many mystics speak of entering into a state of passive receptivity, so Bérulle enters into a mystical servitude that gives him entry into some of the secrets of Jesus' own servitude itself.

Here is a portion from possibly the "thickest" and yet one of the more crucial "elevations" in the *Grandeurs:*

[The] secret...[the] divine invention is to strip the humanity of Jesus of its own ordinary subsistence....[God] substituted the heavenly graft, the divine subsistence, the very person of his Son in place of the human subsistence, which had been negated....For everything in Jesus Christ has its foundation in the hypostasis of his divinity. The eternal Word, as the substance and divine suppositum of this human nature, is the proprietor of all its actions and sufferings.[15]

Bérulle sees how Jesus' humanity has undergone a thorough "kenosis" of itself, not in the sense that the humanity has disappeared, but in the sense that it is in its very being a total receptivity to the action of the Word: "thoroughly emptied of itself and so worthily clothed in the Word." Like a "slave" in a sense, for now the "person" of the Word has the right and power to dispose of Jesus' human actions.

Bérulle even appeals to Plato's image of the human person as an "inverted tree" whose roots are in heaven: how much more has Jesus' humanity been so transplanted![16] Readers unfamiliar with the technical theological language of the time should be alerted that "person" (from the Latin *persona*) translates the Greek *hypostasis*, which means roughly "subsistence" or "foundational reality." Thus the meaning is not that Jesus lacks a full humanity; in the language of the times, his human "nature" is lacking nothing. But this nature is "grounded" in the subsistent Word or trinitarian Son of God in a unique manner appropriate only to it. The Word's "hypostatic person" is the ground of Jesus' humanity.

Bérulle will be led to explore and participate in various dimensions of this kenosis or service as it expresses itself throughout the various mysteries and states of Jesus. In this, he is consciously stimulated by the Pauline writings, particularly the "kenosis hymn" of Philippians, as well as the analogies he finds to the states of the Incarnation in the Trinity itself. Bérulle's successor in the Oratory's generalate, Père Charles de Condren, will go on to develop a "sacrifice-mysticism," in which Jesus' service becomes a supreme holocaust of love to the Father, which endures even in eternity. This sacrifice-accent of the Bérullian servitude surfaces in Madeleine de Saint-Joseph too, but let me cite a particularly fine passage from M. Olier, who himself had Father Condren as spiritual director: "Our Lord, in his divine person, is an altar upon which all men are offered to God with all their actions and sufferings; he is that golden altar upon which is consummated every perfect sacrifice, the human nature of Christ with that of all the faithful being the victim, his Spirit the fire, and God the Father He to whom it is offered, and who is adored by it in Spirit and truth."[17]

Service has a way of degenerating into mere professionalism, or duty, or worse, perhaps even manipulating the other for the sake of one's own "messianic" needs. A sacrifice-mysticism, which could take the form of a "vow of host-victimhood," is a way of keeping our service free from narcissism, non-manipulative. By recalling and sharing in Jesus' own selfless passion, something of the passional selflessness of Jesus permeates our own service state. Adoration keeps our service in constant reference to God, too, "saving" it from a subtle self-centeredness. Indeed, adoration and service seem subtly interrelated. Adoration keeps our service selfless and God-directed; service keeps our adoration from derailing into quietism and world-escapism (which is another subtle form of narcissism).

Mother Madeleine de Saint-Joseph seemed particularly sensitive to the need to "protect" our adoration from illusions. Perhaps because it is the "highest" act of religion, we might think it's free from pollution. She tells us that she prefers "the act of adoration to that of thanksgiving because it is more extensive and it exposes us less to the danger of too much self-preoccupation." Here she seems to be noting the reference to God so pronounced in adoration, while thanksgiving always involves a reference back to ourselves and our met needs, for which we give thanks. Still, she seems to think that it's necessary to bring out the dimension of love too, as if she recognizes the subtle forms that self-deception can take in religion. Adoration "does not even deserve to be called adoration...if love is not its soul," she cautions; then "it is only a pretense."[18]

A Sampling of Bérullian Contemplations and Elevations

As I indicated, one encounters among the Bérullians contemplations of the Jesus mystery of both a more extensive and a more intensive nature. The two, surely, cannot ever be separated, but there are contemplations that move through the full range, extensively/chronologically, of the mysteries and states of Jesus, from infancy, the desert experience, passion, death, and on to glory. In these, one aspect of the full range of Jesus' mysteries is singled out for meditative exploration. To pray and study most of them is to range through the "life" of Jesus as the French School understood that reality.

But one can look at Jesus' life more intensively, searching for the inner depth dimension that is then reflected in varying ways throughout the varied mysteries. For example, our contemplations above, on adoration and servitude, are rather more of this latter sort. All the mysteries of Jesus, in their deeper, "interior" sense are adorational and service-oriented, ultimately rooted in the Son's adoration and service of the Father within the Trinity, and they take various forms and modes throughout Jesus' life.

When the cardinal transposes these twin themes into the register of Jesus' consciousness, explicitly alluding to the teaching of Paul and John, we find him stressing how, throughout his life, "the first function of the soul of Jesus was, without doubt, the adoration of his God." This was, for the cardinal, a trinitarian knowledge, for "Jesus is God through this mystery and he saw with the light of glory (which no one denies him) that he was God." Consequently, Jesus grasped the "bond uniting the Father to the Son, and the Son with the Father through an eternal unity of Spirit and unspeakable love." Further, Jesus' own contemplation of his humanity united to divinity — which "establishes the new mystery of the Incarnation and gives the world a new object...of grandeur and love" — becomes his soul's "second object" of vision and happiness. But, we may add, this second theme at least implies that of service/servitude, for in the Incarnation we find Jesus concealing "such grandeurs with his humility," his life of servitude in history. Hence, in the scriptures Jesus calls "himself Son of Man."[19]

If you will, this double state of adoration and servitude, or this double consciousness (in Jesus) of a God to be adored and yet God's hiddenness through humble servitude, is Bérulle's transposition of the traditional theme of Jesus as both "comprehensor and voyager-pilgrim," a theme nicely studied in St. Thomas Aquinas and here incorporated into a more developed spiritual theology and spiritual program. Jesus, God's Son, "in his earthly life... has allowed himself to be, at once, both *voyageur* and *comprehenseur*," and so his soul "simultaneously mixes with the highest enjoyment and vision of God sorrow and sadness," says the cardinal. This "double-state" creates, if you will, a "strange division" between Jesus' "Divinity and the glory of the Divinity!" For that glory remains somewhat hidden during the period of earthly pilgrimage. What we would today call the theme of "kenosis" is clearly in the cardinal's mind.[20]

Jesus' Infancy and Mary

St. Thérèse of Lisieux has made the devotion to Jesus' infancy and childhood known again in our own times. But back of her is Bérulle's own transposition of this devotion, which was highly influential throughout later French spirituality. Bérulle can accent the theme of suffering and kenosis revealed in the childhood state, and in this sense we can see how he finds his theme of "servitude" particularly disclosed in Jesus' childhood. But there is a balance in the cardinal, and we sense that childhood is not only weakness, dependency, and suffering. Speaking of the "God-Child" Jesus who becomes child through love rather than through necessity, he says:

> Can we not see even that power and greatness are captured by love in the powerlessness and in the lowliness of childhood? Can we not see here that majesty is also transformed into love and changed into the benevolence and humanity of a child?
> Let us live in Jesus.... And since love triumphs over God himself, may it triumph over us who are his subjects and his creatures.[21]

Here in this text from the *Grandeurs*' eighth discourse, we glimpse a more positive estimate of Jesus' childhood (the child's "benevolence"), but yet something of the historical realism of Jesus' birth and youth too ("powerlessness" and "lowliness"). And, as always, our own grace-bestowed participation is echoed in the note that love is to triumph over ourselves too.

But loving service is only one side of the infancy mystery. Not surprisingly the cardinal understands it as the mystery of adoration too, for he sees, as we recall, Jesus' earthly birth as the "state" in which he adores on earth — and thus as a focal revelation for us all — his own eternal birth as the "Second Person" of the Trinity. If you will, his birth into earthly sonship is a privileged revelation on earth of his own "eternal filiation" in the Mystery of the Trinity. "And Jesus alone adores through his state" of earthly birth "the persons and divine emanations" of the Trinity.[22]

The *Life of Jesus*, a meditative narrative, appearing six years after the *Grandeurs* in 1629, is a particularly intense celebration of Jesus' infancy that recapitulates these themes, but widens them to explore the role of Mary in Jesus' life more fully than the *Grandeurs* seems to. "To speak of Mary is to speak of Jesus," say Bérulle; "she is the one who is the closest and the most united to him by the state of this new mystery." Her unparalleled union with her son — and Bérulle can go very far in praising this — enables her to participate in Jesus' "interior and spiritual life." In what amounts to a meditative elevation on Luke 2:19 ("And Mary kept all these things, reflecting on them in her heart."), the cardinal can really soar:

> Stuttering rather than speaking, this is what we can say about things that so greatly surpass the human mind and even the angelic mind.... This is the first conversation of Jesus in the Virgin. This is the Virgin's first contemplation, or better yet, this is the Virgin's first ecstasy before the Son of God made Son of Man in her.

Maintaining that it is one of the unrevealed secrets of Jesus as to whether Mary somehow shared in his beatific consciousness, she at least

> ... possessed the angelic light, which reveals to her the soul of Jesus and its sacred activities.
> Happily, she leaves behind her own thoughts and her interior spiritual life to enter into the thoughts of Jesus, into the interior life of Jesus. She enters the love and adoration Jesus offers his Father.
> ... The Virgin's proper role is to be attentive to the interior and spiritual life of her Son and to be a pure capacity for Jesus, filled with Jesus.
> Nevertheless, it is necessary that I discover some humiliation in the midst of these grandeurs, bitterness among the sweetness. I would wrong the author of these mysteries and the truth of this story if I did not present it as it is; if I did not describe truthfully what is happening, either in the state of the Son or in the state of the Blessed Mother....I discover there the cross and humiliation. For our mysteries are for God himself both cross and humiliation.
> She... agrees to be the humiliated Mother of the humiliated Son.[23]

In these Bérullian elevations, we see how Mary is a unique participant in Jesus' infancy, disclosing something of that adoration and kenotic servitude so powerfully entering history now in the Incarnation. For Bérulle, infancy implies Mary's maternity, as the famed beginning of the prayer of the French School puts it, "O Jesus, living in Mary." On Bérullian grounds, one would not be telling the story "as it really is" were one to ignore the route the Son of God took in becoming incarnate: in and through his Mother Mary. Apart from Mary, Bérulle seems to say, one can't appreciate the depth of the kenosis. Apart from her, one can't appreciate the grandeur of it either. Are her humiliation, and yet her singular privileges, signs and even conduits of the servitude and adoration of Jesus himself? Bérulle seems to think so, for "God and the world have considered her the source of blessing for the world."[24]

There is something more about the *Life* too that deserves our attention. Readers of it will find that it never actually gets to the birth of Jesus, but remains meditatively with the conception-prenatal period (Jesus' infancy is understood in this extended sense). This may only be accidental, but a recent interpreter has intriguingly suggested that Bérulle was contemplating — and through his writing wants us to contemplate and participate in — the "interior" of the mystery, the "state" within the mystery, the eternal and enduringly effective dimension of the mystery. "Like creation, the Incarnation is *at* the beginning, more than *the* beginning, of a new world and history." The *Life* is experiencing the "*at*," the moment of eternity in time that changes all time. At the same time, mystic that he is, the cardinal is indicating that "all mystical contemplation finds its origin at this instant." As the *Life* somehow suspends us from the ongoing flow of temporal history in the eternal now of the Incarnation, so the mystic experience searches out the "eternally effective" dimensions of the mysteries of Jesus.[25] Here narrative temporality is taken up into the drama of eternity.

The Desert

Bérulle, and our other principals, have left us numerous meditations upon the various events of Jesus' life — the annunciation, visitation, epiphany, presentation, transfiguration, the Samaritan woman, Lazarus, Jesus' kingship and empire, etc. — and so it becomes difficult to choose among so many options. I do want to give the reader some sense of the range available, but rather more "qualitatively," as I have indicated. And in this respect, the cardinal's meditations on the desert experience of Jesus do perhaps move us a bit more deeply into the mystery of kenosis contemplated by the French School.

Instead of seeing Jesus' desert experience as a "state of contemplation," a kind of angelic state in which Jesus is removed from the world — as the cardinal claims it is presented in his time — Bérulle says that

> ...it seems to me to have to be represented as a state of exile, of banishment....on the cross [Jesus] will be in a state of suffering while this state corresponds to the pain of sin;...it has a rapport with the exile and banishment of sinners.

If you will, on the cross Jesus undergoes something of the *"poena sensus"* spoken of by the school theologians, the physical sense of pain that the sinner undergoes as a consequence of sin. The desert experience, on the other hand, enables Jesus to experience something of the "pain of the damned," the psychological sense of separation and exile from God.

There are qualifications to be made, surely. Bérulle distinguishes between the "pain" and the "fault" of sin. Jesus, while he might want to share as fully in the sinner's lot as possible, takes on only the pain and not the fault. His identification with the sinner is as profound as his sinless state permits: "...he has taken on the pain, the state of sin which could be deified, and if the fault were capable of the same, he would take that too; but not being able, he has desired to assume everything which can be deified."[26] Behind this nuance is both the cardinal's deep respect for Jesus' beatific vision, as well as the nuance of Romans 8:3: the Son is sent "in the likeness of sinful flesh."[27]

And as we participate in this desert state, we ourselves, says the cardinal, will come to experience something of that deification of sin Jesus knew through our own "effacing of the state of sin in which we exist." And more mystically, we might even come to know something of his own state of exile, undergoing a sort of identification with sinners ourselves. "Adore Jesus in this state, refer yourselves to the captivity and interior annihilation [*anéantissement*] which you undergo in homage of this exile."[28]

Passion and Death

In an unpublished "Work of Piety" Bérulle intertwines what seems his predominant view of Jesus' passional state with our own participation in it:

> What are the occupations [of the Son of God on the cross]? Does he perform no more miracles? Is that useless? Instead he brings about a state of the suffering life, not only a state but an order of suffering souls. And as there are some orders on earth, so in heaven. God has chosen some holy souls to establish on earth some orders leading people to perfection. So, as the Son of God creates heavenly orders honoring his states, so he

brings about an order of suffering souls who will render homage to his suffering on the cross....[29]

This new suffering state is a mystical participation in Jesus' own passive suffering on the cross — his own dark night, if you will. That night is the summit of Jesus' servitude experience, planned for from the "first instant" of the Incarnation, and finally rooted in the Son's offering of himself to the Father's will in the Trinity. Jesus is "guided and invited by his very [trinitarian] self where he offers all" to the Father, to offer humanity to the Father. This offering includes the state "in which he can suffer." And such suffering finally means the cross. The offering of the cross finds its trinitarian archetype in the Son's self-offering to the Father. Our share in it is brought about by God the Father himself "who by his deeds can as easily lead a soul to suffering as to joy." Here the cardinal seems to have in mind the mystical theme of *pati divina* (passive, mystical suffering), for he speaks of the Father's operations here as "very holy, very exalted, very divine, and very dolorous," operated in Jesus' soul.[30] The cardinal's accent is his more mystical interpretation of the kenosis theme, which is intertwined in the cardinal's perspective with the theme of the cross as that state from which emanates "grace and glory" for humanity. For here Jesus is the "victim" who suffers for our sins, and even "endures suffering from the Father, but in a fully divine way."[31] Clearly, the cross as the source of redemption is a well known one in the tradition, which the cardinal integrates into his thought. But his mystical orientation enables him to stress the element of suffering, abandoned love in Jesus' experience as another aspect of the interior of the mystery too. The two views — the mystical and the redemptive — are not opposed, for kenosis brings about redemption.

The Burial Period

Bérulle seems to extend this mystical-salvational meditation upon the passion in his brief "Work of Piety" 109 onto Jesus' tomb experience of Holy Saturday. What does one do between the death and resurrection state, this "between period"? The cardinal, following his time, sees the soul of Jesus in a special state: it and the body are united to the Word, but it no longer animates that body, which is now in the "heart of the earth." And Jesus' soul? "In the hands of the Father," this soul's state "implies several things concerning Jesus unknown or less known until now" having to do with the future and "all matters concerning the salvation of souls." And we are offered a list:

...between death and glory... [souls] must be (1) purified, (2) instructed in the diverse matters not yet understood in the present life, and (3) made ready for the interior operations and impressions of the divine effects they are to receive; [and] how many more will be the most holy effects coming from such as the beatific vision, God's chief work in humans and angels?[32]

One can recognize behind this something of the traditional theme of the descent into hell. Jesus is not only occupied with his own beatific vision and "mystical" interior transformation of soul. But he is concerned with the issue of the "salvation of souls." This last touches upon the theme of hell as the realm of the damned and/or dead, and the cardinal remains sensitively vague and cautious. "Insinuated," to use the cardinal's exact word here, are some mysterious matters touching upon everyone's eternal fate. We don't understand these matters very well, but there seems to be a purgative process at work here, unleashed through this "descent" into the "heart of the earth," a salvational purgation.

Bérulle's meditations upon Joseph of Arimathea are a further "sounding" of this mystery of Holy Saturday. In one of them he suggests that Joseph's work on behalf of Jesus' burial represents those who have a special participation in this mysterious state of Jesus. It also symbolizes both the Father's eternal commission to the Son to carry through the "opprobrium" that the Son must suffer, as well as the honor that the Father wants to render his Son on behalf of his suffering. The first aspect brings out the mystery of Holy Saturday as that of completing the kenosis and cross, sharing to the fullest the pain of those in the land of the dead. Olier shares this view: Jesus' burial is his "complete sharing in the corruption of his brothers." The second aspect brings out the love and life that stems from this painful solidarity: that is how the Father honors the Son. Olier joins both aspects when he says that the "state of burial and of corruption signifies the final destruction of being and the bringing forth of an element of new life."[33]

And, as always with the French School, there is a trinitarian foundation to be noted, for "all the works of God lead us to a knowledge of a Trinity," said Bérulle. And as if pursuing this insight, he tells us in another meditation how Jesus' "dwelling place" upon the cross and in the tomb is linked to his "eternal abode" within the life of the Trinity. For "it is the will of the Father, and the love and obedience which the Son renders him, which brings this Son to this death, and to the place of death, the tomb."[34] The "abode" of the cross and tomb finds its trinitarian analogy and basis within the loving and obedient "abode" of the Son in the life of the Trinity.

The State of Glory: Resurrection and Ascension

The French School somewhat confusingly moves back and forth between resurrection and ascension (and Pentecost) in its consideration of Jesus' glorified existence, as if the lines between one and the other are not entirely clear. And this seems quite appropriate in these "particularly" mysterious regions. The "Works of Piety" are our chief source for Bérulle's own meditations, although the *Grandeurs* does touch on the theme. In brief, Jesus' resurrection is his glorification, the experience of his state as "comprehensor" which was somewhat "suspended" by his state as "voyager." To be sure, his humanity is not abolished, but completed and transformed. And so the wounds remain, both of the body and the heart.[35]

> But now he has become completely comprehensor; he has the fullness of life, of glory, of divine life; he has the fullness of effects, all that is due him. We must take care to rejoice in this glory and the authority that the Son of God enjoys over all.[36]

Of course, grounding this glorification of Jesus is the hypostatic union as well as the trinitarian relation of Father and Son: the Word now fully transforming the humanity of Jesus: now "Jesus requests an effusion and communication of this clarity which he has from his Father and in his Son eternally."[37] In the background here is the cardinal's meditation on John 17:5.

Bérulle will "discover" further dimensions as he probes this complex state of glory. In the famous twelfth discourse of the *Grandeurs*, where he contemplates Jesus' "third" birth into glory, he speaks of a separation between the "essence and state" of glory and the "place" of glory, brought on by love, during the interval between resurrection and ascension, as Jesus still spends more time with us. And in a meditation on the ascension, he seems to emphasize the "finalization" of the glorification experience, bringing with it a "spiritual fecundity" unleashing the Spirit and birthing the church.[38]

As we might expect, Bérulle's view of our participation in this state is more "mystical," stressing how, as we come to share in it, we taste that joy and freedom from suffering (impassibility) that the glorified Jesus knows now. I am myself rather fond of Olier's formulation of our sharing in the ascension, which gets at much of what the cardinal wants to say: "A truly wonderful state of the soul, rendered interiorly conformable and wholly similar to God, and, as the saints say, perfectly deiform, that is, all glowing with love, and luminous with the splendor of God."[39]

Mary Magdalene

Clearly one of the richest and most emphasized themes among the Bérullian elevations is that of Mary Magdelene, the cardinal writing a lengthy "Elevation on Mary Magdalene" of twenty chapters, among other meditations on her. Like Jesus' Mother Mary, Magdalene illustrates the Bérullian theme of "special" or "unique" participations in the mystery of Jesus. As Guillén Preckler understands it, Magdalene becomes an example of someone who "carries in herself all Jesus' suffering states." Thus, she is a model of Jesus the "voyager." But also, we need to add that she is a model of what Jesus the comprehensor is through her special participation in the resurrection. If you will, she is an *abrégé*, a sort of concentrated summary, of the "economy" of the Incarnation mystery, of the perpetual effectiveness of the states of Jesus. But all this, without prejudice to the Blessed Virgin, who alone knew the infancy state, and who remains incomparable for the cardinal.[40]

Perhaps the role of Magdalene in Bérulle's spirituality might come from a meditative reading of these passages:

> There [in the scriptures] I discover that the first person you visited in your new life and in your state of glory was the Magdalene.
> ...The first name you pronounced was her name, the name Mary, the name dedicated, in her, to love and penance. The first commission you gave and, if I can speak this way, the first Bull and Patent that you officially issued in your state of glory and power, was to her, making her an apostle, but an apostle of life, glory and love, and an apostle to your apostles.... You make her an apostle not to the world, but to the very apostles of the world and to the universal pastors of your church because you are so pleased to highlight the honor and love of her soul.[41]

Note how Bérulle sees the Magdalene as a special participant in Jesus' love and penance. This is what makes her particularly representative of Jesus as "voyager," whose own servitude (penance) is the result of love. That same penitential love is what enables her to "recognize" the glorified Jesus, thus rendering her an apostle in some sense "superior" to the other apostles: "...the first name [Jesus] pronounced in [his] glory was her name...which enlightens her, which makes her recognize her Lord, which makes her fall at his feet, which restores life to her and fills her with joy and with new love."[42] No wonder, then, that the cardinal admires "all her states" and says that "those who share in her secrets" are blessed.[43]

Eucharist and Church

Unlike contemporary exegetes, the Bérullian meditations do not usually dwell upon the theme of the kingdom of God, although — we have noted it above — there are some meditations on Jesus' "empire." Rather, like John and Paul — the French School's preferred biblical source — one finds "equivalences" to the kingdom symbol. Surely the church — taken in its full extent as the church suffering, militant, and triumphant — is one such equivalent symbol. The eucharist, too, in its many aspects, becomes also a concentrated expression of Jesus' kingdom.

Basically we should recall Bérulle's notion that the eucharist is one of the "principal" mysteries forming that chain of love: Trinity, Incarnation, and eucharist. If you will, trinitarian love flows through each of these three, uniting humanity to God. The cardinal will also speak of the Incarnation as "the exemplar for the other sacraments, which, following its example, are all composed of two natures in relation to the incarnate Word, who wished to depict and represent in his works and in the sacraments of his church the mystery of the Incarnation, which is the sacrament of sacraments."[44] The implication is that the church and the eucharist are two-natured (interior and exterior) "sacraments" of the Incarnation.

Unlike most the other mysteries of Jesus, however, the eucharist enables us to participate in the fullness of the glorified Christ. Thus, all the enduring states of Jesus — now making up Jesus Risen — are communicated to us in it. This is its specialness. "For here...we are given his life and death, his joys and sufferings, his glory and shame." And, with a typically mystical tonality, the cardinal goes on to say that Jesus' "dolorous and glorified wounds, always alive and life-giving, are applied to and imprinted upon us," provided our dispositions in receiving the eucharist are good.[45] Note the mention of the sufferings and death of Jesus as present in the eucharist. This recalls its sacrificial nature, a theme surely known to the cardinal but especially developed by Condren's and Olier's "sacrifice-mysticism," in which Jesus eternally sacrifices himself in some true sense. The priest, too, greatly celebrated by Olier, is called to a special conformation to this eternal sacrifice: he is par excellence the living representative of the eternally effective "holocaust" of Jesus.[46]

Let me end this survey of Bérullian elevations and contemplations with a portion from Olier's famed "Acts for the Divine Office." Here he looks at the mystery of the church on earth as one flowing from Jesus' interior and called to participate as fully as possible in the heavenly saints' perfect participation in Jesus' interior. It is one of the most lyrical writings of the entire French School, and surfaces its ecclesiology.

> May the church, O my Lord Jesus, dilate what you contain in yourself, and may it express outwardly this divine religion which you have for your Father in the secret of your heart, in heaven, and upon altars. Oh! What a heaven! What music, what holy harmony in these holy places! Oh! May faith enable me to listen in on the marvelous canticles in these tabernacles, which the soul of Jesus Christ sings to God with all the angels and the saints who accompany him![47]

Contemplative Participation and Critical Theology

The modern christologian, looking back over these elevations and contemplations, will either be thrilled, repulsed, or something else in between. The "thrilled" theologian and student of theology will perhaps find here much that he or she feels has been missing in more "modern" theologies. At last, he or she might say, we have here a christology that doesn't artificially separate Jesus the human and Jesus the divine. And a christology that moves the whole person, heart included. And that seems sensitive to the spiritual life, and the faith/church context of a confessing/believing style of theology. And much more besides. And the "repulsed" thinker? Perhaps such a one will find the "mystical" interpretation a form of projection, lacking any historical basis in the text. Perhaps, too, not enough of the struggling, growing, perhaps unknowing humanity of it all, and of Jesus as well, might come through for this person. History, if you will, seems smothered in mystical dreaminess. And the concerns of political and liberation theologies? Where is there room for that in this highly individualistic reading of Jesus? And much more!

Many of us, though, will probably find ourselves somewhere between these postures. We are perhaps attracted to much of the above, maybe even all of it, but we wonder. Am I perhaps being swept away by a kind of nostalgia? Has solid and thus somewhat "boring" scholarship, especially of the historical variety, left my heart so starved that I'm hungry for almost anything that smacks of the mysterious and "mystical" in this sense? Am I, deep down where I don't like to wander too much, perhaps frightened and even threatened by more political and social approaches to christology, while in the Bérullian elevations I enjoy a serenity that is possibly too serene? As a colleague more or less put it to me, "It's beautiful, but is it true?"

Clearly we have many legitimate questions here, which we cannot dodge, even if we can't answer them all satisfactorily. Let me at least try to work through the ones I consider basic.

Methodical Concerns

As we noted in our last chapter, modern theology, and christology within this, is very method-oriented. We have a heightened methodical consciousness, at least in the West. Let us begin with this, then: What are the methodical contributions of the Bérullian tradition of participating in the mysteries of Jesus? Surely we cannot separate method issues from content issues, for as we noted earlier, every good method is simply an articulation of the better and best ways of getting toward the "object" or subject matter of concern. And so the subject matter — the reality of the revelation-experience of Jesus the Christ — is the content that finally must occupy the central focus. Whatever method we choose must finally serve that "object." If you will, christology's method is made for Christ, not Christ for christology's method! The subject matter leads, method follows, to recall to mind a thought of David Tracy's. Within those limits, then, what might some method contributions be of the French School's christocentric tradition of contemplation?

First, I would suggest that, without being simply "unmethodical," the French School does "hang loose" to some extent with method. It represents a not unwholesome sense of suspicion of the tendency to make more of method than it deserves. But it is not unmethodical — let's start with that first. There is evidence that the principals of the French School represent something of a critical reaction to the abstract, propositional form of scholastic theology "in possession" at its time. The turn to mysticism and spirituality, not without its own dangers, is an attempt to reroot theology in faith-experience. The science of the saints is an attempt to keep these two — the scientific and the spiritual (symbolized by the "saints") — in balance and relation. So, our school is methodical in the sense that it is in search of an alternative approach to theology and spirituality. And every now and then the critique of the more propositional style of theology breaks through. For example, Bérulle, in a passage where he is speaking about the relations between knowledge and love in this world, laments: "What a strange condition (if we can say this in passing) found even among the most eminent and knowledgeable Christians, who can never know God as he is in himself, but can love him as he is in himself, and yet they work much harder to know him than to love him."[48]

Still, the French School hangs loose with method, if I can put it that way. One will search in vain, among the principal authors, for any extensive analysis of the method of meditating or participating in Jesus' mysteries. The text cited above from Olier is about as much as one will get, and it is remarkably flexible, warning that it

65

is to be followed only if one's own personal inspiration is not forthcoming. Surely one reason for this is the enormous respect of the French School for God's "incomprehensible mystery." In fact, the element of "respect," "reverence," indeed, of "adoration," is greatly intensified in this tradition. Recall the citation above about entering into the mystery with reverence first, and the desire for clarity second. I would read this, in our own terms, as a protection of a "manifestation-disclosure" or "luminosity" model of truth, rather than simply a "sense model." It is analogous in our own times to Gadamer's suspicions about "method" in his own *Truth and Method*.

Perhaps a second motive operating here with respect to this "methodical reserve" is the heightened sensitivity to the individual person, and his or her unique assimilation of Jesus. The more personal the assimilation, the less of a carbon copy and the more "personalized" that sharing in Jesus must truly be. At the same time, as Hügel persuasively indicated in our own times, the richer the personality (as in Jesus), the greater the variety in unity of that person. And hence, the more we should expect a wide variety or plurality of attempted assimilations of him.[49] On this, recall from above the French School's insistence that, beside our general participation in Jesus' mysteries, we have each our own unique participation within them.

Now there is, in my mind, a very fruitful back and forth movement between the methodical and the suspicion of method in our "School" that fosters that notion, so helpfully emphasized by Tracy, of "the subject matter" leading and "method" following. Something of an inversion of these two had resulted in that propositional theology from which Bérulle in his own time, and some of us in ours, were suffering. Note, too, particularly in Bérulle, the most "theological" of our principals, how the truly critical and "scientific" nature of theology is maintained, yet it is very much a theology in service to a much larger reality.

Secondly, the French School is explicitly an example of what we called in our last chapter a "contemplative-trinitarian" theological model of conversation. Thus, for those of us finding that an attractive avenue to pursue, we should accordingly find much that is congenial for our christological endeavors in the French School. As Olier rooted all genuine conversation in the conversation of the Trinity, so the French School sees our meditative participation in Jesus' mysteries as a sharing in and "dilation" of that trinitarian conversation too. The Divine Mystery (Father) is an ocean of Truth (Son) wanting to be shared (Spirit). The Transcendent (Father) is both meaningful (Son) and participable (Spirit). In the Incarnation, God becomes present, says Bérulle, with "a presence that imitates the eternal indwelling, repose and communication of God in himself."[50] The sharable Logos is the ground of our own ability to enter into "conversation" and "participation" with Jesus. This Logos grounds our ability to converse-participate, stimulates it, and guides it through the Spirit. If you will, the Logos of the divine conversation is inviting us through the Spirit into the conversation that participating in Jesus' mysteries is too.

Let me try to highlight some of the features that the French School, and particularly Bérulle, seem to bring out especially well in this, a christological model of conversation imitating the trinitarian conversation. The intensified focus upon adoration and servitude seems particularly significant. Adoration, the act of special reverence for God alone, keeps the conversation-participation truly open, receptive, and especially non-manipulable by our own often petty and hidden desires, motives, biases, etc., which all too often impede the flow, the genuine entering into the "conversation." In adoration, the focus shifts from ourselves to the Other: it is the response to the attractive pull of the mysterious Other. I believe that something of this is indicated by Mother Madeleine de Saint-Joseph, when she tells us to "adore his Father with him [i.e., Jesus] and with his own adoration." To enter into his adoration is to "follow his movements, unite ourselves with his intentions, his thoughts and his activities."[51] At the same time, servitude or service keeps the conversation-participation genuinely incarnational, a sharing in the service of Jesus who emptied himself in service to the world. Adoration stretches us "vertically," if you will, as far as we can be stretched; servitude, more "horizontally" in service to others.

At the same time, I would think that the intense focus upon adoration especially, but also the element of *anéantissement* (self-abnegation) implied in the kenosis of servitude, fosters a certain "inequality" among the partners to this christological conversation. As we noted earlier, the source and goal of every genuine conversation or dialogue must be the "truth," and not properly the "personal feelings" of the participants. In fact, at times those feelings can get in the way of the genuine flow of the conversation. And so, we saw Tracy saying that at times the personal friendship factor must yield to truth's pursuit. Well, the "truth" of the matter within this trinitarian conversation is that God and the human partner are not on a level of equality. And it is this that adoration emphasizes. Adoration keeps the "divine Logos" both source and goal, and by so doing insures a constant transcendence of the kind of self-interest that can cripple a genuine participation in this trinitarian conversation. This non-equality, for the participants in the christological conversation, seems to preserve God's over-againstness, and therefore the divine ability to "surprise" us in ways we don't expect — namely, the Incarnation. Again, the element of God's kenosis — servitude — and our sharing in that seems to modify this non-equality: the non-equality doesn't come from a God of tyranny. The Divine self-limits the God-Self for our sakes. But if the Divine is not tyrannical, the God-Self is still free, and thus "personal." And the adoration we render God is the echo, within us, of that plenitude of personal freedom that God is and that the Incarnation points to. Here we can appropriately remember Bérulle's lines: The Incarnation "is the work and the triumph of uncreated love, in which fortunately love triumphs over God himself."[52]

If you will, the characteristics just sketched — a willingness to participate in adoration and service, with all that each implies — bring us into the flow — the "economy," to use the favored word of the *patres* — of the trinitarian-christological conversation. I use the word "flow," for these qualities, or "states," foster just that: the flow, the movement, the transcending of the biases and other hindrances getting in the way of this particular "conversation." Plato might have thought of this as the *eros*, the attractive pull of it all, about which Voegelin has written so eloquently, as we saw in the previous chapter. Now I would like to turn to some further factors that add a bit more "shape" to our participation in this conversational movement, factors further fostered by the French School. I'm not sure what to call these "factors." Gadamer would consider them, on a hermeneutical level, "prejudices" in his special sense of "prejudgments" that enable us to enter the hermeneutical conversation with more or less refinement, sensitivity, ability to inquire and discriminate, and so on. Ricoeur would see all of these elements making up that complex reality, "understanding" or *verstehen*, that initial whole that we are and with which we enter the interpretation process. For much traditional theology, this would be the "prejudgments" of a "faith informed by charity."

So let us consider all of these the "prejudgments" fostered by this particular contemplative tradition. Adoration and service are such prejudgments too, and the ones to follow are further specifications or refinements, if you will. Perhaps we might fruitfully recall Bérulle's "chain of love" — Trinity, Incarnation, and eucharist. For the cardinal, these are interrelated realities, the one "implying" or "implicating" the other. The trinitarian "society" of shared communication grounds the possibility of the sharing of God with us in the Incarnation and its continuation in eucharist/church. Well, the French School's "prejudgments" form something of a chain of love too, each implicating the other. A sensitivity to one will or should promote a sensitivity to the other.

That triad or chain of Trinity, Incarnation, and eucharist (church) is surely one such prejudgment. We can look at these either from a method or a content perspective; the former is now the focus. Here I would note the "place" of the Incarnation: it is between Trinity and church, pointing back to the one and forward to the other. I understand this to mean that, for the French School, each of these realities lights up the other and coimplicates the other. Incarnational faith will suffer or at least wane if trinitarian and ecclesial faith suffer too. Obviously these are enormously difficult areas here, but hermeneutically trinitarian and ecclesial faith function like guides enabling us to understand dimensions of the Incarnation. This means, too, that we should look to the faith experience of the church and its teachings as an avenue giving us access to the Incarnation. The church community is part of the "history of effects" of the Incarnation in history. The life of shared community found in it is a hermeneutical sensitizer toward grasping the meaning of the Incarnation itself. The implication here is, clearly, that one will miss aspects of the Incarnation if one does not participate in the church's life, and share its faith. If you will, the mystery of communication that the eucharist-church is "signifies" for us the mystery of self-communication that God has become for us in Jesus. In the eucharist, says Bérulle, God "imprints in our bodies by his divine and sacred touch, as the fathers say, a power that disposes us...and communicates to all."[53]

Trinitarian faith experience is a similar "hermeneutical" sensitizer. Inasmuch as the Incarnation is rooted in the Trinity's inner mystery of self-communication, a sensitivity to the latter cannot help but illuminate the former. And so we have found the cardinal exploring analogies between the mystery of the Trinity and the Incarnation. To take a further example, the cardinal argues that the hypostatic union is "the highest of all the orders" made by God. How does he know this? He sees it as rooted in the trinitarian mystery: "For just as there is only one begotten Son in the bosom of the Father, so also did God desire that there be only one Son of Man who was Son of God." Perhaps we might say that the Son is the unique personalization of God, now made known to us in Jesus. Through him God brings to completion "the unspeakable communication of himself."[54] Here we note how coming to appreciate Jesus' "supreme uniqueness" is hindered if one's trinitarian faith is correspondingly truncated.

We noted in the previous chapters something of the interrelated roles of truth/theory, practice, and even the forms of expression or symbolization used in theory and practice. Questions of method or interpretation are primarily theory questions, to be sure. Theory is concerned with exploring what kind of theoretical enterprise theology and christology should be, and we are trying to make a case for its fundamentally meditative-contemplative nature. Clearly, this is one of the key emphases of the French School's science of the saints. But theory cannot be separated from practice, since it is, as Tracy so helpfully says, "an abstraction from, and an enrichment of, our concrete experience. Theory necessarily abstracts from actual practice to highlight certain salient, sometimes essential, but never exhaustive features of that practice."[55] If you will, good interpretation follows the movement of life. That is why Tracy goes on to say that good theory is itself a kind of praxis, "to be tested by the practice it serves."[56] Here I would only note that the French School keeps itself linked to practice quite consciously — note Olier's "Jesus in our hands" — chiefly through its willingness to explore both the "general" and the more "special" states of participation to which the individual is called. Participationist knowledge is a committed form of knowing, and there should be a kind of consonance between knowing and doing.

Theory looks to the "true," and practice looks to the "good." What, now, about the "beautiful," the particular "forms" through which the true is known and the good is expressed? We noted earlier, too, that there is a complex interrelation between form and content, expression and thought/deed. Where, indeed, is the thought or deed not expressed in form, not embodied? Perhaps one of the most promising insights in contemporary interpretation theory today is its attentiveness to language — the forms — through which truth is disclosed and, I would add, deeds are expressed. The symbolic form if you will, if it's not merely an artificial ornament, is cogenerated by the truth and deed themselves and helps guide us into a fuller participation within them. We recall our comments about how participation in the form brings about participation in the content.

Here I would suggest that the French School, while not providing us with a theory of symbolic forms, is particularly creative, in the sense that it has generated its own rich symbolic forms. And one senses that this was a kind of conscious reaction to the conceptual style of theology to which it sought to be an alternative/corrective. The *Grandeurs*, from which some of the above elevations were taken, is itself a special kind of genre, mixing or blending prayer and reflection, adoration and the call to service, mystery and thought. It goes back and forth between science and sanctity: the metaphysical probings of Bérulle as he explores Jesus' privation of a human "hypostasis," now replaced by that of the Logos, are conjoined to the elevation movement of lyrical "O's"/"Oh's" and praise and adoration, thus keeping this metaphysics humble, rooted in spiritual experience, attentive to mystery. Indeed, the preference for the symbolism of "mysteries" of Jesus, with their profound "interior" beyond their "exterior," as well as the constant rooting of theology in the scriptures, particularly Paul and John, shows this sensitivity to what Ricoeur calls the more originary sources of revelation, which theology serves, but does not replace. Note, too, how the French School has structured into its special genre(s) its leading symbolisms/metaphors. "Adherence," "regard," "relation," "praise," "adoration," "*anéantissement,*" "mystery," "state," "elevation," "elevate," "reference," "refer," etc., "contaminate" one another, bringing out deeper aspects of the "interior" of these "exterior" experiences. These metaphors also repeat themselves like a litany, lending a doxological and interiorizing flavor to this school's literature.

The "mixed genre" of the French School might be called a "theodoxology," or "doxological discourse," in order to bring out the two dimensions of theology (discourse) and doxology (adoration). The doxological dimension is particularly expressed through the "elevations," which actually "lift us up" (metaphorically), not unlike the Preface of the Mass inviting us to lift up our hearts. They intensify the vertical, transcendental dimension of revelation, but also imply the dazzlement we feel in the gracious presence of the Beyond drawing near to us. They give us the sense of God, not simply as beyond, but also incarnate, dazzlingly present in Jesus' humanity. The lyrical "O's" and "Oh's" seem to promote the sense of "savoring" the Divine, the sense of somehow experiencing a taste of eternity now, for which we give thanks, praise, and adoration. Merely passing chronological time "vanishes" in a prolonged, "unending" (eternal) now. The focus shifts, in adoration, from the self and its gifts to the Giver: it seems to intensify the "objectivity" of divine revelation as a gift from the Beyond.

But this is joined with "discourse," "commentary," "analysis" — the theological dimension of the genre. Divine revelation is not simply an unknowable Mystery. It is the Word incarnate, becoming knowable for us, in which we can participate through the Spirit. And so lyrical apostrophes turn into theological insight and practical behavior. Negative "theology" is joined with "affirmative" theology, if you will. This theological dimension is particularly appropriate to the christocentric stress of the French School, whose special charism is to highlight the *revealing* and *saving* role of the incarnate Word.

The French School generally, I would say, employs some form of this mixed, theodoxological genre, at least among its principals. It knows the letter genre, too, which brings out the personal, "direct address" character of Christianity. And this is surely appropriate for a school stressing how we are all called to unique participations in the mysteries of Jesus. And it knows the narrative/autobiographical genre as well. Olier is well known for his *Mémoires,* and we have already mentioned Bérulle's *Life of Jesus.* This latter is a doxological narrative, to be sure, but in it the eternal finds its balance in the temporal, the flow of time so well expressed in narrative.[57]

Hopefully by now the christologian is sensing that there is much of great value in this tradition for christology itself. But, of course, much of modern christology — as seems somewhat normal for a theological "science," after all — has pursued another route, finding a preference for more "austere" historical and "anthropological" approaches. It is less of a meditative-contemplative reflection, and more of a debate or dissecting analysis that often seems to take place in christological circles. To return to the favored terms in interpretation theory, it is rather "explanation" (*erklären*) than "understanding" (*verstehen*) that seems to receive the stress. The *verstehen* moment, especially when (re)conceived along these meditative-contemplative lines, has a reputation of being vague, obscurantist, lacking in controls, "mystical" in the not totally undeserved pejorative sense of "misty."

And as I argued previously, I agree that there is a role for argument, explanation, sustained analysis, and even some forms of "hermeneutics of suspicion" in theology. Especially does this seem helpful when the theological conversation breaks down and gets interrupted, as Tracy so helpfully says. Participating in Jesus' mysteries, if it shares the trinitarian structure of a conversation, is still, from our side, a finite conversation. The flow of it all can be obstructed and it can almost always use greater differentiation and clarity. So, yes, surely, understanding need not, should not ordinarily proceed without explanation (in our widened sense). In our experience they're much more closely related, as we saw earlier.

Here I would only suggest that many of the meditative-contemplative traditions, especially our French School, are aware of these things in their own parallel ways, and indeed that they have much to contribute to sharpening our explanatory skills. But first I must say that for them the explanatory moment is secondary, always in service to the trinitarian conversation in which we are called to participate, whose fullest ramifications always exceed exact "objectification." The Mystery remains. Also, I would suggest that there is a fundamental optimism in the great contemplative traditions: we do share in the Logos through the Spirit. Despite our closure, the "conversation" always remains both possibility and inchoate reality. A hermeneutics of suspicion that would elevate negativity over trust and affirmation is, I think, giving in too much to a kind of hermeneutical Jansenism and moral pessimism. Christologically it's elevating sin over salvation, or at least equalizing them — which, I believe, is known as Manichaeanism. "Hermeneutical Jansenism or Manichaeanism" may be a bit odd, but I think they hit the mark!

Here I would suggest that we recall that the dimension of "asceticism" is one element at least allied with the explanatory moment in theology. Asceticism implies a regime, a discipline, a somewhat ordered program to facilitate one's getting somewhere. The various schemes of spiritual development (abstracting from certain difficulties we can legitimately have with them) — from beginner, to proficient, to perfect; or from purgation to illumination and on to union; or the dark nights of the senses and spirit, etc. — are the equivalent in many ways, in the spiritual life, of what explanation is in theological science. Explanation is a disciplined, more worked out, manner of getting toward the objective of theological insight. It functions as theology's "asceticism." And here I would suggest that the ascetical practice of the contemplative tradition might have something to teach the ascetical-explanatory practice of theology.[58]

The French School "hangs loose" on its ascetical moment, in the sense of articulating it into an ordered, systematized program. At least among its originators. The rather rigid systematizing that occurred later, as with St. Ignatius Loyola's methods, illustrates the kind of formalism authentic mystics always rebel against, and especially the French School. Recall its great stress upon the "interior," upon the unique call of the individual, upon the mystery, etc.[59] Still, there is a regime of *anéantissement* (self-abnegation) and adoration, ecclesial service, meditative and thoughtful exploring of Jesus' mysteries in all their facets and lyrical elevations and apophatic silence, and a struggle to move toward ever greater depths of interiorization and practice that characterize our tradition here. The *anéantissement* moment, that painful "no-saying" to anti-Jesus attitudes and actions on all the levels of our being, reaching down to the depths (the *fond*), is even a kind of spiritual hermeneutics of suspicion, surely with some relevance to theology.

Perhaps the key point I want to make is that the French School is aware of illusion as well as superficiality, and it takes steps to avoid both. Deep from within the bases of the contemplative tradition here there is an openness, even an eros, toward submitting oneself to disciplined development and critique. This is also why our principals will refer to the *patres* and to the "doctors" of the Schools, especially Thomas Aquinas, seeking to learn from them and refine their own meditative insights into the various mysteries. The French School fully participates in the patristic and biblical revival of its time, in addition to its mining and translating of the great mystical teachers.

So, the French School knows something of what the theologian might call the explanatory moment in theology. And that school can be appealed to as a source and precedent, which refuses to separate deeper motives and foundations (the "understanding" moment) from the disciplined need for refinement and appeals to warranting criteria

73

(the "explanation" moment). In fact, given the profound nature of the mysteries under consideration, not to mention the great demand they make upon us personally and socially, there is all the more need to submit oneself to a kind of asceticism. Still, and this seems very valuable for us in our "methodological" age, the asceticism involved in explanation remains secondary and in service to a much greater reality.

Contributions to Christology's "Content"

Keeping in mind the back and forth relationship between method and content, what might some of the more important content considerations be from our survey above? What follows is simply a sampling of some of the more fundamental christological themes of the French School, especially as illustrated in Bérulle. They are not listed in an order of priority — all seem to be relatively important themes coming from the profound meditations-elevations of this spiritual tradition.

First, there is a resolute "refusal" to separate divinity from humanity in the mystery of Jesus, throughout the entire span of his life, earthly and glorified. To fool with this would be, as the cardinal says, to fool with "the basis of Christianity, whose treasure and foundation are the actions and the sufferings of this humanity, not simply as humanity, but as the humanity of the Word."[60] The French School is, somewhat like the tradition of Teresa of Avila, emphatically centered on the humanity of Jesus. But it is a humanity whose "hypostasis" is the Word. Here we have to keep in mind the rootedness of the Incarnation in the mystery of the Trinity: the divine trinitarian dialogue spills out, as fully as can be, in Jesus. Jesus is that dialogue in its fullest personal way in human history.

Yet the French School knows that the divinity-humanity is not always manifest in the same manner throughout Jesus' entire career. One of the functions of the "Jesus the voyager" and "Jesus the comprehensor" distinction, borrowed from the School theology, is precisely to preserve an element of discrimination here. Prior to resurrection-ascension, Jesus' divinity-humanity takes the form chiefly of a kenosis whose deeper meaning is "veiled," the more "glorious" unveiling coming later. We have even seen how the cardinal, daringly for his time, interprets Jesus' temptations (the desert experience) as experiences of real solidarity with the pains of the sinful and damned (but not their guilt). Here the kenosis and veiling of Jesus' identity seem particularly harsh. In the Thomas Aquinas of the *Summa theologiae*, at least, Jesus undergoes the temptations more as an example to us of our ability to withstand sin than as a form of solidarity with the damned.[61] The attentiveness to the infancy of Jesus, too, greatly stems from this sensitivity to the kenosis and voyaging-pilgrim status of Jesus.

Here it may be useful to ask whether a rehabilitation of this "voyager-comprehensor" distinction might be preferable to the frequent use of the categories of "the Jesus of history" and "the Christ of faith" among contemporary christologians. So far as I can tell, there's a diverse utilization of this latter categorization. For some it's a way of de-divinizing Jesus, arguing that the Christ of faith is a later and unfounded projection of divinity onto the simply human Jesus. For others, the distinction is more epistemological: it has to do with the disciples' lack of grasping Jesus' divinity until after resurrection. Among these, but a bit more radically still, the distinction cuts across, not only Jesus' disciples, but Jesus himself: he, too, "grasps" his divinity "later."

As we can see, not all of these can be correct. We need to keep in mind that there is a distinction between the "historical Jesus" and the "historian's Jesus." Granted, we can never grasp the former without some "historian's labor." Still the distinction holds. The really historical Jesus is the fullness of Jesus, in his divine-human unity. There is room and necessity for discriminating between Jesus' pre- and post-resurrection existence, but the divinity of Jesus, and Jesus' own real if not always reflex consciousness of this divinity, span both phases of his career. He is, in other words, the "Christ of faith" throughout his career, even though this seems grasped in varying ways, in both phases of his career, by the way.

My own preference at this point is to find the "voyager-comprehensor" set of categories less misleading and more adequate to the full reality of Jesus. It trusts the New Testament. At least as used by the French School, it can embrace the intent of Karl Barth's proposal, namely, that Jesus' entry into "comprehensive" glory is not the leaving behind of the loving kenosis of Jesus' pilgrim phase, but is that kenotic love's clear revelation and definitive empowerment as God's triumphant being, revelation, and work in him.[62] It is elastic enough to be open to a legitimate spread of views on the issue of just what precise kind of consciousness of divinity Jesus possessed during his pre-resurrection existence. It is also elastic enough to embrace differences in faith-awareness among disciples in both phases of Jesus' career. For example, should the Blessed Virgin Mary's and Mary Magdalene's "fidelity" to Jesus already in his pre-resurrection phase be equalized with that, say, of Peter? Recall Bérulle's outstanding "Elevation on Mary Magdalene" and some of the insights coming from contemporary women's theology about the role of women in Jesus' ministry.[63] In other words, interestingly this older set of categories is balanced enough to meet the legitimate concerns of those

75

using the more "modern" categories, without misleadingly fostering a positivistic separating of divinity and humanity in Jesus' personal being itself.

Secondly, I would suggest that there remains much of value in the French School's subtle use of a distinction often expressed as the difference between the "interior" and the "exterior" of the mysteries of Jesus.[64] Despite its "rough" nature and at times Neoplatonic tendency to separate unduly what should remain interrelated, still the distinction guards us against the kind of reductionism that reduces history to its more "sense-apparent" level, denigrating the meaning and truth dimensions thereof. We could say, in our own terms, that the interior of the mystery points us toward a luminosity model of truth and revelation. Where this gets lost sight of, the study of christology sinks into a kind of listing of chronological and somewhat "biographical" details robbed of their deeper significance. "Everyone should have within him the interior life that the exterior mysteries represent as well as the grace acquired by these same mysteries," said M. Olier, meaning by the "interior" the "dispositions and sentiments that our Lord had in these mysteries."[65] It's clear how this is related to the discussion we just completed. Without some appreciation of the "interior" of the mysteries, there can be no faith apprehension of the divinity of Jesus, surely. If you will, this distinction flows from the French School's *sensus misticus* or "spiritual sense," and ultimately is rooted in a richer and indeed mystical view of Christian and human experience.

There is perhaps more that we can learn from this set of distinctions too. For while the entire career of Jesus in all its phases is relevant in christology, not all aspects are relevant in the same way or in the same degree. Surely we are in need of some tool of discrimination, whereby we can make the kinds of discriminations we need in this area. Thus, I would suggest that the category of the "interior" of the mysteries, at its best, does not denigrate the "exterior," more spatial-temporal ("brute-factual"/somatic) aspects of Jesus' career, but helps us to focus upon the degrees of meaning and disclosures of revelation coming through these. If you will, the attempt to "conform to Jesus' interior dispositions and sentiments" is a way of recognizing that not every spatial-temporal detail of Jesus' life is equally meaningful, and in fact many of those details remain "hidden" or at least "dim." The "interior" directs us away from a fact-fetishism, even with respect to Jesus' career, pointing us toward the revelatory disclosure breaking through the "exterior, sacramental" aspect of Jesus' mysteries. For example, somatically many have died on a cross. But the "interior" of the exterior mystery of the cross of Jesus involves the kenotic/adoring love of the Man-God Jesus.[66]

At the same time, the interior directs us toward the deeper, under-lying "unity" of the God-Man mystery that keeps us in touch with every aspect of Jesus' career and yet limits us to no one single aspect. The Bérullian feast of the "Solemnity of Jesus"[67] was a way, I think, of keeping in focus this deeper unity of Jesus amidst the diversity of his states and mysteries. Finally, I would suggest that this notion of the "interior" promotes a sensitivity toward those dispositions and sentiments of Jesus that remain somewhat "unknown," as the cardinal says.[68] Some of what remains "unknown" to us is surely relevant to christology and to our salvation. The depth dimension of the God-Man surely involves much that transcends our "reach." This, too, needs surfacing in christology.

This is perhaps one of the areas most challenging to contempo-rary methods in christology. Where, for example, are the controls of the *sensus misticus*, this "interior" dimension of the mysteries? The French School provides no simplistic answer, but seems to recognize a back and forth movement between exterior and interior, historical "surface" if you will and the deeper world of disclosure struggling to emerge through the historical surface. The "controls" seem to come from both directions, with the influence of the "interior" occupying a kind of primacy.

Perhaps another important challenge to contemporary christology posed by the French School is its stress upon Jesus as not only our model, but also our source and our goal. As the cardinal put it,

We should exist and dwell perpetually in him, just as he exists and dwells in his Father. We should always live and act through him and for him, just as he lives and acts through his Father. For he is both the source and goal of our existence and our life.[69]

We recall the Bérullian teaching upon the "states" of the mysteries of Jesus. The God-Man is now truly an effective power of transforma-tion and "deification" (salvation) for all of us, enabling us to enter into the mystery of adoration and service that he is. And we, too, should aim to participate in and imitate him not only in our passing actions but in our "stable state of being" too, "the way that is constant, solid and permanent," honoring "the state and the life into which the Son of God entered through the sacred mystery of the Incarnation and in which he perseveres eternally in heaven."[70] We recall, too, the sub-tle idea that while all of us are called to participate in the mysteries of Jesus in a "general" way, we are also called to unique modes of participation in accord with God's unique call to each of us. And only a very subtle process of discernment, whereby our "interior" is attuned to Jesus' "interior," can enable us to know the unique config-uration of our call. Jesus' interior, consisting of "the intentions and dispositions by which God could be honored," says M. Olier, "must be always before our eyes as the source and model of all the interior life of our souls."[71]

Here I would suggest that contemporary christologies dwelling more upon the "surface" or "brute-factual" dimensions of history, suspending or ignoring the "interior" or depth dimension of it all, tend to miss this aspect of christology. At most, Jesus becomes a kind of "model" or "super-brother" throwing before us ideals we may or may not want to imitate, or offering us a message to explore. But this contemplative approach, attempting adoringly and with a sense of service to explore the God-Man mystery, recognizes in Jesus an act of God that lives on, a divine yet human-incarnate source of saving love within our history. Jesus is surely our "model," in a mode appropriate to our humanly common yet unique destinies. He is the "*Logos*," the "Image," the deepest meaning of humanity imaged forth in incarnate form. He is also our "source," inasmuch as through him we have access to an "adoptive" filiation and salvation. But he is also our "goal," inasmuch as eternal life with the Father through the Word in the Spirit remains a participation in the Word *become incarnate*. Note, too, how this connects with pneumatology, for it is the Spirit who enables us truly to participate in Jesus, interiorizing his presence for us, while at the same time preserving its distinctness. Again, when a theology of the Spirit is missing, so too, it seems, is a sense of the presence of the risen Jesus. "Just as the Holy Spirit is the termination ... for the love of Father and Son, ... in the same way Jesus is the termination" of the Trinity's "love operating outside the Godhead, ... the fecundity of his Spirit," Bérulle says.[72]

Here we can begin to see how all of these issues, hermeneutical and more topical, are deeply intertwined. The *Logos* incarnate is the ground/source through the Spirit of our participation in the mysteries of Jesus, enabling us to respond by our own "inner word" to the great "Word" that he is and that he has revealed throughout his many mysteries. Because he is source and goal, we can participate in his mysteries, both in a way common to all, and in a more special and unique manner appropriate to our own unique *attrait*, an *attrait* appropriately nourished and respected by a God "triumphing over the God-Self in love." This helps us grasp as well why it is, as Barth argued, that we cannot distinguish, with absolute decisiveness, Jesus from the believing community and the New Testament witness to him. Holding this unity in focus, and reflecting upon it in a careful manner, is one of the great contributions of the French School. Karl Rahner, it merits mentioning here, said toward the end of his career that theology had hardly begun reflecting upon questions dealing with our "personal relationship to Jesus," but that there were "a few exceptions here and there, as, for example, Bérulle, a representative of the French school of spirituality in the seventeenth century."[73]

The theme of kenosis or service is one that has received renewed attention in our times. Here is an area where both more traditional christologies and more contemporary kinds seem to unite. Of course, the theme of kenosis brings out the compassionate nature of Jesus as one in solidarity with the forgotten, and so it resonates with christologies wanting to surface the sensitivity to the human, and especially the oppressed, in the life and ministry of Jesus. We should recall Bérulle's analogous stress upon this theme, one that he surely came to appreciate through his own deep spirituality of self-abandonment (*anéantissement*) and servitude. And in this he is followed by his principal disciples, such as M. Olier, Mother Madeleine de Saint-Joseph, and St. John Eudes.

Perhaps, however, what is not so stressed in contemporary christologies is the theme of adoration, and it is through this that the French School might be able to infuse some fresh insight into our contemporary concerns. There is a fascinating and "pregnant" comment in Père Denis Amelote's biography of Father Condren, Bérulle's immediate successor as the French Oratory's superior general, which might help us get at this freshness from the adoration theme:

> [Bérulle] is the one to have raised up this buried virtue [of respect]....
> ...it is certain that, in this century in which so much sanctity appears, we see in souls more familiarity with God than reverence, and we find many Christians who love God, but few who respect him....
> ...but should one penetrate to the depth of spirits, he will doubtlessly confess that respect for God is hardly known, and that children aren't raised with a profound adoration of his grandeur, but only with a freedom toward him. This is the source of the neglect of the Holy Sacrifices, the esteem for apparent austerity, and the scorn of priests.[74]

Building on this, we might say that the contemporary emphasis upon kenosis is like the emphasis upon love noted by Amelote above. Love is surely a rich theme, the great theme, and it seems entirely appropriate to stress it in christology, especially in an age like our own that has grown increasingly sensitive to it. But adoration adds a nuance to love, which does not detract from it, but brings out its deep meaning and in fact protects it from degenerating into a kind of sentimentalism or excessively humanistic narcissism. To adore God is to refuse to manipulate the Divine Self in our love: the love remains reverential of the More, "obedient" in the New Testament sense. At the same time, stressing that it is an adorable kenosis with which we have to do in Jesus brings out the properly divine depth of that kenosis, its radically free, gratuitous, grace-bestowing nature. It is so difficult to keep these two — service and adoration — in a complementary focus. Service brings God "down" into the city, and involves Jesus in our struggles. This is why it surely is a congenial aspect of christology in our modern era. Adoration lifts us "up," "elevates" us, in a sense beyond our cities and ourselves. It presents us with a Jesus who discloses the "Adorable More" forever worthy of adoring subjects. Push the first, service, excessively, and it will lead inevitably toward a "low" christology. Push the second, and it will lead to a simply "high" and increasingly separatist christology. Maximize the mutual complementarity of both and you have the God-Man unity that the French School fascinatingly tries to bring before us.

This rich theme of adoration, to which we will devote an entire chapter, implies much more, of course. Bérulle seems to accent the transcendental otherness of God intensified in this experience. But he also strongly notes that it is the Incarnation that reveals the truest form of adoration. As we will see, adoration seems to involve both transcendence and immanence, divine otherness and incarnational presence. An adorably sovereign subject has the personal freedom to reveal the Divine Self personally. And this, in its supreme form, is what the Incarnation is. If you will, God is always adorable, but if we are to grasp this, it must be revealed to us through the adoration offered by the Incarnation.

This theme also connects with the trinitarian dimensions of christology, which I would consider another particular blessing for christology from the French School. We have already noted the rooting of the Incarnation mystery in the Trinity so typical of the French School. This is why it is considered a form of exemplarism; that is, the Trinity is considered by this school the exemplar-cause that creatures, including Jesus, in varying ways "exemplify." To return to the notion of adoration, Jesus' own act of adoration in the Incarnation is itself rooted in the act of adoring homage which the Son renders the Father in the trinitarian life. In the Incarnation, Jesus "offers all created reality in homage to God," says Bérulle, "just as in the Godhead, he offers to God his Father all that proceeds and is uncreated at the same time." It is Jesus' very trinitarian "self" that guides and invites him "to enter into a new state [the Incarnation] for the glory of his Father."[75]

This is but one of the many ways in which the French School links incarnationalism with trinitarianism. The crucial thing is that they are so linked, and that our principals expend enormous energy in searching out the analogies between the chief exemplar of the Trinity and its supreme earthly "example" in the Incarnation. Contemporary christologies, I think, have only begun to probe the mutual enrichment that comes from this kind of back and forth between Incarnation and

Trinity. In Bérulle, somewhat challengingly for our times, it throws light upon the unique mystery that the Incarnation really is: "For just as there is only one begotten Son in the bosom of the Father, so also did God desire that there be only one Son of Man who was Son of God."[76] The uniquely differentiated and personal love between Father and Son finds its earthly revelation in the uniquely personal revelation that the God-Man is. Bérulle, of course, goes on to say that the Spirit makes it possible for us to participate in that unique relationship between Father and Son. If you will, the mysterious reality of the Spirit seems to point to a God whose love is never exclusive, but always participable.[77] Still, the Spirit does not take away the singularity of the Father-Son relationship revealed in Jesus. Through the Spirit we share in it, but it remains the uniquely supreme reality that it is. The Spirit grounds our sharing in Jesus, but in a manner "protecting" both Jesus' singularity as well as our own unique charisms.

Taking a clue from Bérulle, we might well ask the question of what happens to incarnationalism when trinitarianism wanes? It is perhaps not accidental that a radical "demythologization" of the one goes along with a radical demythologization of the other, as Brian Hebblethwaite has recently and persuasively reminded us.[78] Perhaps the French School will aid us in being cautious here. A simply unitarian trend in theology would tend to depersonalize God, I think, and make it impossible to understand the hypostatic union as God's fully personal (definitive) revelation to us in history. It would be a more prepersonal vision of the Deity, and one, then, that could not bring out the depths of God's personalization — or "humanization" — for us in Jesus.

Let me touch briefly on another area where the French School may offer some illumination. I am thinking of soteriology/salvation. Christology and soteriology are not the same thing, of course, but they are surely related and mutually illuminate one another. In a broad sense, salvation has to do with the general impact of the Incarnation event upon humanity. In a more specific sense, it treats of how the Incarnation redeems us from our sins. Bérulle seems to move back and forth between the wider and the more specific senses. On the one hand, in the Incarnation Jesus "wishes to be, in a new way, a living and eloquent image of the grandeurs of God." He is what happens when God goes outside the Divine Self to fully communicate with us. At the same time, given our fallen state, Jesus "wishes to repair in us the image and likeness of the divinity imprinted in our nature and erased through sin." In this way he "wants to transform his own natural filiation into a living source of adoptive filiation."[79]

In many ways, the French School is not original here, but simply transmitting the tradition, particularly that of the early fathers and the New Testament, for whom christology and economy are inter-twined. Still, several emphases have a kind of "freshness" about them, which may prove helpful in the construction of contemporary chris-tologies. The great stress upon reverence and adoration may perhaps remind us that salvation is a being saved from our *sins*. One doesn't properly have a sense of "sin" unless one has in view, not only the damage caused ourselves in our immoral actions, but also the of-fending of God. The heightened theocentrism, symbolized through the stress upon adoration, helps us recognize that salvation is the bringing about of the ability to really adore. Mother Madeleine de Saint-Joseph's formulation of this is particularly helpful:

> Adoration is what God looked for from the beginning in his creatures. ...However, since angels and men failed in this...he wanted to choose a worshiper as great as himself and as little capable of failing as he would be. Thus he decided upon the mystery of the Incarnation, where a God would adore God.[80]

It is perhaps the other element of salvation stressed by Bérulle, that of kenosis/service, that receives more emphasis today. Again, service quite properly brings out the divine condescension into the "city of humanity," the divine compassion. So that Bérulle's con-stant stress upon the Incarnation as an event in which true kenosis now becomes possible is quite refreshing and congenial. But I would suggest that both of these elements — adoration and servitude — complement one another, and even "protect" one another from being abused in a reductive sort of way. Service keeps the adoration that of a God who loves us. But adoration keeps our service something more than a social work professionalism. It infuses something of that non-manipulative reverence that we adoringly offer to God into our work.

Just as we noted that christology itself suffers when one exag-gerates one of these — adoration or kenosis — at the expense of the other, so now we can see that salvation also suffers when one does this. Adoration and service need one another, and perhaps we could even suggest that their fissure creates the artificial separation of christology from salvation from which some forms of christology have suffered in recent memory. That is, stress the service element while forgetting the summons to adore, and we absorb salvation into a this-worldly, human project of social and personal betterment. The more we do this, the more salvation loses its links with the God-Man, who adores and is adored. Stress the adoration at the expense of ser-vice, and we get a skewed vision of Christ and God as getting along quite nicely without the bother of this vale of tears. Here christology becomes wrapped up in itself, cut off in turn from salvation. Surprisingly, adoration and service enable us to keep each — christology and salvation — interrelated while distinct. Hopefully the above will be enough to give the interested and sympathetic reader cause to look more deeply, if not at the French School, then at least at other contemplative traditions that may prove rich resources for the building of a contemporary christology. That of St. Teresa of Avila, or St. Ignatius Loyola, or St. Gregory Palamas come immediately to mind. And there are surely rich christological and especially soteriological mines in a John Wesley, Jonathan Edwards, Martin Luther, and John Calvin coming from a more "contemplative" style of theology too. But there are so many more! I am conscious that, even regarding simply the French School, I have only touched representative issues, and that many more may be of immediate interest to my readers.

I hesitate to look back in an attempt to impose an artificial "synthesis" on the above thoughts. A key consideration I have tried to bring out is the interplay between "method" and "content." If you will, the Incarnation is an event primarily of adoration and service, and it possesses its epistemological correlate in our own participation in those experiences of adoration and service. An adoring and serving consciousness and life help us share in the Incarnation mystery, and that mystery is the "state" and "ground" of our consciousness and life. The "conversational movement" between both is a major point I was trying to illuminate. Here is where we intersect with the concerns of contemporary hermeneutics and try to illustrate our "contemplative" perspective on it all.

But the above goes beyond hermeneutical considerations and reaches down into the actual work of "constructing" a systematic christology for our times. The various themes we have highlighted will prove important in that task. Looking back on all of these, we might sum it up by saying that the French School presents us with a forceful, and I think largely persuasive, form of christocentric trinitarianism or inclusive incarnationalism. It is "inclusive" in the sense that it tries to embrace, and hold in contemplative focus, the entire reality of the God-Man Jesus as well as christology's trinitarian foundations. We recall Bérulle's words: " . . . the basis of Christianity" is "the actions and sufferings of this humanity, not simply as humanity, but as the humanity of the Word."[81] Thus the many mysteries of the humanity of Jesus, and not simply the "birth moment," are contemplated and explored here, but never severed from the *Logos*. And we have tried to present a representative sampling of the range of these contemplations. This is rather more the Johannine inclusive incarnationalism that we have here.

At the same time, this school is "incarnational," in the sense that it stresses the wonder of *God* somehow *becoming human*. Recently,

83

Brian Hebblethwaite has perhaps captured something of what this means in his view of incarnationalism as meaning the belief that "God himself, without ceasing to be God, has come amongst us, not just in but *as* a particular man, at a particular time and place."[82] This is the intent of the emphasis upon the singularity and supremacy of the hypostatic union, so pronounced by our principals, as we recall: "the order of the hypostatic union, which is the highest of all the orders," says Bérulle. And elsewhere: "When I say a new man, I mean not simply a just man, or a holy man; not an angelic or divine man, but a Man-God who sustains, rules and delights heaven and earth."[83] Incarnationalism asserts the most personal encounter between God and humanity possible: God becomes personally present to us, and so in a really uniquely differentiated manner, rather than more vaguely and in a relatively less personal and individual manner.

Recall our earlier comments, in the section on Jesus' infancy and Mary, about Bérulle's *Life of Jesus*. The way that work never gets beyond the conception stage, and the way it emphasizes the "moment" of the Incarnation, are ways of stressing the "eternal" in the "temporal," an eternity responded to by Bérulle's own contemplative ecstasies in which time seems for a moment transcended. Not so unlike the gospel of John, with its sense of the "eternal *was*," which has now "*become*" in time.[84] Well, it would seem that part of the power of Bérulle's style of incarnationalism is to linger over just this marvel and tension created by the becoming of the Eternal in time in Jesus. The kenosis movingly brings out the becoming; adoration, the eternal. Remove either, or relax the "tension" between them, and you remove the depth of the divine condescension in the kenosis, on the one hand, as well as the compassionate love in the adorable God, on the other. Here narrative's temporality is caught up in adoration's sense of the eternal.

At least on the points stressed above — which are only representative of many more — I would urge that contemporary christology has much to learn from the French School. This is not to say that there isn't room for "refinement" and "development" coming from greater historical and philosophical/theological insight. All of this is necessary, and the French School's own inner dynamics demands it. As we have seen, contemplation demands the "asceticism" of both a detached life of service and adoration and one of openness to theological critique. But always within the larger perspective of a contemplative hermeneutics. The theological moment of "clarity" grows from the contemplative *fond* of reverence.

For example, today we may want to question whether the language of the deprivation of Jesus' human "person" and its replacement by the Logos' "person" is alone sufficient to proclaim the unique hypostatic union.[85] The French School itself perhaps shows us a way forward here: not by doing away with the formulation, which is, after all, consecrated by tradition and conciliar in its authority. But the French School searches for a reexpression of the traditional formula, even while continuing to use it; namely, the Incarnation becomes, with Bérulle and his disciples, a supreme and unique revelation of adoration and service. Part of the traditional formula's greatness is to protect the unique reality of the "being" and "constitution" of Jesus himself as not simply assimilable to the presence of God in others, whether they be saints, mystics, holy people, etc. God's own reality finds its uniquely supreme personalization in Jesus.

And there are, of course, other developments needing to be considered. The concerns of feminist and psychosocial forms of theology have their appropriate contributions to make, for example. And one must take up, on an individual basis, historical-factual issues having light thrown upon them by contemporary research. But, in the main, one senses in the French School a powerful and persuasive presentation of the compatibility between a true incarnationalism and the legitimate concerns of a truly contemporary christology. But it is a christology seeking to be "contemporary" in the sense of the contemplative hermeneutics of our previous chapter.

Bérulle, with his principal disciples, it may be helpful to conclude, seems peculiarly and providentially well placed to help us navigate in these difficult christological seas. Somewhat like the great St. Teresa of Avila, he was for a time insufficiently attuned to the importance of the humanity of Jesus. Apparently he was influenced by a tradition of what is called "abstract mysticism," that is, the tendency to view the spiritual life as one of ever greater advancement toward the "spiritual" and away from the "earthly" and "material." And the humanity of Jesus was sometimes included in those latter. In any case, we do know that the cardinal underwent a "christocentric conversion," to such an extent that Pope Urban VIII named him "the apostle of the Incarnate Word." This does not mean that he completely rejected the concerns of this abstract mysticism, with its sensitivity to the transcendent and the "apophatic" dimension of the faith. His approach was more integrative.

This turn to the christocentric, a mystical grace for the cardinal, is a grace for us too. In his own time, that of the dawning Renaissance and its growing anthropocentrism, we can see why some, perhaps alienated from the new pluralism and daring tendencies of the time, might fall back upon a reoccurring tendency to take flight in the "spiritual" away from the "temporal-material." Transposed into christological terms, this would be a taking flight in the Logos beyond and apart from the humanity. To some extent, perhaps, the later Jansenists were doing precisely this.

But there is the other tendency too, namely, to plunge oneself into the anthropocentric to such an extent that one loses a sense of one's "nothingness" apart from God. Transposed into christological terms, this would be to take flight in Jesus' humanity, but apart from the Word.

Our own times seem to know both of these tendencies in varying shades too. And as Bérulle with his associates steered a course between both through an appealing stress upon the humanity of the Word — Christianity's basis is "this humanity, not simply as humanity, but as the humanity of the Word,"[86] said the cardinal — perhaps they can help us steer that course still.

CHAPTER FOUR

On "Christologies from Above and from Below"

"Almost all contemporary thinking about Jesus Christ begins not 'from above' but 'from below,'" Gerald O'Collins said in one of his helpful surveys.[1] Some of us, for reasons that will become clearer, to some extent "resist" being aligned along these kinds of axes. But still, O'Collins is expressing what many in the christological craft do hold or might well want to hold. In some plausible fashion, many, maybe most, modern christologians could be characterized as fashioning a form of "christology from below." And perhaps many of these would want to be so characterized. The 1984 document of the Pontifical Biblical Commission, *Bible et christologie*,[2] finds the characterization useful as a way of describing many of the major approaches in christology it surveys. The nomenclature has reached the "official" levels of the church. Given what appears to be the widespread use of this "from below" approach to christology, it will be helpful, for purposes of clarification and possible contrast, to study the issue a bit more closely and explore its relationships with the kind of christology being pursued in this book.

The Critical Moment

A great diversity exists among "christologians from below," on any plausible rendering of what this means. But we encounter a relatively strong emphasis on the need to critique the seeming inadequacies of the so-called high or descent, christology of the great councils of the church. The characterization "from below" implies this critique of the "christologies from above" found in, say, Ephesus and Chalcedon. We are all familiar with the basic pattern of the latter, which has its roots already in the New Testament, particularly the Johannine prologue: The Holy Mystery, which dwells "above" the heavens (at least metaphorically, if not quasi-literally for some), "descends" to the earth "below" for the salvation of humanity. "...who for us human beings and our salvation came down," says the Nicene Creed of Jesus.[3] This Johannine and Nicene pattern "from above to below" is used as the basis for making the distinction between christologies "from above" and "from below."

Not everyone, of course, is attracted (or equally attracted) to some form of critique of the councils. For many, the "traditional" and "classical" horizons still hold firm, or their "cracks" haven't been too fully pondered. Others, perhaps, may be "bothered" by the traditional framework, but find it preferable to alternatives, at least at this point. For this reason, they may not push the critical moment any further in their imaginations. At least not yet. Others (perhaps many of the Eastern Orthodox tradition?) are trying to evolve their own contemporary adaptation of the councils without going through the kind of "deconstructive" moment many or most christologians from below have undergone. In contemporary Catholic theology, perhaps the retrieval of the traditional *Logos* christology by Hans Urs von Balthasar by appeal to an "analogy of love," whereby the Logos expresses the self-emptying divine love in the uniquely singular Jesus, belongs to some extent in this genre.[4]

Christologians moving from the "from below" perspective, on the other hand, tend to be deeply influenced by the cultural and intellectual emphases that have rocked the European-American countries since the late Renaissance and Enlightenment. To a great extent, it is the "early" Enlightenment with its human subject-centered turn and scientific fascination for the natural world that has been the dominant influence here, stimulating theologians to fashion christologies that are attuned to these "novel" sensitivities. Karl Rahner often spoke of "anthropocentrism" as *the* characteristic of modernity, and clearly this is a crucial influence upon christologies from below. It may be *the* most powerful influence, although the fascination for modern science has played some role among modern christologies (think of Chardin and christologies of the process philosophy kind). In any case, let us look at one of Rahner's own critiques of the traditional christologies. It offers one of the more sophisticated and balanced examples of what I am calling the "deconstructive moment" or "critical moment" of our christologies from below. Dwelling with it for awhile may sensitize us to this critical facet of our subject.

While suggesting that the Christian theologian must remain in fidelity with the traditional christology, Rahner proposes, not a denial, but a critical reinterpretation of the councils. Except for a radical minority, this is common. Deconstruction is *a* moment, in the service of a more positive reconstruction of the christological heritage of the church. Rahner variously speaks of the normativity and the irreplaceability of the conciliar christology, and of the need to develop a mutual correspondence between it and more modern types. "It would be a reproach to ourselves, and to our own spiritual and mental laziness," says Rahner, "the stuntedness of our historical sense, and our bondage to a fashionable present which is not aware of its paltry limitations," were we to cut off continuity with the councils.[5]

Still, the traditional christology tended to present us with an idealized view of Jesus' humanity, Rahner thinks. This is not the same as a denial of Jesus' humanity. One cannot read the scriptures and the entire patristic discussion and come away thinking that Jesus' humanity was denied. Every seminary graduate has at least heard of the notion, so typical of the *patres*, that what was not assumed was not healed. Many remember the "really's" and "truly's" of Ignatius of Antioch, as he sought to defend Jesus' humanity against those thinking it was "only an illusion": ". . . truly born of Mary, who ate and drank, was truly tried by Pontius Pilate, was really crucified, and died. . . . "[6] Nonetheless, Rahner thinks there was a tendency to ignore the full implications of the really full humanity of Jesus, or to be uneasy with it, moving in a kind of monophysite direction, or at least lending that direction some fuel. Surely Jesus *the man's* believing, hoping, being tempted, and searching (to mention some of the qualities underscored by Rahner) do not receive as much attention as many moderns might like, at least in the decrees of the councils and in much of the textbook theology of later periods (Rahner excepts popular piety, and I would tend to except much of the patristic literature that undergirds Chalcedon: viz., Leo's famous "Tome," the writings of Athanasius, Cyril, Theodore of Mopsuestia, etc.).

Is this "idealized" view of Jesus' humanity not still a strong factor among us? Many teachers have often experienced a kind of resistance among their students to a more "concrete" and realistic appreciation of Jesus' humanity. This may be, in part, a reaction to some of the more secularistic or reductionistic views of Jesus "on the market." But it may also be a residue of the "monophysitism" Rahner has in mind. This latter is, understandably enough perhaps, rather strong in our tradition. For example, we recall that St. Thomas Aquinas, in his treatment of Jesus' temptations, seems to have trouble entertaining the thought that Jesus was actually vulnerable to human weakness (not sin, of course). The four reasons he offers for why it was fitting that Jesus be tempted have very little to do with Jesus. The temptations of Jesus seem, on Aquinas's view of them, mainly *for us:* to strengthen us in our own moments of temptation, to warn us, to give

89

us an example, and to fill us with confidence.[7] Thomas speaks of Jesus' "wishing" to be tempted, as if he were staging this for our benefit. Now St. Thomas's achievement is magnificent in many respects, but it seems less than adequate on this score. Thomas's handling of Jesus' *human* knowing seems more balanced to me, admitting an authentic human mode of knowing for Jesus. But even here Thomas wants this to be always "in a perfect form of actuation." One wonders about mistakes, for example, wrong hunches, wrong approaches to issues, etc.[8]

As late as the 1964 statement of the Pontifical Biblical Commission, "The Historical Truth of the Gospels," we are told that "[Jesus] followed the modes of reasoning and of exposition which were in vogue at the time. He accommodated himself to the mentality of his listeners...." In some ways this statement represents a breakthrough, for it seems to admit the historicity of Jesus' teaching at least. But if we dwell with it awhile, we will notice that it hesitates, and is indeed ambiguous. As Raymond E. Brown put it, the document "recognizes a limited worldview on Jesus' part, even if it delicately attributes this to accommodation. Most Catholic scholars would speak more openly of Jesus' own limited knowledge of his time."[9] The "idealized" portrait of Jesus' humanity still lingers, it seems. In our efforts to reappropriate, perhaps through imagination, Jesus' concrete humanity, we need not descend to the banal and distasteful. Jesus' humanity still remains holy, sacred, sinless, and extraordinary. But as the christologians from below add, with much persuasiveness, all of these latter attributes seem to coexist with a really growing and struggling and vulnerable humanity too.

Rahner adds a number of further criticisms that seem to be corollaries of this first one. For example, he suggests that the classical christology fails sufficiently to bring out the connection between the Divine Logos and his function as an earthly mediator of salvation. If you will, the vertical (divine aspect) and horizontal (the level of salvation history) remain too abstract. And for this reason, the soteriological, functional side of Jesus' work remains too widely separated from the aspect of the Divine Logos. It is through the life, and especially the death and resurrection, of Jesus that we are saved. The birth, the "instant" of the "assumption of flesh," is insufficient here as an explanation. An appeal to the "popular" satisfaction theory, Rahner thinks, remains too abstract too. What is it about Jesus' death that actually satisfies for our plight? A mere fiat by the Father isn't much of an explanation.[10]

Others have added their own peculiar twist to this type of conciliar criticism, and Rahner himself has interesting and slightly different approaches throughout his writings. A frequent topic of discussion is the need to find a language that enables us to grant a full human "personhood" to Jesus. Most scholars wouldn't argue that Chalcedon or other councils intended to deny such a thing to Jesus in our own modern sense. But it remains unexplicated in the councils. I should mention that the criticism hasn't only been concerned with reappropriating Jesus' full humanity. Reenvisioning God also is involved. Some want the kenoticism of God, or the divine ability to somehow enter into history and somehow participate in change and suffering, to be brought out in a fresh and more adequate manner.[11] Additionally, Schleiermacher long ago spoke of the inappropriateness of speaking of two natures in Jesus without further nuances, for it gives the impression that they are on the same level (or equal). But of course the "divine nature" is the ground and presupposition of the human. Walter Kasper, for example, said that to "speak of two natures is in any case problematic, because...the term 'nature' cannot be applied equally to God and man, and...an ethical or personal relation is thereby misinterpreted in a physical sense."[12]

This last point, about the reenvisioning of the Divine, deserves a little more attention. It helps us appreciate that, in the main, the critique of the councils is oriented toward deepening our knowledge of God, and our spiritual relationship with the Holy Mystery. Truncated views of Jesus' humanity seem to lead to truncated views of the Divine. A God who competes with the human, or curtails it, or makes it a masquerade, is offensive and blasphemous. The really Holy Mystery who grounds Jesus' humanity remains a *holy* Mystery that really gets along well with authentic human subjects. As Pope Leo's famous "Tome" put it, "What [God] did was to enhance humanity not diminish deity."[13] It is perhaps not accidental that it is precisely this kind of balance that we find in Karl Rahner's theology. Few among modern theologians have stressed as much and as powerfully the "incomprehensible Mystery of God." And the authentic humanity of Jesus.

Let me mention, too, before moving forward, that there is a further "conciliar critique" stemming from sociopolitical christologians. Still in their beginning phase, these thinkers tend to be more influenced by the so-called late, or second, modern Enlightenment (the generation roughly between 1890 and 1930: Freud, Marx, Jung, Durkheim, Weber, etc.). They tend to query the sociopolitical horizon and implications of conciliar doctrines. What kind of praxis (a term that usually means "activity that has been reflected upon") do these teachings tend to foster? Here, of course, one would ask whether the biblical summons to struggle on behalf of the poor, the miserable, the suffering, etc., comes through sufficiently strongly in the traditional christologies. For example, is the somewhat idealized Jesus of Chalcedon too removed from the miseries of the suffering? The connection between this kind of criticism and the earlier notion of Rahner's about the need to surface the soteriological dimension of christology is obvious. Here one might fruitfully explore the Roman-Byzantine imperial structure and whether/how it might have fostered a somewhat "imperialized christology." Reading some of the liberation or political theologians can begin to sensitize one to this fascinating area of research, but there is actually very little work done on the christological councils themselves from this point of view.[14]

"Constructive" Dimensions

It is easier to summarize the critical moment. A greater degree of consensus seems to exist on the need, at least in countries deeply affected by the Enlightenment, to rethink the councils culminating with Chalcedon in a contemporary way. When we pass to the constructive moment, the actual proposals put forward by christologians, a greater diversity emerges. First of all, not even the use of the category "christology from below" is used by all (as we will see, there may be important reasons for this). Rahner has employed the term as a general description for many (but not all!) of his christological proposals in his *Foundations*, and Wolfhart Pannenberg has followed suit in his *Jesus* book.[15] And as we have noted, O'Collins and even the Pontifical Biblical Commission have used it too.

So far as I can tell, the category embraces a rather large continuum. On the one extreme, a christology from below might be said to be equivalent to a "low christology," in the sense of a christological proposal that seems to deny, or blur, or ignore the "divine dimension" or divinity of Jesus. Thomas Sheehan's *The First Coming* seems, to this writer, a clear and maybe the most recent example of this kind of "low" christology. The reader will be able to think of other examples. My impression is that these kinds of "low" christologies are peculiar to the Enlightenment experience of the modern West (They don't strike me as equivalent to the heresy of adoptionism known to the early church, seeming to be more influenced by modern Western deism, atheism, etc.). And they seem to be typical of non-Christian scholars who have ventured into Jesus studies: I am thinking of Erich Fromm's *The Dogma of Christ* and Milan Machovec's *A Marxist Looks at Jesus*.[16] I do not have the impression that christologies from below, as found in noted Christian christologians, are really disguised forms of "low" christology. For all practical purposes, the reader would do well to get this distinction clear.

Another possible option is that of combining the christologies from below and above. This becomes a mixed "genre," which views christologies from below as in the service of helping to make contemporary the received and still normative christological, conciliar tradition. Karl Rahner, we have seen, is clearly within this camp. So, too, has Hans Küng explicitly aligned himself with this group.[17] And the Pontifical Biblical Commission's *Bible et christologie*, while noting unresolved questions, has said that "all attempts to unite a *Christology 'from below'* with a *Christology 'from above'* are on the right track."[18]

Conceptually between these two options might be said to be those who are not as clear as they might be on the relationship between the christologies from below and those from above. Those, for example, who argue that they only want to begin with the human and/or historical reality of Jesus, not moving on to a consideration of the grounds for his "higher," more exalted status among Christian believers, might be said to belong here, at least logically, provided that they never arrive at a consideration of the latter, or leave it ambiguous. Or, they might introduce the "divine dimension" too late in their consideration of Jesus, or too thinly, in a way that makes one wonder whether the full heritage of the christological councils is being reappropriated. I do not have the impression that this "logical possibility" is very common among noted and published Christian christologians.

Let me mention here that biblical scholars who work in the area of Jesus research sometimes become vulnerable to the charge of being aligned with this third category. Sometimes they might seem to work with an excessively "secularistic" brand of the historical critical method, only allowing themselves to speak about so-called purely human and historical facets of Jesus, coming to the brink of the more "dogmatic concerns" of christology, but carefully remaining "this side" of those concerns. In this case, they may need to rethink some of their own deeper philosophical and theological assumptions about the nature of history, about its theological dimension, about whether there is a purely "human" reality (meaning by this one devoid of a divine dimension), etc.

On the whole, I have the impression that biblical scholars in the area of Jesus research fall, rather, into our second category of the mix between high and low christologies. The "high" dimension surfaces, perhaps, in the use of the notion of at least an implied continuity between the "reconstructed" historical Jesus and the "kerygmatic" Christ of faith. Even Bultmann argued for this kind of implied continuity, and he was one of the more radical employers of the historical-critical method! Interestingly, the Pontifical Biblical Commission says that "those [christologies] that concentrate on Jesus' relation to God the Father can rightly be called 'Christologies from above.' "[19] Surfacing the unique filial relation of Jesus to his Father-

Abba is another way of articulating the "high" and "divine" concerns of the christological heritage of the church.

By now the reader will have drawn the conclusion that christologies from below all start in some way with what is thought to be "below" and accessible to our human experience, namely, the human person of Jesus. Perhaps they never get beyond thinking of just that "human" person (= low christologies), or they move between his humanity and divinity somewhat simultaneously (= the mixed genre), or they are somewhere between. But nonetheless, they all start with what they think the human properly to be. As a rough approximation, this will have to serve us for now as a description of christologies from below. We can readily see here the concerns of late, post-Enlightenment, Western human beings. In a world that has largely turned to "experience" (at least in some sense) as the norm for discerning truth, we now have christologies making the same experiential turn. Starting with the "humanity" of Jesus is thought to be starting christology in the only place many modern people think everything must start!

We can start with the "human" in a more philosophical and speculative way, in the manner of a philosophical anthropology. The "earlier" Karl Rahner is often credited with this approach. His groundbreaking "On the Theology of the Incarnation," noted earlier,[20] sketches a vision of the human being as a living openness to the Infinite Mystery that, in a graced universe, lovingly offers itself to us: we become human precisely to the degree that we give ourselves away to the Infinite One, as our ground and goal, who, in grace, offers and gives the Divine Self "away" to us. Rahner had worked out this "graced" anthropology in his sketch of a Christian alternative to Immanuel Kant early in his career. One can sense the "mystical, patristic" feel of it all. It amounts to a post-Kantian and critical reappropriation of the anthropology of the fathers and mystics. The "person" of Jesus is, Rahner suggests, the unique, most intensive and definitive radicalization of this "conjunction" between openness to the Divine Mystery and that Mystery's loving offer of self-communication. Anthropology (properly understood, and in a graced universe) finds its culmination in christology. One can sense especially the vision of Rahner's beloved "father," St. Ignatius Loyola. The Ignatian "being open to God as ever greater" is really the foundation of Rahner's anthropology and christology.[21]

I am using Rahner as one example of this more speculative approach (which in his case is clearly of the "mixed genre" type). The speculative aspects of a Walter Kasper (while adding nuances) and of a Wolfhart Pannenberg owe explicitly a great debt to Rahner's own breakthrough work in anthropology. And there are many more examples of a more speculative, anthropological approach, all of which strive to bring out the divine-human unity in Jesus as a privileged instance of what it means to be human before God. In the hands of "centrists" like Rahner, Pannenberg, and Kasper, the concerns of both christologies from below and above are accounted for. In the hands of others, perhaps we meet with greater ambiguity and perhaps even a "derailment" into simply "low" christologies.[22]

Quite frequently christologians are thought to follow the "from below" perspective when they pursue a more "historical" approach to biblical christology, participating in one way or another in some form of the "quest for the historical Jesus." Others, particularly systematic theologians, will strive to combine the results of this historical scholarship with speculative anthropology/christology. The later Rahner did this, as well as thinkers like Schillebeeckx, Kasper, Hans Küng, John B. Cobb, Jr., and a "younger" generation of American christologians. Thus, Schillebeeckx draws heavily upon Jesus' unique filial relationship to his Father-Abba, something widely accepted among New Testament scholars. He then tries to interpret the new kind of relational being Jesus seems to be in the latter part of his massive book *Jesus* (in part 4), drawing upon a sophisticated analysis of post-Enlightenment notions of what it means to be a "person." He prefers to let the historical reality of Jesus guide his sketch of an anthropology to undergird his christology. Somehow Jesus manifests to us a God who is *humanissimus*.[23] One of Schillebeeckx's points is that what we mean by the "human person" is fluid and open. There is no need to lock ourselves into the individualistic and non-relational notion of the "person" so typical of much post-Enlightenment thought. And what we find in Jesus is a new stretching of our view of the person, a new breakthrough in what it means.

These are but a sampling of those seeking to engage in this kind of "combined" christology. Not all of them necessarily consider themselves christologians "from below," but their work may be viewed as such by some. In the main I have the impression that they follow pretty much the main lines of consensus about the "historical Jesus" that have been emerging since the writings of Käsemann and the beginnings of the "New Quest"; they view the later, explicit christology of the kerygma and councils as at least "implied" (in varying ways) in the Jesus of history; and then they seek to interpret this divine-human reality of Jesus attested in the tradition through some anthropological-speculative analysis that might be plausible before the court of human reason and experience. The aim is not to fall into a reductionistic kind of christology, but to bring forth warrants in experience for a reality such as a God-man unity. The success of each christological proposal must, naturally, be individually assessed in every instance. One of the advantages of this "combined" approach is that it enables one's speculative anthropology/christology to be informed by and worked out in the light of the historical data of the tradition. This serves as a safeguard against the temptation to interpret Christ in the light of an *a priori* philosophy.[24]

O'Collins had noted the appeal to nature (natural philosophy?) as another form of christology from below.[25] One perhaps thinks of Teilhard de Chardin, who somewhat poetically sketched out a christology in terms of modern paleontology and evolutionary theory. Chardin's *The Divine Milieu* is still a powerful reappropriation of Paul's biblical christology, particularly the "cosmic christology" of the later Pauline school, only transposed into an evolutionary register. The forward dynamism of evolution is grounded in the cosmic Christ, for Chardin. The "transcendental movement" of the universe toward not only intellection but love, requires a transcendental ground of love, Chardin suggests. This use of natural philosophy (or its like in science) is not too common in contemporary christology, although one might argue that some forms of process christology are deeply indebted to Whitehead's ultimately scientific vision of the universe. Contemporary ecological concerns are causing theologians to surface some of the aspects of christology that are of interest to ecology: Jesus' attitude to nature, especially as found in his parables; the incarnation as a divine "celebration" of flesh/matter, etc. But at most this ecologically sensitized christology is a motif in a larger christological program.

"Concluding" and "Second" Thoughts

Christologies from below have spawned their share of criticism. In some cases, this criticism seems in the genre of a "corrective." For example, someone like Johannes B. Metz questions the abstract anthropology of Rahner, suggesting that it ignores the concretely sociopolitical and narrative aspects of reality. Perhaps we get too much of a Western, "middle-class" christology in speculations like Rahner's? Openness to the Infinite and Gracious Mystery needs to be filled out with partisanship for the suffering and oppressed, thinkers like Metz (and Latin American liberation theologians) would argue.[26] Feminist christologians might want to see feminist concerns surfaced more clearly: What was Jesus' own practice in this regard? In what way do the later christological doctrines reinforce misogynism, etc.? The current struggle in Catholicism over whether only the male priest can image forth the Christ is a christological issue: In what way is Jesus' maleness of truly christological significance? Ruether's *Sexism and God-Talk* and the work of Elizabeth Johnson are quite helpful for a beginning appreciation of some of these concerns.[27]

"Correctives," however, do not call something fundamentally into question. I have the growing sense, however, of something of a "post-modern" unease with the category of a "christology from below." I have personally registered my own dissatisfaction with this category several times in my works, and I sense a similar dissatisfaction among others.[28] In any case, I have the suspicion that the characterization "from below" plays into the hands of the restrictive notion of human experience and history common since the late Renaissance and Enlightenment. To think of human experience as simply "below" perhaps too easily fosters a reductionistic vision of experience, failing to surface its divine depth in this graced universe that we Christians believe we inhabit. As we have seen, this is not the intention of many of its users. But here I am speaking of the appropriateness of the category. Perhaps it surrenders more than it should. If I understand it correctly, the trend of many, perhaps most, speculative theologians since the Enlightenment has been to remake the case, perhaps on a second level of naivete, for a theophanic or theocentric notion of human experience, particularly when these theologians believe that the universe has been "graced" in Jesus. "Below," of course, is a metaphor, but the point is that human experience reveals a depth to it that discloses the "above," the "Divine." What we think is simply below isn't really simply "below." The International Theological Commission put it this way: " ... deification is the truest and ultimate hominisation of man." At the same time it recognized that we must strive to preserve the specialness of Jesus, working "out anew in terms of their mutual analogies" the possible "relationship between anthropology and Christology."[29] Karl Barth's term "The-anthropology" was his "final" attempt, based on the Apostles' Creed third article of the Holy Spirit, to overcome an autonomous view of the human and nicely captures the thrust of my comments here.[30] The term avoids both reducing God to the human and emptying the human of its relationship with God.

Not only do many revisionist anthropologies call this characterization "from below" into question. So do the prevalent christologies. If I understand them correctly, they all seem to indicate that Jesus the Christ is the overturning of simple dualisms like "above" and "below," transcendence and immanence, divinity and humanity. Remember Schillebeeckx's *Deus humanissimus?* Jesus reveals to us a God who is present in human experience and history. Dermot Lane in his popular *The Reality of Jesus* already seemed uneasy with the characterization "from below" when he proposed his mixed "descending-ascending" christology.[31] But the Christ calls the category "from above" equally into question. That, too, plays into the hands of an aloof, abstract divinity. What some would consider the rigorously transcendent Deity of Arianism (who, because he was

97

above humanity really couldn't become man) fits a "christology from above" more adequately, it seems.

Something of this breaking through of dualisms seems to underlie the entire period of the patristic debates, and to have categories that don't do likewise might well be a regression from the standard set by the patristic heritage. "He has not ceased to be God by reason of becoming human, and he does not flee from things human because he is God," said St. Athanasius. "... it is as one who is God that he took on flesh, and it is as one who was in flesh that he divinized the flesh."[32] I grow more convinced daily of the crucial importance of studying the heritage of the *patres*, particularly from Nicaea on through to Chalcedon and even Constantinople III. Cyril of Alexandria, of course, had already recommended recourse to the fathers, if we want to avoid scandal and "open up" the "healthful teaching of the Church." "We [should be] eager to make much of them," he said,[33] and I agree. Particularly in this area of christology they explored the major routes, the dead ends, and the promising avenues. They are a paradigm for the christological explorer, as it were.

Much of our "modern dualistic thinking" (which is more extreme than anything the fathers encountered, of course) was already decisively (in principle) broken through by the great councils and by the likes of the Cappadocians (Basil, Gregory of Nyssa, Nazianzus), Maximus Confessor, Athanasius, Cyril, Pope Leo, Patriarch Flavian, etc. The patristic struggle over the God-man mystery of the hypostatic union was precisely this struggle over how divinity and humanity transcend the categories of opposition and antagonism. Surely after Chalcedon it is impossible to think the God of Jesus and not think also of humanity, or to think humanity and not think also of divinity. And this is but a matter of fidelity to the New Testament: "No one has gone up to heaven except the one who has come down from heaven, the Son of Man" (Jn 3:13; cf. Eph 4:9).

Now I am not suggesting that all users of the category of "christology from below" can be charged with the above dualism without qualification. Clearly this is not true, especially of the "mixed genre" types, like Rahner. Not a little of Rahner's great achievement has been to break through the kind of dualisms and antagonisms I'm speaking of here. (Think of his brilliant "axiom": "[human] autonomy... does not decrease, but increases in the same proportion as dependence on God."[34]) The very attempt to mix the "above" and "below" dimensions of christology illustrates this struggle to find categories breaking out of our dualisms too. Why not, now, admit that perhaps the categories we are employing do not fit the reality?

I hope the reader will sense my sympathy and respect for the "balanced" objectives of a christology from below as practiced by the "mixed genre" types, which combine both the "above" and "below" dimensions of christology. They have braved the struggle of entering into a confrontation (and sometimes a dialogue) with the tenets of modernity, and they have attempted to enable the christological heritage to remain contemporary. We stand on their shoulders, and the very modest "critical proposals" I am suggesting are in their debt and, I think, will forward the movement they have largely initiated for the rest of us in christology.

The christology we are pursuing within the pages of this book, like the "mixed genre" form of christology from below, wants to try to appropriate the full humanity of Jesus. But it wants to do so in a manner that will not foster the kind of dualism between God and humanity that a graced universe and the full drama of the Incarnation mystery have overcome. At the same time, it wants to avoid this dualism without also collapsing or shrinking the Divine into the human. To some extent this is a matter of language, but the particular vocation of the theologian is the "care" of our language. If we avoid an abstract notion of anthropocentrism, or of experience, and work with a more narrative notion of experience — "experience" as transmitted to us in the "storied" form of the New Testament and in the "stories" of the church community — we arrive rather at a notion like Barth's "The-anthropology," which results from our graced participation in the God-man unity uniquely and definitively disclosed by Jesus. A narrative christology, or a christologically narrated notion of experience, would seem to be at least one promising way to integrate the legitimate concerns studied in this chapter into a perspective that avoids regressing to the kinds of dualism that the age of the fathers and mothers sought to overcome.

Another way to come at this is trinitarian. For we have tried to indicate that the dialogue of Father and Son is inclusive, through the Holy Spirit. "We" are participants in that inner-trinitarian conversation, linked with the Son Jesus through the Spirit. That Spirit guides us, in a way appropriate to each of us, to the supremely unique Son-Jesus, who saves us from our sin and suffering. Here we should recall Barth's proposal that the third article of the Apostles' Creed, the doctrine of the Holy Spirit, makes it impossible to ponder God's relationship with humanity without at the same time pondering humanity's relationship with God. This trinitarian mystery, which grounds the mystery of christology too, again cautions us against the dualisms of below and above. For the Spirit pours the Son out into the Incarnation of Jesus. Again, a trinitarian based narrative of Christian experience seems a sounder basis for our christological explorations.

What we need, it seems to me, are christological proposals that try to surface as much of the full reality of Jesus the Christ as possible, as much of the "rich experience" that Jesus was and remains as concretely narrated by the scriptures. This reality is so rich that we should expect a great "diversity" or pluralism of approaches, a diversity in unity not unlike the person of Jesus himself. This is what we have in the New Testament and throughout the greater history of ecclesial devotion and reflection. The modern "christologies from below," particularly in their more moderate, mixed form, seem to me to be a part of this rich diversity of christological exploration, a return to this greater pluralism. For many of us, they have enabled us to try to reappropriate the narrative-experiential nature of christology and soteriology. These latter have become a good deal more "real" for many as a consequence.

CHAPTER FIVE

Adoration's Centrality in Theology and Christology

Our study of the French School has intriguingly suggested the richness of the theme of adoration for christology. The Son's "reverential regard" for the Father within the Trinity's inner life finds its clearest earthly analogy, it was suggested, in the incarnate Savior's adoring obedience to the Father's will. God was always worthy of adoration by humanity, but this was not adequately known, and even sinfully unattended to, until the Incarnation. Jesus, the God-Man, the "God adoring God," has revealed the adorable glory of God. The Incarnation "displays," if you will, the Son as utter "regard" and "surrender" to the Father. Through the Holy Spirit we are invited into this mystery of "giving the self over" in adoring love to the Father. The theme of adoration lands us on the most fertile soil upon which christology grows, where its deepest roots are to be found: in the "inner" life of the Trinity itself. Accordingly it will serve us well if we take a further look at this rich phenomenon, searching out more of its dimensions, and even seeking by grace to develop our own adorational "skills."

I have chosen the thought of Baron Friedrich von Hügel (1852–1925) as this chapter's chief focus. He was one of this century's leading Catholic philosophers and theologians, deeply committed to the pursual of a "thinking" theology, and at a time when that was not at all easy (the "modernist" crisis). But he was also committed to theology's interchange with spirituality, devoting his central study to the theme of the "mystical element" in Christianity. It is not surprising, then, that he often thought about adoration. His later writings especially accent the theme, his last, posthumous work declaring that "religion, at least among the mystics (and I believe that, on this point at least, the mystics merely dive deeper into and bring out more

---

101

explicitly the sap or central core of the religious passion), consists centrally in the sense of Presence — the sense of an overflowing Existence distinct from our own and in the Adoration of the same." A typical example of spiritual advice to his niece Gwendolen Greené simply says: "You can't have religion without adoration."[1]

A further advantage of turning to Hügel is his narrative style of theology. His major work on mysticism's role in Christianity emerges from a study of the lived drama of Catherine of Genoa. This was deliberate, for he consciously sought to "correct" the unhistorical, abstract "school" theology of his time. His choice was always for the more originary, participationist style of theology, yet without sacrificing the "analytical" element. The baron did theology out of the narrative of his life and the lives of those he pondered.[2] Accordingly, this chapter will be more narrative in nature too: the drama of Hügel and the drama of those he learned from are one cloth. Hügel strikes me as virtually unique, or at least belonging to a relatively special group, among "modern" speculative theologians and religious philosophers who accord adoration the kind of primacy we find in his thought. In our own contemporary times, one will come across a nearly similar stress on the theme in the spiritual and especially the later "theological" writings of Karl Rahner, as well as in the thought of Hans Urs von Balthasar. Similarly, we can say that Karl Barth's theology has an adorational tone to it, going back to Luther and Calvin. And not surprisingly, Balthasar and Barth are theological soul-friends. Let us not forget Kierkegaard, too, whom Hügel considers the great defender of divine transcendence.[3]

Adoration: Elements of a Description

One will search in vain for a precise definition of adoration in the baron's published works. This is probably not surprising for a thinker who was suspicious of the "definitional" style of much of the scholastic theology of his time. After all, he tells us that the Abbé Huvelin, his spiritual "director," advised him to "see truths, realities, as *intensely luminous centres*, with a semi-illuminated outer margin, and then another and another, till all shades off into utter darkness."[4]

Probably Hügel's lengthiest "exploration" of adoration's many mansions is found, in *Eternal Life*, in a passage studying Kant's "deficient" understanding of eternity. "Religion," it says, "indeed, has ever been, at its fullest and deepest, *Adoration*, hence apprehension and affirmation of, and joy in, what already is; and the Prevenience of God, His part in the religious act, has consequently, by the Prophets and Psalmists, by Jesus and St. Paul, by St. Augustine and Pascal, been dwelt upon almost to the exclusion of our own part."[5] Here we find reaffirmed a number of traits of the adoration experience that Hügel repeatedly mentions in his writings.

For example, adoration is an experience, concrete and real. Philosophies of experience that make no room for it are, however helpful in various respects, deficient in this regard. Hence, Hügel's difficulties with Kant, who seems to accord only a kind of "hypothetical" legitimacy to God and to worship, viewing these latter as merely pragmatic rather than cognitively legitimate. "But who ever found the religious soul hypothetic?... it is doubtless this grand sense of Givenness, of Grace, which, as much as anything, won the humanity of the Roman Empire."[6] The adoration experience played not a small role in helping Hügel avoid the tendencies toward the narrow sort of empiricism that would win over Loisy and other "modern" thinkers of his time. This experience is of the sort that, surely not leaving behind the senses, illustrates that we humans are more than the senses: we are apprehending, affirming, and enjoying beings, all of which are responses to the givenness of God. Hügel also suspects that there are tendencies to subjectivize this givenness. Hence he surrounds his descriptions of the adorational experience with other "reality-enforcing" descriptions: it is objective, the "sense of Presence," "distinct from us," and so on.[7]

Adoration is not simply any religious experience, but one that intensifies the experience of God's prevenience: the over-againstness of the religious experience, the "grace" dimension. It recognizes "God's part" in our experience (as he put it above), the "divine environment ...the all-in-all of God."[8]

Here in the *Eternal Life* book Hügel offers us some few corollaries of the divine prevenience. For example, it means an intensive awareness that our action is the result of the divine action and invitation. This heightened sense of divine transcendence reaches a remarkable pitch in the "passivity" (in activity) of the mystical states of quiet. It also means the divine kenosis: the sense that God "has deigned to limit Himself in order to leave us the kind and degree of liberty He has chosen for us" as we freely respond to his presence. And all of this implies the divine "personality": the freedom offered and actuated in experiences such as adoration are not "mere symbols of a stream or tendency; they are now, not less but more, conceived as expressive of the religious Personality which lived them, and such a Personality again is recognized as the vehicle and manifestation of abiding, self-conscious Spirit."[9] Hence it is out of such adorational experiences that we fashion our notion of divine "eternity" as a reality of non-successive, self-conscious plenitude.[10]

The discussion in *Eternal Life* also surfaces what we might call the christological, anthropological, and ecclesial dimensions of the adoration experience, in addition to the more properly theological

103

dimensions so far noted. The brief christological reference will need to be supplemented by other insights, but still the appeal to Jesus in this central passage on adoration is critical and links up with an earlier section of the work in which we are told that "it is not man or men, but God Who... is the beginning, centre, medium, and end of the whole of [Jesus'] life."[11] A key motive for the Incarnation is adoration, this passage indicates.

One may not notice the anthropological element, and this is to be expected. After all, the focus in adoration shifts emphatically to the God pole of the God-human relationship. But the self does not disappear; nor is it annihilated in what Hügel regards as "authentic" adoration. We will see how he has developed some very helpful categories in this area in his major work on mysticism in Catherine of Genoa. For now, I want to stay with the *Eternal Life* book as much as possible. Here the self appears and is known as emphatically receiver even while doing, profoundly free because freely encountered, and even more. "The Givenness, and the sense of Givenness, will infuse a special character into all the virtues." And the baron mentions here: the heroism of forgiving enemies, which requires "a realm of Divine Prevenience and generosity." Or the appropriate humility of never more than moral certainty about the truly supernatural character of our acts. God is not controlled or manipulated by us. Hence, too, the attempt to make "discriminations between Nature and Grace."[12] Surely these virtues bring with them their struggles, their pain. But note the element of joy too. This was a profoundly crucial component of the experience, something particularly taught to him by Catherine of Genoa.

I would see the ecclesiological component present in the reference to adoration as *religion's* central act. In this same passage Hügel mentions cult and worship (key functions of religion), and the notion that it is the divinely prevenient Grace that stirs up acts of cultic worship. Hügel is well known for his emphasis upon the ecclesial-institutional nature of religion and Christianity, and he explores it from various angles in different writings. Here it is not so much the organic, social dimension of humans but the sense of divine presence that he has in mind. That is the deepest ground for our gathering in worship. It is, perhaps, not inappropriate here to mention his frequent "visits" to the Blessed Sacrament, recorded frequently in his diary. The cultic dimension of adoration was a deeply important aspect of his experience. This facet seems to bring out the "givenness" of the Divine Presence itself as one that actively arouses in us the longing to worship and adore.[13]

Finally, we should notice that adoration is accorded a kind of primacy here in Hügel's thought. Just how this might be related to love, which simultaneously seems to occupy a primacy, will require some further attention. The two "primacies" aren't necessarily incompatible. In any case, here adoration is the "fullest and deepest" act of religion, and by this he seems to embrace breadth and depth. Every other religious act is a partial manifestation of it and tends toward it. A gauge of religious experience's fullness is whether or not it moves toward adoration. And this seems to be why Hügel associates it with mystics, for they are the ones who swim more deeply and fully in the religious current of life. This especially applies to Jesus: the primacy of adoration and the primacy of Jesus are of a piece. But this is more assumed than explained here.

Further "Clarifications" of the Adoration Experience

It is not surprising that we find a description of adoration in a book on eternal life, for "eternity" calls to mind the "Reality" of an overflowing fullness arousing in us the free response of praise and adoration. But other writings as well supply insights. In a passage in which he warns against the "immanentisms" and "sentimental anthropocentrisms which fill the air" — thus somewhat confirming the view that the baron came to accent adoration under "pressure" from the opposite direction — Hügel reminds us that "the positions between God and Man, and between Man and God, are entirely uninterchangeable." He appeals to the "greatest doctor" and "practicer" of "overwhelmingly adoring prayer" — St. Augustine — as a key example of one who never forgot the "non-equality" in the "relation between God and man." Here he adds another corollary to the divine prevenience: God is not just first, but supreme. Even though adoration reveals the personal element in faith — God's and our own personal, free exchange — still, this is not an exchange between equals. Hügel is saying: mutuality, yes; equality, no. The divine personality is a plenitude beyond our own. Although uncited, we have here the teaching of Lateran Council IV: "... no matter what type of similarity we find between Creator and creature, it is always outstripped by a greater dissimilarity."[14] (But, as we will see, the Incarnation unites this dissimilarity with a surprising "similarity" too.)

And so, in the same passage, we have the "cultic" corollary drawn: "Hence the most fundamental need, duty, honour and happiness of man, is not petition, nor even contrition, nor again even thanksgiving; these three kinds of prayer which, indeed, must never disappear out of our spiritual lives; but *adoration*." Note here the elements of human need as well as happiness. This latter is that profound sense of joy that Hügel greatly learned from his beloved St. Catherine of Genoa.[15]

The appearance of these "human" dimensions means that the human self never vanishes in the act of adoring, but rather experiences, somewhat paradoxically, greatest actuation at the moment of greatest self-effacement before the Mystery. One has the impression that petition, contrition, and thanksgiving aren't so much left behind as sublated in adoring: cauterized of that aspect of self-regard that might forget its unequal dependency upon God-regard.

But as Hügel emphasizes the essential non-equality between God and humans, he does not lose sight of God's "personality." In fact, the very factors that cause us to stammer before God in adoration also bring home to us the awareness of the appropriateness of referring to God as a "person," but a plenitude of personhood in which we in varying ways "only" participate. This is important to hold in mind, for there is often a tendency to "depersonalize" God the more we become rapt up in adoring wonder. It is as if we find the categories, and indeed the experience, of the "personal" inappropriate in these regions. But not a little of Hügel's contribution is to link these two aspects. The qualities that cause us to attribute personality to ourselves — freedom, sensitivity, insight, and so on — are qualities that we recognize in their "plenitude" in God. And so we adore. It is that "plenitude" that gives rise to adoration. Hügel notes that this finds its ground within the interpersonal life of the Trinity itself. For because God is an interpersonal sharer interiorly, so can God be exteriorly. These texts would be representative of the baron's thinking in this regard. First, as regards the divine "personality":

> Qualities, such as reality, transcendence, presence, existence — these are not apprehended as abstractions floating in the air, or fancied in the mind; such qualities, or the impressions of such qualities are, however confusedly, however unuttered even to itself by the apprehending mind, felt and loved as effects and constituents of a Reality distinct from the apprehender, and yet a Reality sufficiently like the human spirit, when thus supernaturally sustained and sublimated, to be recognized by this human spirit with rapt, joyous adoration as its living source, support and end.

Now as regards the trinitarian dimension of this "personality":

> For can anything be more certain than that [the trinitarian doctrine's] root-causes were the two utterly concrete realities, apprehended in the most realistic ways — the real God of the Jewish prophets, now most completely revealed in His most rich reality by Jesus of Nazareth, and this same real Jesus, so richly real in His life and death, His teaching and His persistent power? The roots of the doctrine were these two realities and the need somehow to co-relate them, as well as possible, . . . and to protect this richness of the life of God as against all absolute co-ordination with the world. . . . If we take so utterly daring a teacher as is

St. Catherine of Genoa of man's Pure Love of God as man's perfection, since it alone imitates and reciprocates the Pure Love of God for man, as part and parcel of God's essential nature, we discover that God is found so lovable and so love-impelling, precisely because He who has no essential need to be loved by finite spirits,... nevertheless does love them far better then ever they can love themselves, and invites their love of Him.... [16]

"Earlier" Thoughts of the Baron: "Comparative" Comments

The Mystical Element, a modern classic explaining the theological significance of the mystic's mission, is a deeply contemplative work in the most "ample" Hügelian sense. By "ample" I have in mind Hügel's capital distinction between a form of "pure mysticism" in which contemplation derails into world amnesia, and a more "inclusive, incarnational" type that shows how the mystic stays with the world even while transforming it. It is the contemplation of the latter that attracts Hügel, and that seems most consistent with the incarnationalism of Christianity. But while this is an "amply" contemplative work, it is contemplative nonetheless, and so one is led into a brilliant exploration of Catherine of Genoa's mystical experience of painful yet joyous pure love. The "yield" for christology from our study of this work will be direct and indirect. Direct, because the kind of incarnational mysticism studied has its ground in the Incarnation. Indirect, because it is through the narrative and drama of Catherine that we see reflected an incarnational "image" of the incarnate Jesus himself. Catherine's incarnational adoration links us with the Incarnation. Let us see how, in this, the earliest of the works by Hügel that we will explore.

A first question to ask is whether the relative lack of accent upon adoration means anything and can contribute anything to our appreciation of the adoration phenomenon.[17] By way of hypothesis I would suggest that it does. Hügel seems to go through a development in his thinking on a number of interrelated fronts — adoration among them — and paying attention to these will enable us to grasp a little more precisely the particular nuances that the later accent upon adoration gives to his theology. I am speaking of a development here, not a revolution, in Hügel's thought. And this seems to be how he would have viewed it. For recall the remarks in the 1923 "Preface to the Second Edition." "[God's] Givenness is the central characteristic of all religion worthy of the name," which means philosophically that "Critical Realism" is the appropriate philosophical perspective on Christianity, he very emphatically tells us now. And he explains that this insight is "no more than a full development into a quite conscious decision of what, in 1908, was already predominant but not yet persistently articulate and comfortably final."[18]

We are speaking here about a shift that is ever so "slight" and delicate, a transition that doesn't overturn the insights of *The Mystical Element* but rather pursues them a bit more doggedly. So there is much continuity between the "later" and the "earlier" Hügel; more continuity than discontinuity. This means that the accented themes of *The Mystical Element* largely function as structural equivalents to adoration, "doing" much of what Hügel thinks we need to do when we engage in adoration. Still, the slight but new accent upon adoration in the "later" writings does gives us insight into what adoration brings to christology. Let us study this more fully now by way of a comparison with some of *The Mystical Element*'s key themes.

Maurice Nédoncelle, in his largely appreciative study of Hügel, gives us a place to start when he tells us how much the baron emphasizes "the development of personality" as the goal of the enriching yet painful friction between the famed three elements of religion (the intellectual, institutional, and mystical). The greater that friction in the integrational project, the richer the personality. And then, in a comment somewhat "critical" (and I think misleading), Nédoncelle says (thinking of Hügel): "the development of personality is the final goal of the world, for which even the heavens wait."[19] This is misleading, because it largely passes over "developments" in Hügel's thinking, and also because it needs to clarify more emphatically that what Hügel means by "personality" in *The Mystical Element* is worlds removed from any kind of reductionistic humanism. Still, Nédoncelle's comment does point us in a direction that might be helpful. I would suggest that the movement toward pure love is perhaps the great goal that Hügel emphasizes in his *magnum opus*. And it is this "pure love" that he finds so compellingly actuated in Catherine of Genoa's life.

"Pure love" calls to mind the quietist controversy, with the difficulties between Fénelon, Mme. Guyon, and Bossuet. And Hügel deals, nearly definitively, with these difficulties. Simplifying, as I unfortunately must, Hügel wants to argue that pure love is radically disinterested or non-egotistical love. We could also call this "purified" love, inasmuch as all tendency toward manipulation of the self or other, including especially "The Other" (God), has been eradicated from our love-thinking and love-doing, insofar as this is possible on this earth. And it is eradicated through the mystical entrance into a state of utter "passivity" or "abandonment" to God. Now it was this "passivity" that was largely the battle front of the quietist controversy, and Hügel, I think convincingly, wants to free the mystical passivity from all self-annihilation (and also

108

institutional-and-church-annihilation). Deep oneness with God purifies our energies rather than destroys: "...such 'Passivity,' or Action, is in reality the condition in which the soul attains to its fullest energizing."[20]

Properly understood, such "pure love" will lead to adoration, and the references to adoration at various other places in *The Mystical Element* would seem to imply this. But adoration is not the focus of Hügel's discussion here. My own suggestion would be that pure love refers to the complete actuation of the richly complex and able-to-be-differentiated reality of the God-human or revelation-faith interrelationship — a kind of continuum — and that adoration tends to accent as emphatically as possible the passivity/receiving/gift-recognizing dimension of the always passive yet energizing nature of such love. Each of these dimensions interpenetrates and is accordingly essential to the other. Oscillations in the one affect the other. And so derailments in the one can cause derailments in the other. So, drawing this out, should the passivity moment derail into a kind of inactive self-annihilation, this would contaminate the adoration dimension, too. The more the energizing, action-producing reality of God is obscured, the less God can be "adored" as the plenitude of personal, freely responsible "action."

The discussion on pure love in *The Mystical Element* tends rather to focus upon the energy-enabling, faith-arousing dimension of love, and so focuses a bit more upon what God effects in human persons, bringing them to fullest actuation. Hügel's own somewhat "anthropocentric" epoch, as well as the need to free pure love from the charge of quietism, probably are behind this focus. In this sense, Nédoncelle seems correct in noting a stress upon the human pole in the God-human interrelationship. But this tendency is ever so slight and imperceptible, as the Second Preface indicates. Stressing either dimension of the dipolar aspects of pure love seems appropriate at various times, and I think certain existential pressures toward immanentism led Hügel to intensify the adorational pole in time. But in coming to that intensification, perhaps he also came to a greater clarification of the nature of pure love itself.

A historical analogy I would point to is the case of Bérulle. I am not arguing here for any necessary borrowing by Hügel from Bérulle. I am only looking to the case of Bérulle as one that might illuminate the deeper meaning of Hügel's eventual stress upon adoration. (However, close readers of Hügel will notice that Bérulle and his two disciples, Condren and Olier, do surface occasionally in his thought, thus indicating some degree of knowledge of the French School. I am inclined to think, however, that Hügel came under the influence of the French School chiefly through a later "adaptation" by Huvelin,

Grou, and Fénelon. The importance of St. Augustine is another common link between Hügel and Bérulle.[21]) To return to Bérulle now, we will recall the celebrated passage in Père Amelote's biography of Father Condren in which Bérulle is praised as the one who has "raised up [the] buried virtue of [respect], the one to have renewed the sense of adoration in children," and so on.[22]

Here Père Amelote describes Bérulle's charism as one of discovering respect and adoration in an age intensely alive to the reality of love, including the love of God. One thinks, for example, of St. Francis de Sales's teaching on love (Bérulle and the saint shared a mutual regard for one another) — were some drawing the wrong conclusions, derailing more into "familiarity" than reverence? Using the terms above, were some overstressing the self-actuation dimension in the gift-recognizing and energy-producing moments of pure love? Perhaps Hügel came to recognize a similar tendency in his own time? Adoration, looked at in this way, "defamiliarizes" our love for God (and also for others in and through God), and so fosters the refusal to take for granted, to cease to marvel; it encourages us to be thankful, and so not to manipulate because one has dulled one's sense of being gifted. It perhaps recaptures and intensifies what Thomas Aquinas would have called "filial fear" (as distinct from "servile fear"), such filial fear remaining even in the bliss of eternity. A text in St. Maximus Confessor strikes a similar note. The saint argues that there is a kind of "fear" even in eternity, but that it "is coupled with love itself and constantly produces reverence in the soul, lest through the familiarity of love it become presumptuous of God."[23]

So far as I can tell, Hügel never precisely worked through the relationship between love and adoration. He seems to distinguish them, but never to separate them. It would seem sound, on both logical and theological grounds, to accord love the primacy. After all, our ability to adore presupposes God's loving relationship with us as its ground of possibility. And Hügel seems to indicate this in his "trinitarian" passage above, where he appeals to Catherine of Genoa's teaching about our love as grounded in God's inner trinitarian love. If this be sound, then adoration is a moment, a dimension, of fully Christian love. In this way, we are also able to agree with Hügel's notion of the primacy and centrality of adoration. Love and adoration can both be primary, if the latter is a "moment" of the former. And love surely seems the more "inclusive" notion. Love becomes adoration when its gift-bestowed nature breaks through into the consciousness and action of the adorer. We might say that a love for God without the adorational moment can derail into manipulating God, while an adorational love without love's intimacy can depersonalize God.[24]

For a moment, let me return again to the example of Bérulle. As I have indicated, his work breathes an adorational air continuously. "Each day," he tells us, "requires three adorations of the Trinity: ...in the morning we adore him as source...at noon as our being's perfection...at evening, as [its] end." And side by side we find references to love, but again the interrelationship between these two remains incompletely articulated. We perhaps will recall that the cardinal's soul-friend, Mother Madeleine de Saint-Joseph, brings them together, rather remarkably, in a celebrated letter. Like Bérulle, she exalts adoration: "Adoration is what God looked for from the beginning in his creatures. . . . " And because it could only be done imperfectly by creatures God "decided upon the mystery of the Incarnation, where a God would adore God." And she intriguingly glosses: "What is most important to understand is that not only is adoration imperfect without love, but that it does not even deserve to be called adoration, nor is it welcomed by God as such, if love is not its soul and its life, if we can speak thus." Interestingly, we also come across a passage in Bérulle where he admits that he needs to pay more attention to love. Could it be, as one scholar has suggested, that the Mother was the crucial influence over the cardinal?[25] In any case, it is interesting: Hügel first seems primarily to focus upon love at its "purest" and most disinterested, and then is brought to accent its adorational moment; Bérulle first accents the adorational moment, and then resensitizes himself to love's dimension of intimacy.

This discussion, then, clarifies the link between adoration and love. We can plausibly argue that Hügel's "later" stress on adoration is not a radical departure from his focus upon pure love as the deepest actuation of Christian personality, the theme probed in *The Mystical Element*.[26] Adoration is what happens to love when it reaches sufficient depth. Adoration also brings to explicit clarity the Divine Reality who has aroused our movement toward pure love in the first place. It would not be difficult to connect these insights with Hügel's later views on the cultic and anthropological dimensions of adoration, studied above. Christology is not really the focus of *The Mystical Element*, but it is in the background, Jesus appearing as the unique but definitive exemplar and source of pure love. But this is enough to help us see why Jesus' adoring obedience to the Father is considered by Hügel in his later thought to be the key legitimation of his growing emphasis upon adoration.

The relation between religion and ethics is another theme that *The Mystical Element* studies through the lens of Catherine of Genoa. It also casts a certain amount of light upon Hügel's later focus upon adoration, providing us with some of the more practical reasons behind this growing focus. Hügel was criticized for not choosing a "normal" saint, like Teresa of Avila, for his focus. This choice was partially the result of grace, of a "mystical *attrait*," as Hügel would say. But he also defended his choice by arguing that he "wanted a heroic Christian who was almost a Neo-Platonist, an institutional who, in some ways, hung loosely on institutions; a deep thinker beset with much psychophysical disturbance, etc." In other words, he wanted to take in "as much as possible of real life — to show very exquisite spirituality having to live on largely in this rough world." And so Catherine had her ecstasies in and with her deep thoughts, her marital obligations, and her profound service. Her life of intense action was "experienced psychically as a surprise and seizure from without, rather than as a self-determination from within."[27] It pointed again to the divine prevenience. And the baron's colorful image of a "seizure from without" nicely coheres with the objective over-againstness of a God who startles us into adoration.

Hügel appeals to Catherine's experience of religion as a "seizure from without" to indicate that in her experience "Ethics are englobed by Religion." Hügel, reacting to the Kantian ethics, refuses to reduce religion to ethics. Ethics would tend to stress duty, responsibility, law, the rational growth of the human person in understanding and affirming moral values. But Hügel insists that the two forces of the mystical and the ethical hardly ever develop at the same rate (one can be quite mystical and rather "primitive" in values, and vice versa). And the religious element englobes ethics in a "fuller" context: of, namely, "Trust, Grace, Heroism, Love, Free Pardon, Spiritual Renovation." All of these are traits much in evidence in Catherine. As Hügel develops this elsewhere, religion is mainly about "Isness," not "oughtness." In James Kelly's helpful analysis of Hügel, "Religion is primarily evidential, it intimates a supernatural world and reality and it affirms a real contact with this reality which is felt to be within and yet beyond our experience."[28] This distinction, then, between ethics and religion serves to underscore religion's sense of "givenness," an experience brought to intensive expression in adoration. In the light of this, it is not a particularly long step from Hügel's meditation upon Catherine to his later emphasis upon adoration. Like love, ethics also breaks out into adoration, if it reaches sufficient depth. This easily links up with Hügel's interest in the anthropological aspects of adoration. It is also not hard to see the link with Jesus. A rationalistic or ethical (in Kant's sense) christology seems weak in comparison with the incarnational and adorational style of ethics practiced by Catherine of Genoa.

Some other ideas in the *magnum opus* also cast a little more light upon why Hügel increasingly came to accent adoration. Surely the non-parity between the mystical element, as pointing to the ground of the other two elements (the institutional and the intellectual), and the other elements reminds one of the non-equality between God and

112

creatures, the "Divine Dwarfer" emphatically indicated in adoration. God "it is Who, however dimly yet directly, touches our souls and awakens them, in and through all those minor stimulations and apprehensions, to that noblest, incurable discontent with our own petty self and to that sense of and thirst for the Infinite and Abiding."[29] Hügel's extensive critique of pantheism, as abolishing the over-againstness of God, illuminates the same reality, as also does the moving analysis of the bliss of heaven, which does not abolish the divine incomprehensibility, but brings it home more perceptibly.[30] These are major themes running throughout *The Mystical Element*, which intersect and illuminate the adoration theme, and which are pregnant with theological and christological implications.

Adoration and the Three Elements of Religion

Now I would like to widen the discussion and probe how this analysis of adoration might illuminate the major dimensions of Christian existence as Hügel understood them. This will help us sum up the major theological and christological dimensions involved in adoration. It will also help us "develop" our adorational skills. To do this we must look at Hügel's celebrated "three elements," elements that are most synthetically treated in *The Mystical Element*, but that remain always present in his thought, receiving an increasing depth as he "matures." We can use these elements as organizing principles, since they would seem to cover, if we would but sympathetically transpose them into our own "modes" of thinking, the major dimensions of our Christian existence. This will involve some repetition of the anthropological, ecclesiological, and christological dimensions of our theme, as treated so far. But hopefully this will be a repetition that clarifies and develops, rather than bores.

Hügel begins his Catherine book with a discussion of the three elements and then returns to them at the very end. It may be useful to note the influence of Maurice Blondel and particularly Cardinal Newman, his fellow countryman, in his formulation of these elements. The first helped him develop the notion of the person as a dynamic-active interpenetration of these elements. And through Newman's "Preface" to the third edition of the *Via Media*, Hügel was sensitized to the church as a dynamic interrelating of the priestly (spiritual/mystical/devotional), kingly (institutional), and prophetic (doctrinal/intellectual) elements. Hügel "transmutes" these sources in his own unique ways, developing a landscape of the three elements as the "three chief forces" of Western civilization, of religions, and of all persons individually. They are distinct rather than separate and ought to be conceived dynamically and interpenetratingly, with one or another being under- or overstressed, with corresponding reactions and attempted corrections, and so on. Reactions to all this will vary by different readers. As I have said, to the reader well disposed and alert to Hügel's qualifications, these elements do seem to cover the broad scope of the major constituents of human, religious, and Christian existence. In this sense, they are actually enormously helpful in maintaining a feel for life's complexity, avoiding simplicisms, without completely giving up on the quest for unity. In fact, for many, myself included, these insights are the fruit of an intellect that knew its moments of true genius.[31]

A survey of Hügel's writings relative to these three elements indicates that his "move" into the depths of adoration was not a kind of flight into angelism, but rather went along with a tenacious holding to that need for richness through the unity in multiplicity that comes from the oscillations between these three elements. The writings in which the stress upon adoration occurs indicate no retrenchment of his earlier "struggle through balance." And we are entitled, I think, to draw the conclusion that the adorational accent had its special contribution to make to this great balance, through reinforcement and greater clarification and intensification.

We have very strong evidence for this with respect to the intellectual element in life and religion (the analytic and synthetic faculties). For Hügel told us in his "Preface" to the second edition of the Catherine volumes that he had come to a greater clarity on the divine prevenience, a clarity that brought him intellectually to a form of "critical realism" against all forms of Kantian and Kantian-derived subjectivisms. It is helpful to notice that the intellectual (or epistemological) correlate to adoration is some form of critical realism. "Critical," because Hügel recognizes the "human subject humanly apprehending." But "realist," because "givenness" remains the "central characteristic of all religion worthy of the name." And so it is that "the central and final philosophic system and temper of mind which is alone genuinely appropriate to the subject-matter of religion is, I cannot doubt, some kind of Realism." In fact, our mind's turning "to realities other than itself" is an intimation that "adoration appears to be essential" to us, at least at a very embryonic level. And the adoration of Christianity, sensu stricto, utilizes this penchant for the "objective," the over-against. Adoration, we could say, transcends the famous subject-object dichotomy of subjectivisms and "narrow" objectivisms. It points back to a more totalistic notion of experience in which the "plenitude of experience" stimulates the subject into wonderment and analysis. The "ad" of adorare, if you will, points to the objective real; the "orare," to the subject in responsive prayer

114

and recognition.[32] The self is "relational" and "interrelational," if you will.

Hügel's life and work exemplifies this combination of adoring prayer and hard thinking. Like his mentor Newman, Hügel never depreciated the role of the intellectual in life generally, and in religion particularly. There is no evidence that he "retracted" his views in the autobiographical segment of his Catherine book:

Born as I was in Italy, certain early impressions have never left me; a vivid consciousness has been with me, almost from the first, of the massively virile personalities, the spacious, trustful times of the early, as yet truly Christian, Renaissance there, from Dante on to the Florentine Platonists. And when, on growing up, I acquired strong and definite religious convictions, it was that ampler pre-Protestant, as yet neither Protestant nor anti-Protestant, but deeply positive and Catholic, world, with its already characteristically modern outlook and its hopeful and spontaneous application of religion to the pressing problems of life and thought, which helped to strengthen and sustain me, when depressed and hemmed in by the types of devotion prevalent since then in Western Christendom.[33]

Thus, as Lawrence Barmann has recently reminded us, among Hügel's models was Nicholas of Cusa, in whom "the depths of faith, and the clarities of reason, the vigour of action, the warm life-welcoming and life-giving expansion and embrace of love" meet. Even during the miseries of the modernist period, Hügel maintained his intellectual balance, refusing to retreat into a kind of fideism (a sort of "pure" mysticism) or legalism (a kind of exaggerated emphasis upon the institutional element). He surely grew and developed, "purifying" his understanding through articulating his critical realism (his life of prayerful adoration is central here). But this is quite different from retreating into an intellectual obscurantism. His adorational intellectuality, I would suggest, promoted that kind of reflective distance needed to steer between both fideism and gnosticism. Adoration cannot abide the gnostic temper; it rather stimulates the wondering gaze of the theological inquirer. This is, perhaps, what Hügel meant when he spoke of "that queen of the intellectual virtues — perfect sincerity of mind, which, surely, is a kind of fruitful virginity of soul."[34]

Few writers can match Hügel's sensitivity to the institutional and historical element of life in general, and of religion in particular. His appreciation of the scientific temper of mind, concerned for the "thing-like" and the "factual," is celebrated throughout his writings. And the religious correlate to this is, of course, the institutional church, with its "thing-like" mediations of the religious spirit. Here I don't want to rehearse all that Hügel has had to say on these themes. I only want to point to the correspondences between his adorational theology and his sense of the historical-institutional. The key, again, is provided us by that oft-quoted passage from *The Reality of God*, in which he tells us that "it is the external world and our apprehension of it which furnish the religious sense with certain uniquely valuable supports." This, the baron holds, in opposition to those who want to overstress the "interior world as the sole home and satisfying support for the religious convictions." We recall that there is a kind of "embryonic adorational attitude" — with proper qualifications — built into the human being, inasmuch as we "hunger for Reality, Presence, Existence, something to lean upon because it resists, because it is not our own mind, nor this our mind's projection, but because our mind can, and does, apprehend it as rational, as increasingly penetrable, yet always as distinct from this mind which penetrates it." This it is that furnishes us with an intimation of the way to the Other through others. Adoration directs us outward, if you will, to the Other.

Thus, it is important to note that Hügel links adoration with religion. "Religion," that expression going back to Augustine in the Christian tradition, calls to mind the Roman tradition of structure and law, of institution and cult. It expresses, by its externality, the objectivity, the over-againstness of the religious Reality. Hence cult and dogma have a dimension of "authoritativeness" to them that is the echo of the objective Other recognized in adoration and obedience. "Religion is indeed authoritative, since *only if felt and accepted as not of our making but of God's giving is it religion at all*." But note, too, that religion derives its authority not from itself, but through leading to the Other, whom it serves. The "Beloved Community" would remain "vague and weak," without its sense of "a distinct Christ and a distinct God."[35] And so, as adoration finds its epistemological correlate in a critical realism, so it finds its correlate in the sphere under question in a critical ecclesialism. Interestingly, adoration neither abides the triumphalist temper nor the anti-church virtuoso. It generates saints like Catherine of Genoa: an institutional who can "hang low" on institutions.

The intuitive-volitional ("ethico-mystical") element is, of course, the deep, grounding reality through which our spirit intersects with Divine Spirit, the "fundamental," grace-bestowing ground. It is the "experimental" ground which is "articulated" and always in some manner encountered institutionally (culturally-linguistically) and intellectually, but transcends them both and always points us to and meets with the Greater More. This is clear from the beginning in *The Mystical Element*, where Hügel makes it clear that the production of personality "begins with" and "ends in" what is really the "determination of the will."[36] But it is even more emphatically clear as that work progresses, exploring the centrality of the mystical as the ultimate ground in Catherine's life. And as we have seen, it becomes

116

even more emphatic as Hügel stresses adoration as the central and fullest reality of religious experience. By its very nature, adoration highlights and even intensifies the mutual yet "leading" role that the mystical dimension in existence must play.

Hügel is not saying that the "mystical" element cannot derail. It can and it does. The volitional and experimental aspects through which this element expresses itself make it peculiarly liable to "over-charge," and not a little of *The Mystical Element* is concerned with illustrating the difference between a "pure" or almost "raw" "mysticism" that has lost its contact with the other elements, and a more "inclusive" or incarnational mysticism that maintains the friction yet richness of interpenetration through the other elements. Here I would only want to indicate again that, as the mystical element becomes "adorational," its tendency would be to remain within the more "incarnational" kind. There should be, and there is, a correspondence between how adoration leads to a balanced if costly focus upon the intellectual and the institutional, and how it leads to a balanced, incarnational style of mysticism.

At first, this seems surprising. Should not adoration lead us to a profound sense of the God who transcends institutional and intellectual mediation? It surely does, as the Hügelian accent upon the prevenient, over-againstness of God makes clear. Thus Hügel has a profound respect for the "negative style" (*via negativa*), which affirms our inability fully to "penetrate" and explain the Mystery: the "surplusage" of dimness over clarity "is at its highest in connection with God."[37] Still there is a "logic" implicit in adoration that joins the *via negativa* with the "affirmative" tradition in Christian existence. For the adorational stance is one that looks to the "objective," the over-against, not the isolated ego, for growth, development, stimulation, as we have seen. In and through the others of our existence we will be brought to an adoring encounter with the Other.

In this respect, I would particularly point to Hügel's comments on the Trinity and the Incarnation as pertinent. As we saw above, he suggests that the doctrine of the Trinity is a way of "protecting" the over-againstness of God: God is a rich plenitude of personality, a multiplicity in unity, which needs no other for completion. It is this plenitude that, as grace, gives rise to our adoration, and yet it is also this plenitude of personality that promotes in us the sense of our own personalities as a participation in God's own. If you will, adoring the divine multiplicity in unity promotes our own striving for multiplicity in unity.

No doubt the living soul is not a whole made up of separate parts; still less is God made up of parts. Yet we cannot apprehend this Unity of

117

God except in multiplicity of some sort; nor can we ourselves become rightly one, except through being in a true sense many, and very many, as well. Indeed the Christian Faith insists that there is something most real actually corresponding to this our conception of multiplicity even and especially in God Himself. For it as emphatically bids us think of Him as in one sense a Trinity as in another a Unity.[38]

If you will, our own person-developing process of unifying the multiple elements of the mystical, the institutional, and the intellectual is itself based upon our own adoring attunement to the rich multiplicity in unity of the Divine Life itself.

I would also suggest that it is God's own adoration-evoking plenitude of personality that forms the link between Incarnation and adoration, causing the latter to tend in the direction of incarnationalism in religion and life. It is because God is personal as such that the Incarnation can happen and has happened. Hügel has made this explicit. A "Pure Mysticism is but Pantheism," for it leaves "no place for a distinct and definite God, for Sin, for Contrition, ... and for Adoration." And he argues that any attempt to interpret Jesus along the lines of a "pure (pantheistic) mysticism" would run aground on the fact that "all the words and deeds of Jesus ... are the deed of God, the immensely Personalist Power, and not the work of mankind, still less just the operation of the world-whole." It is this "Personalist Power" that brings into being the "supreme revelation" [of Jesus], "in unique fashion and degree, in such and such years, and months and days and hours, and in such and such places, of human history."[39]

Ad Jesum per adorationem — Hügel considers adoration the road to christology. It enables us to appreciate the uniquely supreme "condescension of God" in Jesus: only a distinctly personal (and so free) God — who can thus summon forth our adoration — can become freely personal for us in history. "There exists, not only God Pure, but also God Incarnate, Jesus Christ." And yet we recognize, in and through our adoration, that God remains more even while being incarnate. Walter Kasper has recently suggested that this is one of the meanings behind our attribution of the quality of "person" to God in the eminent sense. God is the "sovereign subject," not to be manipulated by us. Hügel would welcome that understanding of the matter: "But God is God, already apart from His occupation with us," he said.[40] But he simultaneously enables us to grasp that it is this sovereignly non-manipulable person that makes it possible for the Incarnation to happen too. The "personalization" of God in Jesus points us to the plenitude of non-manipulable personality in God.

The link between adoration and christology is a particularly compelling insight of Hügel's, enabling us to entertain the notion that adoration is an essential experience for those wanting to explore the

Incarnation at its deepest. Where adoration suffers, then confessing the Incarnation suffers too. God unincarnate — surely adoration recognizes that. But a God incarnate too — that also ultimately requires the adorational experience. This is not so readily seen. We might put it this way. In the Incarnation, God the adorable becomes God who is adored, the non-manipulable Person who is God discloses to us the mysterious and non-manipulable nature of the divine personality as and in the man Jesus. Only a God who is "adorably" free and sovereign can freely, uniquely, and fully personalize the Divine Self for us. That "freely bestowed love" is what "person" means in its fullest sense, and what we acknowledge in the Incarnation.

If we were to return to the Trinity as our principal analogue (Hügel leaves the trinitarian foundations of his thought sketchy), we might suggest the following. Adoration enables us to participate in the mutual relation between Father and Son, through the Spirit. On the one hand it is a sharing in the Son's adoring homage of the Father, and in this sense adoration stresses the divine transcendence and otherness. On the other, adoration is a sharing in the Son's kenosis, his openness and surrender, his love for the Father. And in this sense adoration has an "incarnational pull," for Jesus' own becoming human — and especially the cross and descent to hell — is his earthly expression of his trinitarian kenosis and love itself. The "becoming human" of God is that trinitarian kenosis of the Son in human form. And all of this is through the Spirit, the bridge, enabling what is radically "other" to become penetratingly "present." These are not Hügel's categories. They are rather more those of the trinitarian exemplarism of the French School. But the links are clear.[41]

Hügel's treatment of adoration is subtle, richly differentiated, yet unified, not unlike that multiplicity in unity that he believed to be the deepest nature of personality, and that he confessed at its plenitude in the multiplicity in unity of the Trinity, and in its supreme incarnate form in Jesus Christ. To be sure, it remains only incompletely defined, and this was probably a deliberate result of his insight into adoration's many (and greatly incomprehensible) mansions. But if it is not tightly defined, it is not incoherent. One senses its "logic," albeit of a supernatural sort. The traditional teaching on adoration is here: the act only properly rendered to God, confessing God's prevenience and so also the divine ability to freely communicate with us. But Hügel has mined this teaching and the experience that is its basis. And it is one of his special contributions to have surfaced the epistemological (intellectual), the institutional-ecclesial, the anthropological, and especially the christological dimensions of this phenomenon. If this teaching is complex, it is because it springs from his richly contemplative experience, and that of the sainted-mystic contemplators he

119

consulted. For the contemplative aims for the whole, the "catholic" in the deepest sense. Whatever limitations Hügel's teaching may have probably spring from what some would consider the somewhat artificial schema of the three elements of religion. I think he had a healthy "detachment" from his own categories, saw their dangers, and built in multiple qualifiers. The crucial thing was that he aimed not to abolish complexity in favor of some narrowly conceived program. In this respect, he didn't reduce all religion to adoration: it was not the whole, but it was central for the whole. We have to get that distinction to appreciate his views. His trinitarian soundings remain sketchy, as we have noted. And it would have been helpful if he had probed the literary nature of the adoration genre. He was sensitive to the symbolic, cultural mediation of adoration, of course (his "institutional" element), but his insights would have nicely complemented the few comments we were able to make of a literary nature in our last chapter.

In sum, we should be grateful to Hügel for "rehabilitating" adoration as a central category in theology. It brings a crucial sensitivity to this book's project of interrelating spirituality, theology, and christology. Hügel's "suggestive" insights about the link between the Incarnation and adoration are also central, and we will put them to good use in what follows. And finally, his ability to relate adoration to critical realism (the intellectual element), to cult/worship (the institutional/historical element), as well as serious personal prayer and a heroic ethics transcending utilitarianism (the mystical element) gives us a good idea of how to go about developing our adorational "skills."

CHAPTER SIX

Saints and Mystics
As Christological Sources

The Theological Significance of the Saints

There is a "logic" behind turning to the saints and mystics now, after the chapter on adoration. For the adorational experience seems to characterize the saints and mystics in a particularly intensified way. Those of us wishing to explore this experience, and its christological implications, a little more deeply could hardly do better than enter into a kind of "discipleship" under these masters of adoration. The saints and mystics will also enable us to remain close to the fuller intensity, drama, living practice, and narrative nature of Christian experience, as we theologically "consult" their lived experience and the often explicitly narrative writings through which they have described that experience for us.

I will be using the two terms "saint" and "mystic" as roughly identical, meaning by these anyone who has been deeply and consciously-explicitly permeated by and transformed by the gospel summons. These are the great contemplatives, who have been "seized" by Jesus Christ as fully as one can imagine in this existence of ours, "seized" throughout the breadth and depth of life. "Canonization," which may or may not be accorded the saints and mystics in all cases, gives expression in a representative manner to their ecclesial and social "mission" (and even deepens that mission), indicating that a truly christified life always in some way pours itself out, like the Lord's blood and water, on behalf of the many. In some sense, all genuine saints and mystics must manifest this mission dimension, which usually stimulates a resonating response on the part of others. The witness that the martyr is expresses, *par excellence*, this christic pouring out for the many. And that is why the lines between the saints, mystics, and martyrs must blur, and why martyrs must be accorded special prominence among all these prominent witnesses of the church.

Many of us are accustomed to speaking of the "attractiveness" of the saints, but we usually have in mind some virtue that they express that we find congenial and appealing to our own particular *attrait* in the spiritual life. Thus, we find ourselves "inspired" by the Blessed Virgin Mary's fidelity, St. Peter's humility, Paul's single-minded courage, the ability of St. Francis de Sales and St. Thérèse of Lisieux to find the extraordinary in the ordinary, Monsieur Olier's profound devotion to the Blessed Sacrament and priesthood, Julian of Norwich's biblical hopefulness, and so on. But here I would like us to think about the possible "theological" and even "doctrinal" attractiveness of the saints and mystics, considering them as a theological and christological source.

The church does just that when it names a "canonized" saint a "Doctor of the Church," assigning him or her a feast that celebrates not only the person's sanctity but also his or her theological contribution to the church. In some cases these saints weren't "professional" theologians in the school sense, and yet the church points to their "learning" as a source of the church's doctrine and teaching. Here the *lex orandi* suggests that theology should be done with a sensitivity to the saints and mystics: *sentire cum sanctis et misticis in theologia.* In recent times, we can think of the role that the saints and mystics played in the very content of Balthasar's theology, one embracing individual theological studies of St. Thérèse of Lisieux, Elizabeth of the Trinity, and Adrienne von Speyr, and going on to include whole volumes on others in his theological "trilogy." Karl Rahner, too, frequently pointed to the theological importance of the saints, and of spirituality in general (of which the saints are the great exemplars). He particularly felt in the debt of the great St. Ignatius Loyola: "I think that the spirituality of Ignatius himself . . . was more significant for me than all learned philosophy and theology inside and outside the order."[1]

Balthasar and Rahner are contemporary examples of an "older" style of theology, which tries to unite learning and sanctity, theology and spirituality, or, metaphorically expressed, "light" and "fire." Cardinal Bérulle and M. Olier would call this the "science of the saints." Père Bourgoing's famous "Preface" to Bérulle's works suggests that the cardinal was quite consciously trying to overcome the "split" between theology and spirituality characteristic of the schools.[2] The fathers and mothers of the early church (think of the desert solitaries, the great monks and nuns, and others, especially the likes of St. Gregory of Nyssa and his sister Macrina, Gregory's greatest teacher in some ways), are privileged examples of this, combining sanctity and theology often in themselves. Is this one of the reasons for their fruit-fulness, their freshness, and their creativity? And let us not forget the preeminent role that the saints have continued to play in the theo-logical traditions of the Eastern Orthodox. For example, St. Gregory Palamas can be seen in many ways as someone who dedicated his life to defending the theological significance of the mystic. But Gregory is representative of many. And let us think, too, of the formative influ-ence of the mystics upon Luther, or upon John Wesley, who can serve us as representative of the theological "consultation" of the mystics among the reformers.[3] Let us try to hold on to these thoughts and, stimulated by great theological thinkers down the ages, let us inquire into this "consultation" of saints and mystics by the theologian.

What is it, more exactly, that might recommend the saints and mystics to the theologian precisely as "theological sources" them-selves? One way to approach this question is to ask why much of the theology of recent times lost contact with the saints, and in gen-eral with the realm of spirituality of which the saints and mystics are the richest "ore." It is generally agreed that much of post-Baroque, Western theology tended toward the "abstract," becoming somewhat extrinsic to experience and its many narratives and other dramatic genres, "rationalistic" in the pejorative sense. A theology that tries to work its way back to the concrete fullness of experience, attempting somehow to recover the "intrinsicist" nature of revelation as a reality arising from God's disclosure through the reality of our human expe-rience (as thought, action, feelings, etc.) — such a theology will find the mystics congenial and even irreplaceable guides in this effort. For the saints learn their theology from their experience. They embody it: the fire of their life is the glowing ember of an experience of the faith penetrated by purification. That is why it is also "light," and so a potentially rich theological source of illumination. The narratives (in a stricter sense now as biographies and journals, rather than in the broader sense of any genre rendering the dramatic nature of human experience) and other "participative" genres through which the mys-tics gave expression to their experience (poetry, letters, plays, prayers, hymns, etc.) — and without which their experience could not occur — are not a "second best" form of theological literature, somehow not quite as good as abstract treatises. The latter, rather, can express only portions of the former, whose texture is much richer, if many times more "compact."

St. Teresa of Avila, representing a "modern" self-reflectivity, put it succinctly: "There was nothing I understood until His Majesty gave me understanding through experience." Olier, penetrated as he was by a Christ-mysticism, put it this way: "Now, the Saints and the just are like echoes, which carry to God the voice of Christ living in them."

I have already cited St. Francis de Sales describing in a memorable way the difference between the "unsainted" and the "sainted" as that between a musical piece "read" (*une musique notée*) and one sung (*chantée*).[4] In each case, it is the lived, the experienced quality of revelation that is being pointed to. And this is why these mystics find themselves attracted to narrative and other dramatic forms of genre, and non-written art forms as well, as the only appropriate mode more or less adequate to the lyrical depth of their experience. No wonder, then, that Balthasar would describe the kind of theological source that the mystic can be as "experiential dogmatics."[5]

It is not surprising, then, that any number of contemporary thinkers have turned to the mystics. Think again of William James's *The Varieties of Religious Experience*. Or of Rudolf Otto's "consultation" of Shankara and the Christian Meister Eckhart. Think also of Henri Bremond's literary *Histoire* of French mystical "sentiment" (which was particularly sensitive to the literary, symbolic-narrative dimension of experience) and Hügel's work on the mystical element in religion, as studied especially in St. Catherine of Genoa, also a piece of narrative theology. And we should remember that the Abbé Huvelin, Hügel's spiritual director, had advised him to be cautious of the abstract theology of the "schools." The "modern" interest in experience was in the air. And there was even something of a "critique" of inherited dogmatisms in this fascination for the experiential. At times this was also accompanied by a growing suspicion of ideologies and totalitarianisms and utopianisms, all of which are rooted in "dreamy abstractions" severed from human experience.

But most importantly, for the Christian, the appeal to experience and its narrative-literary expressions — and so to the saints/mystics — is more than a cultural phenomenon. The very nature of our faith as "incarnational" — revelation as occurring through the human, although not simply reducible to it (God intersects experience, rather than "shrinks" to it) — and as possessing a message relevant to the experience of all demands this constant turn to the fullness of experience.[6] Revelation takes the "form" of the Word Jesus — it has not just remained "vague" and "formless" — with which we are invited to dialogue in the Spirit.

"Experience" is a category we can turn to, then, in our effort to describe what it is that gives the saint and mystic "theological authority." We have suggested how, in the modern context, it can be an ambiguous word — and, in the minds of some, even dangerous. Thus, as a "protective device" against reductionistic tendencies, we should also speak of revelation as "embodied" or "incarnated" in the saints, inasmuch as they witness to it. God's Word is not reduced to experience, but illuminated through it. Or, with Newman, we might think of mystics as profoundly living out a "real" rather than simply "notional" assent. At the same time, we must recognize experience's linguistic-narrative nature, and its culturally mediated nature as well. What seems important is to recognize that "experience" is not a univocal reality, but a complex one, referring to the many levels and aspects of the human in grace-bestowed relationship with God. The mystic's grace-bestowed, spiritual experience of the Divine is every bit as much of a real "human experience" as any other kind of experience. Not a small contribution of the turn to the mystics is to restore to us this "larger" notion of experience, which since the Enlightenment we have tended to forget. Perhaps we could call this a "theocentric and ecclesial-cultural model of experience."

Here I would suggest that we view the mystic's *via purgativa* as an attempt, on one level, to "purify" and "open up" our experience, separating out the illusions, reductions, defense mechanisms, blindnesses — sinful or otherwise — that impede our humanity from becoming the "disclosure" of the Divine, or which impede us from recognizing that disclosure elsewhere. There is a "theological" relevance to this *via purgativa*, for it serves as a kind of Christian "phenomenological" method that invites us to overcome our "illusions" and enter into the greater "depths" of reality. Oftentimes the "Word" that speaks to us in revelation cannot be heard by us, because the "inner ear" of our being is plugged up, and the ascesis of the saints can enable us to open this current of receptivity. Teachers wishing the student to appropriate the fuller experience of revelation would do well to invite the student into the mystic's world of "experiential-linguistic-symbolic exploration" through purgative purification. As our narcissistic blindnesses are peeled away, we find ourselves entering into — better, brought into — a space where the encounter with the Word can occur in the *fond* of our lives.

"Experiential explorers" of revelation — this can serve as a first, "rough" description of the contribution of the mystics/saints to theology in general and christology in particular. If we search how these "explorers" have aided theologians like Balthasar and Karl Rahner in their theological work, we might usefully speak of "appropriate" and "critical" contributions.[7] Balthasar has suggested that the dark night experience of some of the mystics might serve as a bridge to christology, lighting up for us the death experience and "tomb" experience of Jesus, about which otherwise we would know very little. Here the mystic gifts us with an appropriately experiential expression of the heart of christology itself. Jesus' "descent into hell" has light indirectly thrown upon it through the dark night experience of the mystic, whose stripping of narcissism and identification with the forgotten and "damned" seems to be an "experiential analogue" to

Jesus, making sense only in the light of Jesus. Here, too, we come upon the theme of Balthasar's "theological aesthetics": God's glory is revealed in kenosis; the truly adorable is the utterly humiliated and "empty" one. The saint's kenosis is a true act of doxology, derivative from the Son's own definitive doxology through kenosis. The great and numerous trials of the "little" Thérèse would also seem to be potentially rich in this regard, as well as M. Olier's famous "ordeal," which Balthasar notes has been likened to one of the earlier, psychosomatic ordeals of Thérèse.[8]

If Balthasar illustrates how the mystic can provide us with an "experientially appropriate" view or exemplification of revelation, especially christology, perhaps Karl Rahner can illustrate the potentially "critical" contribution — or challenge — of the saints (although each of these great masters illustrates both functions of a consultation of the saints). By "critical" I mean the mystic's ability to uncover "forgotten" dimensions of revelation, to expose narrow and harmful distortions of revelation, and to "promote" a necessary "development" in theology and doctrine. Here I am thinking of Rahner's brilliant retrieval of Ignatius Loyola's "new" and "modern" sensitivity to the unique individual as called by God to discern one's own special mission in history. Rahner finds Ignatius breaking out of a kind of ecclesial collectivism, which views the person as one instance of the collective many. In a sense, Ignatius uncovers something of the forgotten "personalism" of the gospel. In another sense, this is a critique of the danger of ecclesial and social totalitarianism, and a renewal of what Newman would later call "conscience" in the church and John Courtney Murray and Vatican Council II "religious liberty" (properly understood). I find a similarly "critical" discovery in Thérèse of Lisieux's critique of elitism in spirituality and ecclesiology and in her renewal of the priority of grace over works (in a Catholic sense), long before Vatican II. Thérèse's "little way" can be viewed as a Catholic recovery of the priesthood of all the faithful, of ecclesial collegiality, and of the call to sanctity to all. And today we hear her critical comments about limiting presbyteral ordination to males in a new way. Besides "exemplifying" the common view of revelation, the French School was surely "critical" too, bringing to light the high calling of the presbyteral priesthood, renewing the tradition of the priesthood of all the faithful, critiquing the loss of the spiritual/mystical roots of theology, etc.

These examples of how the saints and mystics can be challenges for theology have not explicitly mentioned christology as one of the areas so challenged, but surely it too can be enriched through "critical challenge" by the saints. In a broad sense, this entire book tries to illustrate this challenge. Surely the way that Christian contemplation "sublates" christology's method and the rich retrieval of an inclusive and trinitarian christocentrism in the French School illustrate this challenge. Our next chapter will explore how the study of Mary, Jesus' mother, also deeply enriches and challenges contemporary christology.

Thérèse of Lisieux's Narrative Christology

Perhaps I can appeal to St. Thérèse of Lisieux as one "summary-like" representative of how the mystics both exemplify and challenge the church's christology. I particularly like to appeal to her because one senses in her both the old and the new, a profound fidelity to the tradition as almost literally "carved out" on her body, and yet a daringness, that non-dogmatic openness to the new and challenging that seem to characterize the great mystics. Christologically her "religious" name is very suggestive in this regard: Thérèse "of the Child Jesus and the Holy Face." Thérèse here indicates her "christological" relevance: it is Jesus she will try to exemplify, but inclusively, from childhood through the passion (the Holy Face/Shroud). It is not, however, some idealized Jesus who has been "romanticized," but the Jesus of suffering (Holy Face) and of the forgotten and uncounted (the Child), and a Jesus daring and "precocious" (like the child too). Her "little way" has much more in common with this retrieval of the dispossessed and the daring — the "child" in this sense — than with some romanticized view of children.

Thérèse's christology, discoverable through the narrative of her *Story of a Soul* and her conversations, is traditional, in the sense that it tries to recapture the full divine-human reality of Jesus, but also new, in the sense that it challenges the idealized humanity and near-monophysitism of much of the recent tradition. Jesus' life in the Holy Family "wasn't everything that they have told us or imagined," she said. She primarily rethinks Jesus through the lens of love: he is the earthly revelation of the trinitarian "furnace of love" giving the church a heart "burning with love." This love led Jesus to be victim for all, all sinners included, and Thérèse prays that it will make her a "martyr" of his love too. Her famed "dark night" in the last year and a half of her life becomes for her the entry into detachment from the last remnants of prideful self-reliance and an experience of solidarity with those who experience utter abandonment and alienation. Thérèse's "secret" was the radical way in which she abandoned her life over to Jesus. As she put it in another context, she was a "little zero," which "by itself has no value, but put alongside *one* becomes potent, always provided it is put on the *proper side*, after and not before!" She thought of herself as this "zero" next to and after others, supremely Jesus, working "together for the salvation of souls." But this was the

127

key, I think, that enabled her to discover deeper and in that sense "new" facets of the mystery of Jesus. Here was how she discovered her "little way," which was "very straight, very short, and totally new," she claimed.[9]

This "little zero" metaphor is typical of Thérèse. In one stroke it expresses her genius. Or better yet: our own "participation" in the form of this metaphor enables us to experience something of her genius. It is a playful metaphor, suggesting the playfulness of the child. And thereby we experience something of the child Jesus to which she is so dedicated, devotion to which she thinks is a special window onto the mystery of Jesus. The metaphor also suggests abandonment, and thus the hard path of the cross, calling to mind her devotion to Jesus' Holy Face, the face of the shroud and cross. The playful metaphor is not sentimentalism: it leads us into the interior of the mystery of Jesus — the radical love — yet without becoming "heavy" and burdensome. It also teaches us to identify with the "little," those who don't count: another side of the childhood theme, as well as the soteriological dimension of Jesus' work. Thérèse's writings manifest a profound attraction to rich, originary metaphors like this "little zero," which perhaps helps account for the extraordinary "success" of her mission. Here is another, very well known one from her *Story of a Soul*, suggesting the same cluster of meanings:

> I had offered myself, for some time now, to the Child Jesus as His *little plaything*. I told Him not to use me as a valuable toy children are content to look at but dare not touch, but to use me like a little ball of no value which He could throw on the ground, push with His foot, *pierce*, leave in a corner, or press to His heart if it pleased Him; in a word, I wanted to *amuse little Jesus*, to give Him pleasure; I wanted to give myself up to His *childish whims*. He heard my prayer.[10]

To entertain this metaphor of the little ball requires a lightheartedness: people taking themselves too seriously will find it offensive. And so again we become like the little child — the child Jesus, and children who haven't assimilated the heavy pomposity that won't allow us to laugh at ourselves. But again we are introduced into the christological mystery of abandonment. One can almost feel how completely the ball is at the disposal of the one playing with it. We are back with the devotion to the Holy Face.

Thérèse's entire narrative-autobiography is like these metaphors: as we participate in it we experience something of Jesus the Child and the Holy Face. The "drama" of these two become our drama in a way, and thus we begin to participate in the mystery of Jesus in a way both faithful to the tradition and yet challenging in its newness. For think of the rough, notebook character of the *Story of a Soul*, unpolished and spontaneous (three separate manuscripts, later joined), like the world of the child. How fitting for a work celebrating devotion to Jesus' childhood! And there is also the childish sense of being the center of the universe itself, but somehow this is lifted up into a much higher purpose, which the very form of the autobiography suggests. For it is a "confession," written out of obedience and love, not unlike the Holy Face responding in obedience to the Father's call to the cross. And the fact that Thérèse surrendered it over to her sisters, for them to revise as they would, intensifies the sense of participating in the surrender of the passion. The "leaving nothing in her life unsaid" also seems to come from the sense that her entire life has been delivered over, not unlike her Lord's.

This fascinating interplay between Jesus' childhood and Holy Face, suggested by the form of the work itself, is a theme played out with many variations throughout the book. It meets us powerfully at the end of *Manuscript A*, which takes us up to Thérèse's entry into Carmel. There Thérèse chooses the form of the wedding invitation to express the theme: "God Almighty...and the Most Glorious Virgin Mary...announce to you the Spiritual Espousals...of Jesus...with little Thérèse Martin, now Princess and Lady of His Kingdoms of the Holy Childhood and the Passion...of the Child Jesus and the Holy Face."[11] The context of the wedding suggests that the mystery of love is really what we discover in the child and the face, love under different aspects. And we meet the theme of love in its perhaps best form in *Manuscript B*, which is really a doxology to divine love. This is the famous part in which she speaks of discovering the church's heart as one of love, and her own vocation as one to love. The themes of childhood and Holy Face continue, but on a deepened level. Now they seem to express Jesus' embodiment of a love for the victim, not unlike the suffering servant. She is the "little bird" who wants to be *fascinated* by [Jesus'] divine glance." And she hopes that Jesus, "the Adorable Eagle," will "fetch" her and "plunge" her "into the burning Abyss of this Love to which it has offered itself as victim."[12]

Manuscript C recounts the remarkable dark night during the final part of Thérèse's life (1896–97), in which she experienced the "naked faith" that learns to trust only in God and nothing else, not even one's supposedly "correct" beliefs. The latter for Thérèse was especially the belief in heaven: throughout her *Story* heaven is the place where life's inequities, including the ones she has had to suffer, will be rectified. It is her crutch, so to speak. Still there is not the complete abandonment. But now it comes, this "thickest darkness," which makes of heaven "the cause of struggle and torment." Now God was giving her "the experience of years," and it is fascinating that as she is stripped "naked" of herself, she discovers her solidarity with sinners and wants only to become the servant of all. Childhood does not disappear here either: the "little flower" now gives her celebrated "elevator" metaphor of how the "little way" is the "very straight" and "totally new" way to God, lifting us to God. And she has discovered true littleness in this most intense sharing in the Holy Face, where "naked faith" is her way of experiencing Jesus' utter abandonment.[13]

The last two manuscripts overlap, covering some of the same period. Does this suggest that dark night/abandonment (*Ms. C*) is the real key to doxology and love (*Ms. B*)? And does the retracing of the same terrain indicate the deepened levels at which love moves and the need to interiorize it? Here something of the drama of existence that narrative can explore comes through. Note, too, how the perspective of the author (Thérèse), looking back upon her life, intensifies the sense of the "extraordinary" unfolding in the "ordinary," the attainment of sanctity through littleness. For she "confesses" her life as but a mission on behalf of the "little way." And fascinatingly the reader feels drawn into this most personal of accounts through the addressees (Mother Agnes, *Ms. A;* Sister Marie of the Sacred Heart, *Ms. B;* Mother Marie de Gonzague, *Ms. C*). The movement from "I" to "we" helps bring this about, as well as the sense that these people seem to represent the "official" church to whom Thérèse's life is dedicated. And yet the singularity of each addressee preserves the intimacy and "direct address" character of her mission, which is really Jesus' mission on our behalf.

Much of the power of Thérèse's work comes through the "pilgrimage" with her of her *Story*, which in some sense we "undergo" as we meditatively read it and experience the cumulative effect of the metaphors, very original and playful, like the child, but going deeper into the mystery, as we gaze through the eyes of the Holy Face. Her "christology" and "soteriology," both nicely united here, largely derive their power from the interplay between Jesus' childhood and Holy Face. It is a christology of love, but love can be so easily romanticized and cauterized. The devotion to the Holy Face keeps the love real, costly, and freed of narcissism. The childhood theme keeps it playful, creative, in touch with the forgotten; indeed, even bold, suggests Balthasar.[14] This is not a theologically "scientific" christology, but a suggestive return to the originary springs out of which christology flows, and through it we have a most compelling rediscovery of the theme of kenosis in the scriptures (especially 1 Cor 12–13), with a keen insight into its implications for a church freed of elitism and triumphalism.[15]

Further Dimensions

Father Olier, in his celebrated "Acts for the Divine Office," spoke of the "immense religion" and the "multiplicity of loving sentiments" that the saints manifest in their offering of glory to God. At the same time, he spoke of the "holy harmony" that their religion also expresses.[16] Multiplicity and harmony — these will be the overwhelming experience of the theologian who takes his or her theological questions to the saints. And we need to search the possible "theological" significance of this rich diversity in harmony. Is it that the saints give expression, analogously, to the diversity in harmony of the trinitarian life itself, so that to "consult" the saints is to enter into the "conversation" of Father, Son, and Holy Spirit, hearing the "echo" of that conversation, if I might borrow M. Olier's thought? God's "oneness" is a richly differentiated one, capable of grounding interpersonal richness. And perhaps this rich harmony in diversity is found reexpressed in the immensity of the Incarnation: in Jesus, who "unites" humanity in divinity, the unique self with the community of others, "insiders" and "outsiders," men and women, poor and oppressed, etc. And again, it is reexpressed in the "communion of saints," whose own diversity and oneness echoes that of Jesus and the Trinity.

I suspect that there are many levels of "meaning" to this rich harmony in diversity manifested in the saints, aspects of which each age perhaps especially recognizes. Let me mention some possibilities. We find a pluralism of expressions among the saints, even to the point of what sometimes seems like "wildly" idiosyncratic manifestations, yet there is a deeper harmony in the obedient commitment to Jesus. Might not a consultation of the mystics/saints enable us to work our way through the complex world of theological pluralism without losing our need for a deeper harmony? Their very diversity keeps us attuned to the rich texture and not fully exhaustible reality of revelation. And yet there is a harmony, a correspondence between these many "words" and the one Word Jesus. There is a repetitiveness to the saints too: often they seem to give off the same theological message. Is this an expression of the need to "interiorize" the depths of the Christian message, to stay with it in a contemplative mode, not rushing on to the new and superficial?[17] The saints reveal the "new" to us, surely, but it is a newness with deep roots in the old (with continuity). It is a development in the understanding of doctrine, not a revolution of doctrine, that the saints seem to manifest.

So the saints, analogously, express the unity in diversity found in archetypical form within the Trinity itself. Another manifestation of this analogy between saints and Trinity might be found in the following. The Spirit grounds the rich diversity of the saints, their unique charisms and missions for the church. The Son, who "norms" the Spirit and to whom the Spirit leads, unifies these unique gifts for the truly personal building up of the body of Christ. And the Father, as the inexhaustible source, means that no mystic or saint will ever exhaust, but can only point to, the rich trinitarian mystery of Father, Son, and Spirit.

Since the Quietist controversy we have become aware of the saints and mystics as controversial in the church. Some are probably attracted to the mystics because they sense in them a way of bypassing ecclesial mediations of revelation. One suspects that not a little of the fascination of modern philosophers for mysticism has something to do with a desire to get at the supposedly "pure" core of revelation prior to any institutional "tampering" with it. A "theological" consultation of the saints needs to know this history, which has its own contribution to make to our work in theology. I do not think that Christian mystical experience, when it is authentic, bypasses ecclesial mediations of the faith. It is christocentric and ecclesiocentric in the great mystics. For them, experience is "shaped" by scripture and tradition — as experience is always shaped by culture and language — and always leads to a more profound appropriation of those sources. In fact, the very reality of the saints/mystics calls to mind the "mediated," incarnational nature of revelation, which comes to us through the "witness" and "shape" of those hallowed out by participating in the mysteries of Christ. It is their self-emptying that makes of them finely tuned "receptors" of the sources of the church's revelation.

Still, to "go to the mystics" is to introduce a kind of tension into theology and church: not one arising from bypassing the church and tradition, but from a mystical "purgation" (the mystic's correlate to the cross) of the church and its theology, which tries to free the tradition from narcissistic dross and blindness.[18] I would suggest that this "tension" is rather more of an eschatological reality, a sign that the saints are trying to prod us a little closer to the kingdom in which theology is practiced, not with intellectual blindness, but with contemplative openness. And so, to the theologian, the saint and mystic comes as a challenge, a summons, to explore the "soundings" of the Word being uttered in human existence. And, as a result, they come as a challenge to confront the blockages to the hearing of that Word.

I have been concentrating on the contribution of the saints to theology, but there is the other side, that of theology's contribution to the saints. In its "scientific" aspect theology has its modest but crucial role to play in the process of clarifying, refining, and developing our doctrinal heritage. The saints are not always their own best interpreters, although it is a blessed reality when theology and sanctity coalesce in one. What the mystic sometimes "knows" more dimly and intuitively, the theologian can try to "unpack" more "scientifically." In other words, the theologian should apply to the *locus misticus* the kind of critical hermeneutics he or she applies to all theology's sources. Still, I think the mystic teaches the theologian to keep *intellectus* in the service of *fides;* knowledge anchored in the fullness of spiritual experience, language, and narrative; light at the service of fire. While theological "light" can save us from a pseudomysticism that is little more than a form of "narcissistic vitalism," mystical "fire" can save us from theological rationalism and gnostic intellectual arrogance.

There seems more to it, too. The mystic's willingness to undergo the "purification" indicates that there is a "pull" in authentic mysticism toward submitting one's experience to theology's critical gaze. But having said this, still I think theology is brought to a humble recognition of its "servant" role in the church by the mystic. Mystical experience brings the theologian back to a contemplative mode of knowing, which is the fuller "matrix" from which the more analytic modes of knowing of the theologian develop. "Analysis" is in the service of *contemplatio* and *adoratio*, not vice versa. In this sense, I would suggest that mystical experience and contemplation occupies a certain primacy. It leads, and theology follows. Interestingly, as the lives of the greatest of the saints and mystics illustrate, this "*contemplatio*" transcends the dichotomy of theory and action, embracing both. It is the fecund *fond* embracing both thought and action. With this in mind, I think we can trust that the saints' guidance will lead us to a "balanced" perspective on theology, and even to a renewed sensitivity to the poor and forgotten.

CHAPTER SEVEN

The Virgin Mary
As a Christological Source

Like other chapters in this book, this one will have something of an "experimental" character to it. Here we will be probing the way that the mystery of the Blessed Virgin Mary can illuminate christology. This chapter wants to situate itself within the grand tradition of the church, which knows well the way in which Mary and Jesus "implicate" one another. Cyril of Alexandria, writing John of Antioch in reference to the recent problems with Nestorius's christology, expressed this insight with some solemnity: "You really have an obligation to understand clearly that almost the whole of the struggle on account of the faith was waged because of our conviction that the holy Virgin is the Mother of God."[1] Here John is reminded, if he really needs it, that christological positions are at times arrived at from mariological insights.

The thinking of the tradition about this, the "eminent" role of Mary among the sources of christological insight, is really fairly simple. It has to do with her mission as the *Theotokos*, the Mother of God. The intimacy this involved, on all the levels of her being, biologically to be sure, but also spiritually, gave her a unique bonding with her son unmatched elsewhere. It is this unique love relationship that gives rise to the unique position of Mary in the tradition, constituting her a privileged source of christological insight. For love is not simply a way of being, but also a participative way of "knowing." And Mary *knew:* "And Mary kept all these things, reflecting on them in her heart" (Lk 2:19). "Mary is the means Our Lord chose to come to us and she is also the means we should choose to go to him," said St. Louis Mary Grignion de Montfort. For her "strongest inclination is to unite us to Jesus, her Son, and her Son's strongest wish is that we come to him through his Blessed Mother."[2] It is this "inclination" of her being that seems to make her a source for us, even the eminent source. And so it makes sense to say that her Son's wish is that we come to him through her.[3]

Referring to Mary as the "eminent" or "privileged" source of christological insight needs to be interpreted in an "inclusivistic" rather than "exclusivistic" sense. That is, Mary needn't be imagined as a kind of buffer zone between Jesus and us, a sort of hurdle we must go through to reach Jesus. As Vatican II's rich "Marian chapter" of *Lumen Gentium* put it, she "does not hinder in any way the immediate union of the faithful with Christ but on the contrary fosters it."[4] Mary always "includes" Jesus; Jesus always "includes" Mary. Nor is it a question of thinking of Mary as a source separate from scripture. Scripture remains the privileged source, but scripture "includes" Mary's eminent witness. Vatican II wanted to break new ground in some sense by "correcting" deviations in approaches to Mary and by taking pains to present this more "inclusivistic" christocentric, ecclesiocentric, and bibliocentric approach to Mary. But having said all that, still the council affirmed that Mary in virtue of her mission and by the "merits of her Son . . . far surpasses all creatures both in heaven and on earth." Or, using a nicely compact alternative formulation: Mary "occupies a place in the Church which is the highest after Christ and also closest to us."[5]

In what follows I hope to "interrogate" mariology from a primarily "meditative, contemplative" perspective, understanding by those adjectives the various ranges of meaning they have received from the previous chapters. In order to give a bit more focus to our discussion, and also out of humility for one's limits, I plan to concentrate upon the mystery of the virgin birth (often referred to now as the "virginal conception"), seeking its contribution to our christological insight. It is the "proposal" of this chapter that the *contemplative* approach to christology and theology we've been pursuing up to now has some special light to throw upon the tradition's belief that Mary is a privileged source of christological learning. Our earlier chapter on the French School has been a special inspiration in this regard. More provocatively, it's one of the proposals of this chapter that the "relative" lack of the "contemplative" style in theology has been one of the reasons for the "relative" lack of attentiveness to mariology in christology.

Why do I choose the virginal conception as the object of focus? Let me quite honestly say that I'm not quite sure I can answer this question satisfactorily, to others or even to myself. Perhaps I fear that the widespread indifference to it, or rejection of it, points to an important inadequacy in the way we tend to go about our theological and christological work. As though the somewhat "massive indifference" has, as its other side, a "massive christological inadequacy." In a sense, the issue of the virginal conception has "chosen" me, inasmuch as my work in christology, particularly from a meditative slant, has drawn me toward a deepened appreciation of its significance, mariologically as well as christologically. In any case, at least according to the witness of Matthew and Luke, the virginal conception is the historical way God chose to *begin* the Incarnation among us. Taking a clue from God's pedagogy, it may be the way to *begin* work in christology too.

The Adorational Experience and the Christology of the Virginal Conception

Adoration, we have seen, is the special province of the contemplative. It is what happens to contemplation when it reaches its "highest pitch." So, in a contemplative approach to the virginal conception it is appropriate to return to our considerations on adoration as a port of entry. And this is suggested by both Matthew and Luke, who present us with a doxological narrative in the birth stories. Matthew associates the visit of the magi with the virginal conception, these magi who "prostrated themselves and did him homage" (2:11). Luke has his doxological (adorational) equivalent in the shepherd story of his telling of the virginal conception: "And suddenly there was a multitude of the heavenly host with the angel, praising God and saying, 'Glory to God in the highest and on earth peace to those on whom his favor rests'" (2:13–14). It is as if the mystery of this birth calls forth adoration in the forms of worship and glorifying as its appropriate response in these narratives. As we proceed, I would ask the reader to recall what we have said previously, by way of a more formal nature, about narrative and the doxology genre. The following tries to show how both Matthew and Luke seem to suggest that the narrative of Jesus' birth "unfolds" only for the believer willing to be caught up into a posture of adoration.

Biblical scholars commonly mention the theme of adoration in Matthew's account: the verb translated as "paying homage" being the same one commonly used for "adoring." In fact, Matthew's use of this term *proskunein* has been called a "theological concept," given the seemingly careful way in which the term surfaces in his gospel. This term occurs thirteen times in Matthew (more than any of the other gospels, with John coming close: eleven occurrences; Revelation, not surprisingly, breaks out with its use some twenty-four times), and in at least five places, he has altered or expanded parallel passages in Mark in order to bring out the theme of adoration. That is, in the stories of the leper (Mt 8:2; cf. Mk 1:40), Jairus (Mt 9:18; cf. Mk 5:22), Jesus' companions in the boat (Mt 14:33; cf. Mk 6:51), the woman of Canaan (Mt 15:25; cf. Mk 7:25), and the mother of James and John

(Mt 20:20; cf. Mk 10:35) we find uniquely in Matthew that those approaching Jesus do so with *proskynesis*. Matthew 27:29 leaves out Mark's mention of adoration by the soldiers (15:19) perhaps because Mark is referring to the mockery being made of it by them, while for Matthew *proskynesis* seems to indicate true adoration. This is what makes the devil's claim to it so wrong (Mt 4:9f.).

It seems clear that for Matthew the theme of adoration is meant to indicate the presence of a truly divine mystery here in Jesus, and in our particular case, the birth of Jesus. The *proskynesis* reserved for God alone (Mt 4:9f.) is rendered to him at his birth. This doesn't seem to take anything away from the humanness of this birth, or the humanity of Jesus. Homage (*proskynesis* in this more limited sense) could also be rendered to a king in some sense, and Raymond Brown suggests at least an implicit reference to Psalm 72:10–11 here in the birth story, which would emphasize more Jesus' kingly role as the one spoken of in the psalm who is being honored. There is also perhaps a hint of the passion that Jesus will undergo, even here at this divinely mysterious birth, inasmuch as we have the paradox of Jesus' rejection by many of the Jews and his later acceptance by the gentiles "proleptically" disclosed in the struggle with Herod and the homage of the gentile magi. Not unimportantly for our considerations to follow, the magi also present us with the great evangelical theme of the "reversal of expectations." It is not those who should have known, through their greater familiarity with the scriptures, but those who do not have that familiarity, in whom the element of wonder still lives, who "understand" in reverence the mystery.

As I suggested, Luke's account of the conception seems to contain its adorational equivalent in the theme of "glory" (*doxa*) permeating the story of the shepherds. As Raymond Brown has suggested, the shift from earth as the scene of action (the angel announcing the birth in 1:26f.) to the heavenly host offering glory and praise in 2:13–14 indicates the theophany genre. And the theme of "glory," so typical of theophanies, had been announced earlier at 2:9, when we were told that "the glory of the Lord shone around [the shepherds], and they were struck with great fear."

As the Jewish apocalyptic literature presented the angels praising God in response to his work at creation, so now Luke may be engaged in showing something of a parallel: the new creation in Jesus' birth through the Virgin Mary marks a new moment of angelic praise.[6] And the detail that the shepherds "made known the message that had been told them about this child" (2:17) as well as "returned, glorifying and praising God for all they had heard and seen" (2:20), indicates that this new praise is happening on earth too. Raymond Brown helpfully explains: "There has now begun a praise and glory of God on earth echoing the praise and glory of God by the heavenly host (vs. 20 echoing the language of vss. 13–14)."[7]

Again, in this "exalted" atmosphere, it is suggestive that the theme of glory goes along with that of Jesus' humanity, particularly his *suffering* humanity. Matthew takes a similar view, as we saw. Brown suggests that "the closest parallel to the Gloria [of the birth story] is the liturgical acclamation at the entry of Jesus into Jerusalem."[8] There as he prepares for his arrest and passion, he receives from the crowd the acclamation of glory. Does the glory of his birth point ahead to the paradoxical glory of his crucifixion? Is this another of those evangelical "reversal of expectations," in which divine glory takes the form of kenosis? Of a piece with this is the fascinating observation of René Laurentin that, in the birth story, it is the shepherds who are transformed by God's glory, rather than the child Jesus (2:9). The "divine humility" of the manger is the kind of glory we seem to encounter here.[9]

Brown has suggested another aspect in Luke's presentation that seems to link the divine glory shining through in Jesus with his true humanness, thus further avoiding any christological docetism. Even here, in these exalted moments of divine glory. Brown speaks of "Luke's instinct to get the shepherds off the scene as soon as they have begun [their] praise," likening it to Matthew's "instinct to have the magi depart (2:12) once they have paid Jesus homage." We do not "get lost" in this glory, tempting as it might be. It seems to "push" us outward, toward kenosis. I think this is what Brown means, as he comments on these evangelical instincts: "Both evangelists know that when the public ministry of Jesus begins, there is no surrounding chorus of adoring believers, treasuring the memories of the marvels that accompanied his birth at Bethlehem — this memory is completely absent from the records of the ministry." Except for Jesus' Mother Mary, as Brown also notes. She is "a bridge," linking the birth with the ongoing ministry of Jesus. Her pondering in her heart the events of the birth (2:19) makes of her the model of the one to penetrate and grasp the depth dimension of what is now entering history in Jesus.[10] That is why it seems so important to "consult" the Virgin Mary when practicing christology.

Borrowing Brown's notion of the "instinct" of the evangelists, we can suggest another instinct at work in the presence of this mystery of Jesus' birth, that of adoration (or giving glory). Like the magi, we need to offer homage to Jesus to penetrate this mystery. Like the shepherds, we must open ourselves to the glory of the heavenly host, allowing them to overshadow us. Especially must we be like the Virgin Mary, whose own "heart-pondering" seems, in the view of Luke, to include a profound sense of doxological praise, if we keep in mind Mary's own canticle (1:46–55).[11]

Pursuing this adorational approach, I think we link up, perhaps surprisingly, with one of the major "explanations" for the virginal conception offered by the fathers. But first, let us recall some of the insights we gained into adoration/doxology from our previous examination of Bérulle, Madeleine de Saint-Joseph, Olier, especially Hügel, and, in the background, the lead of the later Rahner, of Kierkegaard, Barth, and Balthasar. Let us recall that the adoration experience points both to the Divine Mystery as an ever greater dissimilarity to the creature and as one who has drawn personally near ("similar") to us in Incarnation. Both dimensions, in the Christian experience of adoration, are present: ever greater dissimilarity and incarnational nearness. God is the non-manipulable More, and so we attribute "personality" to the Divine in the highest sense. For as non-manipulable, God is free, unconstrained and unconstrainable, an ocean of love. To adore God is to recognize the nature of God as "personal" I. And only such a "personal" God can freely choose to share, to communicate, to open the Divine Self to others. The personal Divine I becomes a personal I for us in Incarnation.

The "trinitarian" dimensions of this personal God remain somewhat undeveloped in Hügel, as we have noticed. However, Hügel's thoughts remain strikingly suggestive too. On the one hand, he "reads" the trinitarian doctrine as a pointer to the divine majesty, its greater "dissimilarity" from us and independence of us. God's "Being, His Interior Life, are in no wise exhausted by all [His] outward Action, nor does this action occasion or articulate His character." Here the Baron is emphasizing that "God is God, already apart from His occupation with us." And this kind of insight is what is "specially revealed to us in the dogma of the Holy Trinity — facts of which we have an especial need in these our times." This is surely one of the "aspects" of the Divine Self being "expressed" in doxology and adoration, as the Baron emphasizes, with great insistence. "Our prayer will lack the deepest awe and widest expansion, if we do not find room within it for this fact concerning God."[12] This "dazzling" richness of personality, overwhelmingly drawing near to us in freedom, also arouses our doxology and, within this, especially our adoration.

On the other hand, the trinitarian doctrine points to a richly "differentiated" God too. If the first point we mentioned stresses the divine beyondness — beyond all our attempts to differentiate — this next point of Hügel's stresses the "personalistic" reality of God the Trinity. "However non-compound we may rightly think God to be, we require to think of Him as dazzling in His riches," we find the Baron telling us. We have in God "an immense richness of life" that our term "personalistic" points to.[13] Here, of course, the Baron is thinking of the Divine Self as a richly differentiated reality of "personality" and even "interpersonality," although it does not seem to have been his particular theological charism to pursue this much further. But what I wanted to reemphasize from our earlier presentation is the link between the plenitude of personality in God and adoration. Our adorational awe is aroused by this personal plenitude, and in fact, it is surely only because God freely chooses to allow us to participate in this personal richness that the Incarnation has occurred and that our own free response has in turn been evoked. A totally other God would indeed be "adorable," but only if that God draws near to us in free love can actual human adoration occur.

Adoration, then, is at least in part a free response on our part to the personal self of God — a sort of freely accepted arousal. It points to the Divine Self and links us with this Self. In trinitarian terms more developed than those of Hügel's, Christian adoration links us with the Son of the Father through the Spirit: The Son is the Father's love "personalized," the Father's free expression in love. And the Spirit is that love in its inclusive openness, its ecstasy. Our adoration is what happens to us when the ecstasy of the Spirit somehow becomes our own. And then we are introduced into the personalized expression of God's love — the Son, whose own "unique" filiation is the result of the Father's full and unparalleled expression. There are not two "Sons," for the Father does not freely express his love in halves. Dumitru Staniloae, a Romanian Orthodox theologian, has nicely expressed this insight:

> The initiative of the Father in considering himself represented by another "I" is implied in the act which is known apophatically as the "begetting" of the Son from the Father. The Son is so completely the one who takes the Father's place and reveals him, though always by virtue of the Father's will, that St. Gregory of Nyssa calls the Son another "self" of the Father.[14]

Gregory of Nyssa's notion of the Son as the Father's "other self" calls to mind, as Staniloae indicates, John 14:9: "Whoever has seen me has seen the Father."[15]

Adoration and the unique filiation of the Son — these seem to be interlocking realities. Where adoration weakens or fails to arise, then the experiential horizon within which the Son's unique filiation can be affirmed — indeed, adored — correspondingly weakens or does not exist either. A failure to appreciate the crucial role that adoration plays with respect to the mystery of the Son is, I suggest, one of the factors lying behind an inattentiveness to the significance of the virginal conception too.

Virginal Conception As Sign of Jesus' Unique Filiation

We have already tried to suggest that the adorational experience leads to — better, ultimately arises from — the unique filiation of the Son from the Father. Now I would like to indicate that, if we maintain this adorational "insight" as a hermeneutical entry to the virginal conception, we will find ourselves linking up with a very "old" tradition about that christological and mariological doctrine. And in the process we will be learning something of how the mystery of Mary becomes a source of our christological insight. But the mystery seems to have to be approached in adorational reverence, not unlike Mary's own adorational stance toward her own Son.

This "old" tradition is nothing other than the teaching we've already discovered through adoration; namely, Jesus' own unique filiation from the Father. Some of the *patres* saw this as a key reason for the virginal conception. Lactantius, for example, in the fourth century makes this connection:

> But, in order that it might be certain that He was sent from God, it was not necessary for Him to be born in just such a way as man is born from the union of two mortals, but that He might appear heavenly even in the form of man, He was formed without the operation of a human father. He had a spiritual Father, God, and just as the Father of His Spirit is God, there being no mother, so the mother of His Body is a virgin and there is no father.[16]

In this theology there is a genuine insight into the virginal conception as a pointer to the unique Father, and to the Son as the uniquely filiated one. Tertullian seems to have a similar teaching in mind in a passage on christological themes, where he states that because Christ is "from God the Father, he is surely not from a human father" either. And "if he is not born from a man, then it would follow that it must be from a mother; and if from a mother, it is obvious that the mother must be a virgin."[17] The trinitarian dimensions underpinning these insights have yet to find their proper expression in the history of theology (Tertullian dies, after all, around 220, and although Lactantius is later, trinitarian theology is still in the forming). Still, both *patres* seem to notice in the virginal conception something of a pointer "back" to a deeper mystery grounding it all.

In "contemporary" theology one will occasionally come upon this insight too. Two theologians — whose own writings possess a markedly christological-trinitarian hue — express it, bringing out a bit more fully (than Lactantius or Tertullian) the later trinitarian nuances of church theology. Hans Urs von Balthasar, in a passage on the virginal conception, says:

Mary alone sings her Magnificat. It is quite clear that much more than the question of "biological generation" is at issue here; for we are dealing with the decisive emergence of God as the unique Father, which excludes in Jesus another father-relationship just as much as Jesus' marriage-relationship to his bride, the church, excludes a different marriage relationship to him.[18]

It is of some moment, I think, that Balthasar, whose own writings are so marked by not only a trinitarian but also an adorational-doxological accent, so quickly moves from the virgin birth to the trinitarian filiation of the Son from the Father.

Karl Barth, also — who, by the way, has been so influential over Balthasar — is one of the few great "doctrinal" theologians of modern times extensively to treat the virgin birth. In a detailed passage he asks the question why it is that the Holy Spirit overshadows Mary, and in his answer brings us to a profound insight into the filiation mystery. Again, it is not without moment that Barth's theology also breathes an adorational atmosphere.[19] He says:

The very possibility of human nature's being adopted into unity with the Son of God is the Holy Ghost. Here, then, at this fontal point in revelation, the Word of God is not without the Spirit of God. And here already there is the togetherness of Spirit and Word. Through the Spirit it becomes really possible for the creature, for man, to be there and to be free for God. Through the Spirit flesh, human nature, is assumed into unity with the Son of God. Through the Spirit this Man can be God's Son and at the same time the Second Adam and as such "the firstborn among many brethren" (Rom. 8:29).[20]

This helpfully coheres with our earlier observations about the Spirit as the "overflow" of the Father and Son, the inclusivity of their love: through the Spirit the Incarnation of Jesus occurs, Jesus' supremely unique union with the Son. And a sign, a link, from our side, pointing to that mystery, is the virginal conception. The unparalleled and unique nature of that conception refers us back — invites us, in keeping with the personalism of God — to the unique filiation of the Son from the Father.

Clearly this "reading" of the doctrine as a "sign" of the unique filiation cannot be proven, nor will it be received as equally plausible by all, even the well disposed. Wolfhart Pannenberg, several decades ago, had already taken Barth to task, arguing that "the legend of Jesus' virgin birth stands in an irreconcilable contradiction to the Christology of the incarnation of the preexistent Son of God found in Paul and John." He seems to mean by this that, with the virginal conception "scheme," Luke and Matthew are arguing that "Jesus first *became* God's Son through Mary's conception," while he was already preexistent as Son in Paul and John.[21] But this interpretation seems forced. It seems more plausible to argue that Matthew and Luke are simply confessing that the Incarnation is rooted in the Divine Self, not moving any further into questions of the inner nature of the trinitarian mystery, as at least John seems to be doing, and perhaps Paul too. The virginal conception tradition, in other words, need not deny the Son's preexistence; the reality of the Son remains mysterious and somewhat "undifferentiated": it is the "prior" reality of God that overshadows Mary through the Spirit. The virginal conception is a piece of the incarnational revelation, a moment within a larger mystery that makes more coherent sense only when grasped in connection with the trinitarian revelation as it is unfolded through John and later tradition.

A Sign of a Uniquely Personal Universe

The virginal conception points "back," to the mysterious origins of Jesus in God, mysterious origins that eventually become clarified as the Son's unique filiation from the Father. The "unique conception" symbolizes a "unique filiation" that has now been disclosed in human history. As Barth liked to indicate, it is a kind of protective doctrine, indicating that indeed the inner mystery of God has been revealed now in history. I would suggest that this doctrine points "forward," too, in the sense that it witnesses to the realization in history of a new participation in the Divine Mystery. If you will, the uniquely personal Son, through the Spirit, makes possible a uniquely personal universe. The unique Thou of the Son initiates in the Spirit a universe of thous, each with its own unique specialness, its own particular mission. Mary's virginal conception is a sign of the "special and unique mission" now made possible through the Incarnation. Her specialness (derivative and subordinate) points back to Jesus' specialness and is rooted in it. It points to the truly personal, and so uniquely special kind of communion now possible in history.

Again, there is an "adorational logic" required here that possesses its own power and beauty, but that may not be convincing to a more purely "rational" perspective.[22] Adoration is the posture appropriate to those who refuse to manipulate the Divine Self. That Self remains a "personal" reality, uniquely independent and not simply a "tool" for someone else. To adore is to share in that "refusal to manipulate," that "refusal to depersonalize" revealed to us in the Incarnation. The adorational person in some sense expects to encounter the personal and unique in history. At the same time, the kind of "personal" universe fostered by a supremely personal God does not coerce assent either. The attractiveness yet non-coercive nature of the appeal would seem to be an intrinsic aspect of the actions of an adorable God.

Here we might be able to throw a little light upon the so-called Marian privileges, not only that of the virgin birth, but of the later doctrines of assumption, immaculate conception, and so on. In every instance, surely, these need to be shown to be rooted, genuinely, in the incarnational mystery. We cannot "fabricate" Marian doctrines simply because we would like to. I would only suggest, in a more general manner, that there is a coherence between the idea of such "privileges" and the kind of mystery revealed to us in the Incarnation. The personal God revealed in the Son Jesus does not foster a depersonalized world, in which all is reduced to a common denominator, all becoming the carbon copy of each. It may be that not only Jesus' specialness, but that of Mary, too, points to that realm of the uniquely personal now made available to all of us in history through the Incarnation.

The difference between genuine "uniqueness" and simply "being bizarre" is not always easily adhered to in matters religious, and in the history of mariology too. Something of the battle to maintain this difference was struggled over at the Second Vatican Council, I think. The instinct of that council was one of trying to move beyond what Pannenberg has called a "Mariolatry,"[23] by restressing the view of Mary as a paradigm of true discipleship, illustrating what the rest of us are called to be. In some sense, this makes her like the rest of us, which she surely is. Hence, the council spoke of her as "a type of the Church," to indicate that she is not somehow excluded from the church's economy of salvation. At the same time, Pope Paul VI did speak of her title as the "Mother of the Church" at the closing of the council's third session, and this seems to have been an intuition that the economy of grace in the church is not one in which personal uniqueness is somehow smothered in an ecclesial collectivism. The unique mission of the Son respects and fosters the unique charisms of us all. And why not his Beloved Mother, the one we should expect to share most fully in the charisms of her Son?[24]

The adoration experience seems to enter here again. Let us recall Mother Madeleine's notion that adoration unites love with reverence, the longing for intimacy with a respectful distance. This is why the love does not degenerate into a subtle narcissism with its manipulation of the other for one's own ends. In the history of mariology — as well as christology, let us remember — this wedding between reverence and love hasn't always been maintained. True adoration avoids a gnostic "knowing too much," a sort of theological voyeurism that really transcends the limits of legitimate faith, replacing it with a kind of "quasi-religious" rationalism. A legitimate mariology slides into mariolatry when it becomes gnostic in this sense. On the other hand, uniting love with reverential distance does not mean snuffing out the love and intimacy. And this is probably the danger of more "modern" forms of rationalism. A genuine openness to the always uniquely special mystery of love revealed in the Incarnation is what genuinely Christian adoration seems to entail.

Related Mariological Reflections

We have concentrated on only one specific christological insight entailed in the virginal conception. We have chosen Jesus' unique filiation because it is particularly connected with the contemplative and adorational perspective we are pursuing, and also because it seems a central theme in contemporary christology. But a few connections between our perspective and some of the other "frequently" mentioned christological insights connected with the virginal conception could appropriately be indicated now.

The biblical theme of the "new age" inaugurated by Jesus the "new Adam" can be connected with Mary as the "New Eve." The latter is, in fact, grounded in the former. It then becomes possible to see in Mary's existence the signs of the beginnings of this new age. And some have suggested that the *novum* of Mary's virginity is connected with this *novum* of the eschatological end-time in Jesus. Why shouldn't this be the case, if Mary's existence has been integrally affected by and permeated with her Son Jesus? Here the departure from history's normal way of birthing serves as sign of a new form of the "birthing of grace" in history. Some liken this to the creation at time's beginning. The Incarnation is the beginning of the new creation; like the "first" creation, it has no adequate analogy. One can see the virginal conception as the sign, in this respect, of the overcoming of original sin and its effects in history. A new, "grace-ful" healing is entering history now, and Mary's own unique birthing experience somehow points to this: perhaps its radically "gift" nature turns it into an experience for Mary of the "thanks-inspiring" nature of grace?[25]

This particular constellation of insights seems to highlight the "soteriological" dimensions of christology, the "for us" aspect. In this sense the virgin birth already, in the person of Mary, signs and foreshadows the inseparability between christology and soteriology. The "unexpected" yet "real" nature of the virginal conception sign-ifies the unexpected yet real nature of grace. Historically it is fascinating how quickly the New Eve typology develops, once christology and the virginal conception and motherhood are secure. Here there is a logic from the particular to the general, from Jesus and Mary to the rest of us. Just the sort of logic history leads us to expect.[26] And here we find, it seems, something of a complement to the theme of the unique filiation. The virginal conception, by pointing "back" toward the unique filiation is christological in foundation and significance. By pointing "forward" to us it is soteriological in foundation and significance.

Just here, however, we seem to stumble upon one of those difficulties that, in our modern context, we need to wonder about, if I may put it that way. Surely one of the great stumbling blocks to the appropriation of the virginal conception is its seeming refusal to grant sexual intercourse a "place" of significance, right at the heart of the Incarnation happening. How, in this regard, can Mary be a sign of the new age of universal grace if this important reality is excluded? We are wondering how Mary can sign-ify the new age of grace if sexual intercourse seems excluded from her birthing experience. If you will, we are querying, in a mariological sort of way, the famous soteriological dictum, "that which he [Jesus] has not assumed he has not healed," to employ Gregory Nazianzus's formulation.[27]

Our response to this is to suggest that the virginal conception, simply in itself and considered in a sort of abstract way, is ambiguous. But to view it that way would really be to treat the doctrine unhistorically and unrealistically — even *docetically*. The doctrine should be read in the horizon of belief in God and especially belief in the Incarnation. In the light of these it sign-ifies the incalculable miracle of grace and the unique filiation of the Son. It is the Son who must "exegete" the virginal conception for us. And in the light of this we can say that there is no element of docetic denial of the flesh or sex in Jesus. Jesus is a celibate, surely, and so is Mary. But this does not mean a denial of the goodness of sexuality or the created order. The meaning of this charism must be sought elsewhere, and exegeted, too, in the light of the entire Incarnation happening. It is the God revealed in Jesus that the virginal conception points to, and this God embraces humanity *in toto*.

Walter Kasper, in his justly remarkable "Letter on 'the Virgin Birth,'" has some insights that seem helpful at this point. He argues, with respect to the key sources on this doctrine, that "it is impossible to find... anything to warrant" a bias against sexuality. The patristic struggle against docetism and gnosticism was involved in an effort to defend creation's goodness, including especially that of the body and sexuality, as well as Jesus' full humanity. This is why the *patres* would be uncomfortable, in fact, with the "modern" tendency to treat this doctrine as asserting an idea rather than a biological fact. That would be docetic to them. Kasper continues:

Thus one is able to turn the spear around and to say: if, today, many statements which were originally meant in a realistic sense are now explained as mere imagery demanded by the time in which they were first expressed, and as codes, symbols or interpretation, then Docetism has once more reared its head. Who is actually repressing here: the one who takes the virgin birth seriously as significant in its bodily aspect, or the one who gives it only a symbolic meaning?[28]

Perhaps a further "specification" of this soteriological motif in the virginal conception is the way it sign-ifies the "vocational states" in the church. In a broader sense, this again points to the notion that the "intensely personal" God revealed as Jesus creates a universe of personalism, and so of unique vocations/missions corresponding to our own unique personal aptitudes. This would be a soteriological parallel to the christological insight of the uniquely personal filiation of the Son. Christologically the virginal conception points "back" to the uniquely personal filiation. Soteriologically it points "forward" to a God calling each of us uniquely and personally to our "states in life."[29]

Traditionally, surely, we have seen a special "place" for the callings of virginity and celibacy (and the "consecrated" single state as well[30]) in the virginal conception. Mary's own virginity participates in and models forth Jesus' virginity/celibacy. Here I wouldn't pretend to think that we can exhaustively comprehend the levels of meaning in the celibate/virginal vocation.[31] Again I would recommend a christological exegesis: it takes its meaning from Jesus and his mission on behalf of God and the kingdom. It tries to stake all radically on God and the kingdom, symbolizing their priority over all. It seems to stress the *priority* of the kingdom, and so the need to remain available for all, for that kingdom calls all (Mk 10:29–30; Mt 19:12). Nothing must get in the way, neither family, nor anything nor anyone else. Those "harsh" Mary texts, like Mark 3:31–35, Matthew 12:46–50, and Luke 8:19–21, in which Jesus unmistakably says that the work of the kingdom takes priority over kith and kin, even "mothers," can be understood in this context. In this respect, the tradition of the perpetual virginity of Mary takes on significance. For if she is to model forth her Son's virginity, and if we keep in mind that such virginity is an entire "state of existence," involving a profound embracing and interiorizing of values, then a lifetime of virginity seems the only real possibility.[32]

I doubt that we normally think of the married state in connection with Mary's virginal conception. At least in my own personal experience such an association is rare. But we have to keep two elements together: not only the adjective "virginal," but also the noun "conception." Mary was a mother, a married woman. Our marital existence as Christians also participates in her marital existence and models it forth. Apparently there was some discussion about this in the tradition, for Thomas Aquinas devotes an article in his *Summa theologiae* to whether Mary's marriage to Joseph was a true one. In the end, Aquinas held that it was, because of the "inseparable union of souls, by which husband and wife are pledged by a bond of mutual affection that cannot be sundered." And so he concluded that "both virginity and wedlock are honored in [Mary's] person, in contradiction to those heretics who disparaged one or the other."[33]

I think Aquinas gives us the key clue as to how the virginal conception throws light upon the married state. He locates the heart of Mary's and Joseph's true wedding in their "mutual affection," or we would say, in their "covenantal love" one for the other. Mary's virginity, precisely by being virginal, pushes us right away to the "heart" and "center" of genuinely Christian (sacramental) marriages, love. In Mary's case, this was accompanied by sexual abstinence, because of her virginity. But again, following our christological exegetical principle, we should not read the virginal conception as an attack upon the sanctity of creation/sexuality. So when married couples look to Mary for marital inspiration, they aren't necessarily being called to virginity. They are being called to the one thing needful: agape. Agape is what Christians bring to their sexuality, and this is what makes it sacramental. In this sense, marriage, too, sign-ifies dimensions of the kingdom, which is perhaps why Jesus can liken that kingdom to a "wedding banquet" (Mt 22:1–14; cf. Eph 5:32). Something of the intimacy of love, and its fidelity, shine through in marriage, prefiguring the intimacy and fidelity of the kingdom itself.[34]

Mary's combining both virginity and marriage is also suggestive, inviting us to think about this "combination." Perhaps keeping the two somehow combined — in relation, in mutual interchange — is an aspect of the soteriological mystery to which the Incarnation calls us. Jesus, too, somehow combines the two, but differently from Mary. She was both virginal and married; he was only a virginal celibate. Still he upheld the sanctity of marriage (Jn 2:1–12), liberated the wife as an equal partner with the husband (Mt 19:1–9), and, as we noted, saw in marriage an image of the kingdom. Does celibacy's valuation of the priority of the kingdom over all, and its concomitant stress on making oneself available for all, so as to invite them to the kingdom — do these run the danger of becoming abstract, impersonal, cold? Do they not need the intimacy of marriage to keep them "warm" and personal? And does not the intimacy of marriage always run the danger of narrowing itself into exclusivity, forgetting about those beyond kith and kin for whom the kingdom banquet is prepared? Celibates can help "universalize" the intimacy of the married; married couples can help the celibates keep in touch with the call to learn intimacy.

In this way, each fertilizes the other, and something of celibacy enters into marriage; something of marriage, into celibacy. Each reflects in a more or less preponderant way genuine dimensions of the kingdom offered us in Jesus. And, ultimately, each reflects the trinitarian God who is intimately sharing in love (Father and Son), yet non-exclusively so (the Spirit). The subject who is God (the divine "I") is a reality of deep personal intimacy, but an intimacy always open and unselfish (the divine "We").

Let me surface a further christological and soteriological dimension of the virginal conception, stimulated now by women's theology and criticism. Should one argue that the lack of a human father in the conception of Jesus is a denigration of men, a divine putdown of them? Or, conversely, should one argue from the apparent fact that Jesus' unique filiation points "back" to the eternal Father-God, that therefore a "patriarchal" religion is legitimated in the virginal conception? The first option seems anti-men; the second, anti-women. And both might find in the virginal conception some support for the position taken.

Starting with the first, the possible denigration of men, again I would appeal to our principle of christological exegesis. That is, the virginal conception, purely in itself, can be ambiguous, and it needs to be interpreted against the backdrop of the Incarnation. Given this, I think one will find no support for the denigration of men, or of anything created, in the Jesus event. Whatever else the virginal conception may mean, measured against our "Jesus-hermeneutics," it cannot mean the denigration of men. Perhaps, following an intuition of Karl Barth's, we could say that the virginal conception, in excluding the human male, is sign-ifying not man's "denial" but the gift of God as sheer grace to humanity.[35]

The second issue, that of a "latent" patriarchalism, seems a bit more complicated and difficult, and clearly the Christian community has yet to come to a consensus on the issue. Surely traditionally we have spoken of God the Father as the ground and foundation of Jesus' unique filiation. In this sense, the mystery of the filiation, pointed to in the virginal conception, witnesses to a "Father-principle" in the Godhead. Yet we know that "begetting," at least from our human side, is not simply the work of fathers, but also mothers. In this sense, we could argue for a "Mother-principle" in the Godhead too. And this is further reinforced if we try to "exegete" the issue against the more ample backdrop of the tradition. For the First Testament sees something maternal in God (Is 49:15), and Jesus likens himself in some sense to the maternal (Lk 13:34). In this light, the virginal conception points "back" to the mystery of an eternal begetting that can be pointed to in analogies drawn from human fatherhood as well as motherhood.

Surely the latter has not been given the attention it deserves, and we may hope that women's theology will further this work, bringing a greater sensitivity to how women's experience may be able to enrich our theology of the Trinity.

There may be something more to it, too, again suggested by Karl Barth. By itself, he seems to suggest, the virgin birth seems to denote more the "mysteriousness" of the Incarnation event, "the inconceivability of it, its character as a fact in which God has acted solely through God and in which God can likewise be known solely through God."[36] In this sense, this doctrine points us to a God who transcends our expectations and analogies. It keeps us open, like Mary's *Ecce ancilla Domini*, for God's mysterious self-revelation. But if God is beyond the control of our customary analogies (which for us are usually analogies from men's experience), then God is free to awaken us to the possibility of other appropriate analogies (which in our time seems to mean a greater sensitivity to how women's experience images forth the Divine Self).

Hopefully something of the adorational and contemplative perspective we began with has "glowed" in and through this discussion of related approaches to and corollaries of the virginal conception. The theme of the "new age" entering history through Mary, the New Eve, is another way of speaking of the radically personal and non-manipulable God — and so "adorable" God — inviting us to participate in a world in which we don't reduce one another to mere instruments to be used by ourselves. Our own unique calls/missions, symbolized in Jesus' own unique mission as the Son and Mary's own unique virginal conception, express something of this deeply personal universe of non-manipulation which we can now enjoy. And the new sensitivity to women's experience, and the manner in which it helps us rethink more appropriately our faith, also seems but a consistent application of the principle of non-manipulation to women, and not simply or predominantly to men.

Adoration and Explanation: Some Comments

In accord with the direction of our hermeneutical observations, in which we argued for a wedding between contemplation and "explanation" — adoration's openness to the Mystery implying an ascetical willingness to undergo the asceticism of self-critique — let me intersect now with some of the concerns prompted by modern methods of explanation. Hopefully our contemplative style of theological conversation has shone throughout our treatment above. There has been an effort to move back and forth between the biblical and patristic witness especially, and the sensitivities arising from our own spiritual experience today. But readers will have noticed that the "explanation," such as it was, primarily made appeal to the experience and testimony of the Christian heritage, especially that of the *patres* and those working within that horizon. In other words, the argumentation was mainly by way of an appeal to the "analogy of faith," seeking the coherence and congeniality between the virginal conception and the other primary mysteries of the faith, especially christology and soteriology.

In a more general way, we could complement the appeal to the analogy of faith with one to the "analogy of being," or otherwise put, by an appeal to our general understanding of experience as a whole.[37] Here I don't mean to "descend" into the kind of theological biologism that really offends against the mystery involved, a mystery that Karl Barth especially well in our own times protects. But I would suggest that Karl Rahner's notion of the miracle as not necessarily a suspension of nature's laws might be useful here. Rahner suggests what is really a quite traditional notion, namely, that the laws of nature, while real, also include nature's integration into the "higher," psycho-spiritual dimensions of reality, at least on a theocentric perspective. He explains that "one need not necessarily speak of a suspension of the laws of nature and yet may accept the miracle [here he is speaking of miracles of healing], viz., if one presupposes (what is really self-evident) that every determined level and order of being is from the very start open towards a higher level and order and can be incorporated into it, without its own laws thereby having to be suspended."[38]

Thinking along with this, one can think of the virginal conception as surely miraculous, but this need not mean that it asks us to believe in the absolutely absurd. It transcends nature, surely, but, nature's openness — under grace — entails the possibility of such unique happenings. The fact that this conception does not bypass the mother, but happens in and through the mother, perhaps indicates that nature is not being violated even while it is being surpassed. But I put this last comment forth only very tentatively and hesitantly. Appeals to nature must be very carefully made lest we trespass on the mystery. In a certain sense, the analogy is to the act of creation itself. This "out of nothing" event is pure gift, and we really can't say much about it other than that. In the sense that the virginal conception is a "new creation" (of the order of grace), it represents an even greater "from nothing" which imposes an adorational modesty upon us. Still, the analogy with the original creation is only an analogy. It doesn't completely fit.[39] After all, in the case of the virginal conception, God asks for the consent of Mary and "uses" her womb (in the original creation, there is nothing preexisting). This relationship with Mary seems fitting for the inauguration of the order of grace, which, after all, is an order of free response and personal interchange.

We haven't touched upon many of the legitimate concerns of modern exegesis either. We've pursued the issue of Jesus' conception chiefly from a theocontemplative perspective, believing that it is the ultimately necessary perspective to take. And we did this partly following the guidance of Matthew and Luke themselves. But we must never allow "contemplation" to become an excuse for "soft" thinking in exegesis. Such would be an abuse, a sort of theological quietism. The theologian, within the horizon of contemplative faith, must always be striving to insure that theological analysis flows from the data of revelation, coheres with it, and is demanded by it. On the other hand, our contemplative perspective would clearly object to any attempt to separate exegesis from contemplation, moving into an exegetical positivism. In and through the spatial, temporal, and generally narrative dimensions of scripture the mystery of revelation is going forward for us. The ecstasy of the Spirit, which is after all at work among us, can lead us to the heart of the mystery, and without bypassing hard thought at the same time.

In this regard, I am not aware of major exegetes doubting that Matthew and Luke teach a virginal conception. There is plentiful debate, to be sure, about how to explain it; but the fact that both teach it is assured. It seems to me that the more one allows exegesis to stray too far from a contemplative holding of the analogy of faith, the less one is able to grasp the coherence of this mystery with the other Christian mysteries. I note, too, that it becomes relatively easy to get lost in endless arguments about surface details of time and place when one strays too far from the central doctrinal issues. It would seem that a contemplative perspective tries to keep its focus on the heart of the mystery, and "tolerates" a legitimate openness on issues of "detail."

There is a normal conservatism here, however. The contemplative is not quick and simplistic, recognizes the enormously complex levels involved in revelatory experiences, and allows the Mystery to remain. There is a legitimate doctrinal minimalism that doesn't try to impose more than the faith of the church asks of us on others. Still, the contemplative soul, even one cauterized by "methods of explanation," goes beyond minimalism and remains open to a rich diversity of possibilities in these complex areas. At times, the details of the narratives may seem relatively remote from the heart of the mystery as well as ambiguous and maybe even conflictual. At times, we may be dealing with literary forms that help us grasp theological meaning. And we surely always recognize that there can be no absolute separation of meaning and form. At other times, we may be

152

dealing with elements that may find their rooting in historical events hard to decipher now (the star, the magi, shepherds, etc.) or that may be explained in a way analogous to modern mystical auditory-visual experiences. In any case, one is cautious — which is different from naive — with what one reveres.

The Marian Dimension of Christology

And so our meditative perspective has helped us come upon what the tradition has always recognized: a truly "Marian" dimension in christology. Here I am following the lead of Pope John Paul II's meditative encyclical *Redemptoris Mater*, written for the recent Marian year, in which he speaks movingly of this "Marian dimension."[40] Thinking along with the pope, I mean that our understanding of Jesus Christ is inadequate if it does not include within it a growing appreciation for the significant role of Mary in Christianity's "economy of signs." Significant, in the sense that she seems to disclose dimensions of christology that remain obscure without her. Significant, too, because she models forth for the rest of us essential elements of what it means to live out our life of faith — she is a paradigm of the disciple, as much recent theology wants to say today. But significant, too, in her own special and unique way: she is the "first" and "highest" after Jesus in Christianity, and in this we have the germ of the high mariological traditions, which celebrate her intercessory and privileged role in the faith.

If we take our bearings about this Marian dimension from our little study of the doctrine of the virginal conception, perhaps we could hazard the following by way of a more precise summary. First, we suggested that this doctrine, "obscure" and "ambiguous" in itself, begins to take on meaning only when it is contemplatively approached as an aspect of the Incarnation. The "unique" conception refers back to the "unique" filiation of the Son: what enters history in Mary's womb is the revelation of the unique Son in the womb of the Trinity. Or, complementary to this, the *novum* of the virginal conception signifies the *novum* of the Incarnation. In any case, what this adds up to is that Mary's being *refers back* to Jesus; it is "referential."[41] Or, to recall the words of Cardinal Bérulle, "The Virgin's proper role is... to be a pure capacity for Jesus, filled with Jesus."[42]

To contemplate Mary is to be invited to contemplate her Son. The "miracle" that she is only takes on meaning — ceases being "odd" and becomes truly a "miracle," a "sign" — when we open ourselves to the Incarnation, and through that, to the inner life of the Trinity itself. For the Father sends the Son in the Spirit. In this sense, Mary discloses the mystery of grace, its absolute priority in the order of salvation, its call to us to accept its offer in faith. Here, perhaps, is the "ecumenical" role of Mary today, in helping us heal the break between the Roman, Orthodox, and Protestant-Anglican traditions. In this regard, then, the Marian dimension of christology is the latter's rootedness in the Trinity, its being truly a "miracle of grace" because it is the inner life of the Trinity itself inviting us to communion through the Holy Spirit. Our own appreciation of the profoundly deep invitation to the inner trinitarian life made possible in the Incarnation is obscured when this Marian dimension remains obscured. If you will, Mary can only be a "mother" because she has a "son."

Our study of the virginal conception also opened out onto another side of christology, its "soteriological" side. Grace is not just offer and possibility, but effectively real in human history. Mary's unique birthing "cooperatively" effects in history, and indeed symbolizes[43] the uniquely new reality of transforming grace. Here she is both "New Eve" and "Mother of the Church," while the first aspect perhaps stresses her role as "first disciple" of faith (her maternity is primarily a maternity made possible through her faithful acceptance of grace). The Marian dimension now is the soteriological side of christology, its "for us" dimension. In terms of grace: grace not only as offer, but as transforming reality. The celebrated prayer of the French School, "O Jesus living in Mary, come and live in your servants...," lyrically captures this transformational dimension opened up in Mary.[44] And I would suggest that we fail to appreciate just how "new" this sharing in grace is if we fail to appreciate the "new" displayed in the virginal conception.

Certainly we can draw a number of crucial corollaries from this soteriological dimension opened up by Mary. The fact that grace is now effective in history through Mary highlights the historical dimension of Christian revelation, and with that, the ecclesial dimension. Quite appropriately, the gift of salvation is mediated through Mary's womb (in the extended sense, through her entire being), and that means, through human cooperation, and thus, by implication, through the church. Here the Marian dimension is linked to the ecclesial dimension of christology, and more deeply the pneumatological, each implying the other. It is one of the great insights of John's gospel to have expressed how mariology and ecclesiology are corollaries of christology at 19:25–27, when John (the symbol of the true lover of Jesus — the true church) is told that Mary is his Mother (the Marian dimension passes into the ecclesial dimension).[45] And, of course, John does not fail to bring out the role of the Spirit in all of this either (14–16). But again, the depth of the *novum* of the church, its definitively new nature calling forth our obedient response, is missed when the Spirit's *novum* expressed in the virginal conception remains obscured.

Finally, something of the uniquely personal nature of grace is also disclosed in the virginal conception. The uniquely personal Mediator mediates a uniquely personal grace and love in history. Grace is never abstract; it is intimately personal, since it is a participation in the intimately personal life of the Trinity. The unique "privilege" of Mary's conceiving expresses this uniquely personal form of grace. To rob Mary of her "unique mission" in history is to underplay just how uniquely intimate, personal, and so unique is the grace revealed in the Incarnation. It is, after all, the grace of the uniquely personal filiation of the Son through the Spirit, the giver of unique charisms. In this regard, the Marian dimension of christology and soteriology is its intimately personal nature.

The Marian doctrines, such as the immaculate conception and assumption, and some of the other Marian "theological" traditions (Mary as intercessor, "helper," etc.) might well be able to be understood in the light of the above. To some extent, the tendency among some is to stress what Mary has in common with the rest of us. Thus, these further teachings can be seen as expressions in Mary of what all of us are analogously called to be through grace. The immaculate conception, for example, can be read as an expression of what grace offers to do analogously for all; the assumption becomes a sign of the transforming power of grace in eternity; the cooperating role of Mary, a sign of how the church mediates grace. At the same time, there is the uniquely personal component in grace, too. This is expressed first in the uniqueness of the Incarnation, and secondly, I think, in the element of the unique in the Marian tradition. All of these Marian teachings display something of this component. Clearly in the case of the virginal conception, but also the specialness of Mary's freedom from all sin and her special role as intercessor for us in eternity display her uniquely personal charisms.

Perhaps we can sum up by saying that "grace" — as offer, as received, as personally unique and intimate — is the "Marian" dimension of christology. Or at least an important part of it. To refuse to see it as "Marian" is to refuse adoringly to meditate the uniquely "new" depth of that offer, its transforming reception, and its intimacy. To return to Cardinal Bérulle, this is why "to speak of Mary is to speak of Jesus." It is also why "God and the world have considered her the source of blessing for the world."[46]

CHAPTER EIGHT

Jesus' Uniqueness and
the Dialogue between the Religions

The accent we have placed, with the French School, upon the defini-tive singularity of Jesus, the incarnate Word, an accent just reinforced by the chapter on the virginal conception, meets with varying re-actions in today's cross-cultural atmosphere. For the presence of the venerable religious traditions other than Christian causes many of us to ask how we are to evaluate them, and their originators, given the claims we Christians make for Jesus.[1] It is clear that this issue is one of the more burning ones in christology today. And it is not hard to see why, for in discussing the relative merits of Jesus Christ vis-à-vis the other religions, we are probing the very "substance" of Christian faith itself. The importance of the issue pressures us for as much precision as possible. At the same time, I am continuing to work on some of the christocentric mystics — such figures as Thérèse of Lisieux, Teresa of Avila, Ignatius Loyola, and the French School and tributaries, with their mystics and saints all centered in Jesus (Bérulle, Madeleine de Saint-Joseph, Condren, Olier, John Eudes, Louis Marie Grignion de Montfort, John Baptist de La Salle, Libermann, Chaminade, etc.).[2] To take these people seriously, in a theological way, surely challenges one's own christocentrism, even and perhaps especially in our global age. And I grow more convinced all the time, that a good strategy for Christians is to move into the cross-cultural dialogue only with and in these great mystics.

When we speak of Jesus' uniqueness, there seems to be a more general sense that we could have in mind. That is, like everyone else, Jesus is not simply a carbon copy of everybody, but enjoys the sense of distinctness and difference that characterizes human uniqueness in general. And surely, as consubstantial with us in our humanity, we should attribute this kind of generalized uniqueness to Jesus. But the tradition goes beyond this and wants to claim and confess a uniqueness that is of a qualitatively distinct nature, being unsurpassable, definitive, and with no equal. In some sense Jesus' uniqueness, in this latter sense, is of a cosmic nature, definitively altering the cosmos as a whole. This latter kind of uniqueness "qualifies" Jesus' more general uniqueness, spoken of earlier. Yes, Christians believe he is different from others ("unique," in the first sense), but we believe he is also unique because he represents a definitive, unsurpassable, and unequalled instance of revelation and salvation ("unique," in the second, deeper sense). There are any number of legitimate ways to try to articulate this more radical kind of uniqueness in Jesus. Paul's formulation gets to the point rather well: Christ inaugurates the "fullness of time" (Gal 4:4). Something "pleromatic" occurs in him, constituting the cosmic change of the ages (see Jn 1:16; Col 1:19).

Truly we are before a mystery in the strictly theological sense, and a posture of modesty, reverence, and especially faith-filled adoration, which elevates and humbles, are in order here. In a moment, I will be returning to the significance of this posture. With this as foundation, however, I would like to try, in a concentrated way, to express and probe what is, I think, a legitimate way to understand and "explain" this christological uniqueness. The only originality I wish to have here is that which is faithful to Nicaea and Chalcedon.

Dimensions of Jesus' Definitive Uniqueness

Let us begin by suggesting that the "happening of Jesus Christ," historical and risen, represents the loving personalization of God for humanity. Let us further suggest that this event is, by its nature, a one-time, definitive, and thus unsurpassable and unequalled event, for the cosmos as a whole, but that it is also one that inaugurates and enables a participation within it on the part of others, and on the part of the cosmos as a whole. If you will, this is an *accessus ex caritate*, an "approach from love," but taking "love" in its profoundly divine and agapaic sense. Our approach intends to be every bit as "metaphysical" and "ontological" as arguments for Jesus' special uniqueness framed in terms of his unique self-consciousness. Theologies can use philosophies of consciousness to throw light upon Jesus, but the philosophy of love can also be a theological ally here, if one thinks of Jesus' very being itself as constituted by agapaic love, with his consciousness "reflecting" that being. Here I would suggest that we try to avoid thinking of "love" in a shallow, pop-psychological or merely functionalist sense, as if it were not the deepest nature of reality itself in a Christian understanding of reality.

We have often spoken of the Incarnation as a reality of dialogue

157

and love, manifesting how God becomes a "definitively" human, personal presence for us in Jesus the Christ. But now we need to think through with more precision what is implied in this enormous assertion and confession. First, I think it implies that our awareness of God has differentiated the radical transcendence of God beyond the cosmos. It is because God is "known" in faith as more than simply a numinous, intramundane reality, as distinct from the cosmos and therefore unique, that the Holy One can relate to us in a distinct and individuated manner, and that we can know and appreciate that this relationship is freely bestowed on God's part, asking for our free response in turn (our own personal freedom is a correlate of our awareness of God's personal being).

Thus, a long history of growing awareness of God's transcendence is required before the Incarnation really becomes possible. Finally, at least by the time that a text like Isaiah 45:22 is able to be written in Israel, this differentiation seems to have occurred: "Turn to me and be safe, all you ends of the earth, for I am God; there is no other!" Until this beyond-the-world transcendence becomes known, the kind of radically human, individuated, personalized love relationship with God revealed in Jesus remains impossible. We can speak of a growing history of this awareness or differentiation, in which God's desire to be a fully personalized love-presence for us develops, but I think one has to make the "break" with the cosmos before it can be fully appreciated, believed, and "known." This sense of the break with intraworldly sacrality (anachronistically called "polytheism"), which leads to an awareness of what idolatry means, is implied then in the event of God's personalization for us.

Among contemporary authors, I would suggest that Eric Voegelin's first volume of *Order and History*, entitled *Israel and Revelation*, is superb on this sense of a break with the cosmos. In another writing, his important letter "On Christianity" to the sociological philosopher Alfred Schutz, he makes it clear that one of the crucial factors behind the radical novelty of the Incarnation was precisely the fact that God's otherworldly transcendence had been differentiated: thus God could be grasped as freely bestowing a uniquely individuated love in Jesus. "In the time of Jesus ... god-men were no rarity; a whole set of Hellenistic kings were gods ...," Voegelin tells us. But one of the things that was "new," that "excited people," he continues, was "to have a mediator who was not the incarnation of a God but was God in the monotheistic sense that excludes all other gods." And Voegelin does not hesitate to draw the implications: such a God is "radically universal," and so is this "mediating function." And "its validity remains universal for all times."[3]

Secondly, now, if this fully transcendent God is to manifest a divinely personalized, individuated, distinct, human, and radically self-giving love for us, by its very nature this "theophanic Incarnation" would seem to have to be a one-time, uniquely individuated, radically loving act that would be definitive. Without this, this "love" would still remain general, amorphous, lacking in unique individuation, not known as freely bestowed because autonomous, not a full gift of the Divine Thou to us, and therefore not really the act of the Unconditional Thou. It seems that when we speak of God's human personalization in Jesus, something like this is what is meant. Incarnation doctrine means that God personalizes or clearly individuates for us through freely and fully bestowing the gift of the Divine Self upon us in Jesus. One of the key elements here is that "personal" means "uniquely differentiated." If God is to be personal for us in the Incarnation, it would seem to be a one-time (uniquely differentiated) event. And of course, it is loving too: only a God uniquely differentiated from the cosmos can freely love us like this. And it would seem to be definitive: God's desire to be uniquely personal and loving for us "de-fines" for us through the complete gift to us which Jesus is.

This personalization of God, this act of "amorization," surfaces all over the New Testament in various ways, but with a special force in the Johannine trajectory. And this is one of the reasons for that trajectory's special place in christology. Jesus is in some way the "I am," and we should note the personal pronoun here, as well as the hint of a reference to the divine "I am" of Exodus (Jn 6:35; 8:12; 10:7, 11; 11:25; 14:6; 15:11). At the same time, John grasps the one-time, unique nature of this event: Jesus is the "only Son" (1 Jn 4:9). As well as its loving nature: 1 John 4 represents a staggering differentiation of the kind of personalized love disclosed in Jesus. And of course, the crucified form of love, found in John but perhaps more intensively in the synoptics, brings out the kenotic nature of this love.

The *patres* went through an enormous struggle over this Christ-differentiation. In the light of the earlier differentiation of God's otherworldly transcendence, which had most clearly developed through grace in late Israel, but also had begun to develop in some circles in late Greek philosophy, one can grasp how staggering this "new" one must have been. Once "seen," it meant something unheard of and once-for-all had happened. Hence, Origen would say, "We must ... suppose that some of the heat of God's Logos has made its way to all holy people, but we are bound to believe that the divine fire itself came to rest on this soul in its full reality, and that it is by derivation from this source that a portion of heat has reached the others."[4] And again, with greater clarity, in St. Athanasius we read:

He became human. He did not enter into a human being. It is, moreover, crucial to recognize this. Otherwise... people might fall into this error too and deceive some others, and these in their turn might suppose that just as in earlier times the Logos "came to be" in each of the saints, so even now he came into residence in a human being.... If this were the way of it, and all he did was to appear in a human being, there would have been nothing extraordinary.[5]

Here the notion of God's ecstasy, the loving out-going in dialogue, which constitutes what I am calling divine personalization, is struggling to emerge. With the fathers (and the mothers that we can find to read!) one feels still close to the sense of the radical novelty of what was involved with the Incarnation, particularly with Athanasius. But with him one also feels close to a striking and irreplaceable theological penetration of what it means.

Thirdly, I would suggest that it is precisely because of this one-time individuation of the divine love within history that all the rest of us can come to share in an individualized relationship with the Divine too. Inclusivistic participation is an aspect of the very nature of the Incarnation. And that participation is always derivative from, subordinate to, and dependent upon this one-time Incarnation spoken of. I do not mean that, prior to Jesus, participation in God remained impossible. But I do mean that with and after him it became appropriately individuated and personalized. This sense of qualitatively new participation through Jesus is also clearly felt in the New Testament. Again, 1 John 4:9: "In this way the love of God was revealed to us: God sent his only Son into the world so that we might have life through him." Paul seems to prefer the metaphor of "adoption" to highlight the derivative and especially gratuitous nature of our participation in Jesus the Christ (Rm 8:14–17). Here, too, by the way, we can glimpse something of the difference between the kind of personalized individuation that we find in Jesus, and the kind of narcissistic individualism that we come upon in more egocentric models of the self. The Jesus Christ-self is a radically sharing self: co-constituted by sharing/participation, and indeed empowering participation. As many have pointed out, the kind of self expressed in Jesus is one of personalism, interpersonalism, and selfless solidarity with society's "rubble," even to the point of death. Here is the point of intersection between christology and ecclesiology — the church flows from Jesus the Christ. Jesus' self is truly universal, indeed cosmic, as it should be, since it is the act of the cosmic God. It reaches not only today and tomorrow, but even the past history of humanity (see the descent into hell theme, 1 Peter 3:19, so powerfully explored in our time by Balthasar[6]). Might I repeat that this "universalizing" quality of the christic love in which we share surfaces particularly intensively in our times in St. Thérèse of Lisieux?[7]

The above three elements are, if you will, implications of the agapaic event disclosed in Jesus. This is an "approach from love" for the definitive uniqueness of Jesus. Not surprisingly, we can also see the elements of the trinitarian understanding of God present here. As we have frequently seen in these pages,[8] the love event in Jesus leads directly to the trinitarian doctrine: God as distinctly the Transcendent (= Father); God as individuatedly personable (= Son, to whom it thus belongs in sovereign freedom to become incarnate); God as individuatedly participable (= Spirit). Or, staying with one of St. Augustine's insights in *The Trinity*, which would have to wait for Richard of St. Victor for a fuller probing: "So then there are three: the lover, the beloved, and the love."[9]

Seeing the link in this context between the Incarnation and the Trinity may help us avoid a christomonism while at the same time preserving the specialness of Jesus in divine revelation. For the Incarnation does not deny the "hypostasis" of the Father as the transcendent ground of creation, but depends upon the Father's sovereignty for its own free bestowal in history. It is this divine paternity that seems particularly manifest throughout creation itself (Rm 1:18–22). The "hypostasis" of the Son means that Jesus is the definitive disclosure and personalization of God: God's "Word" become "Word" for us. In Cardinal Newman's terms, "The Son of God became the Son a second time, though not a second Son, by becoming man."[10] We Christians believe that the Father is at work in creation preparing and developing a "context" for the reception of the incarnate Son-Word, but we also believe that the Word has become definitively "audible" in Jesus. The Holy Spirit, as the Father's Spirit, enables all of creation to participate in the trinitarian life (Gn 1:2). But this Spirit is also the Son's Spirit, leading us to our appropriately personal participation with God through the Son. We only know the Son through the Spirit (1 Cr 12:3), and the Spirit guides us to the Son (Jn 14:15–27). This is the Spirit of Pentecost (Acts 2).

So the Spirit "universalizes," in the sense that all created reality is invited to participate in the trinitarian dialogue through the Spirit. But this universalization does not take away from the Son's — and so from the Incarnate Son's — mission as the final Word of God for us. In this sense, the Spirit "particularizes" by leading us to the concretely particular Jesus. And here is where we can link the Spirit — the "pentecostal" Spirit — with the church, as the foundation of the church's specific missionary mandate. The Spirit also "particularizes" in the sense that our relationship with Father and Son is in a mode appropriate to our own "particular" uniqueness as individuals as well.

For in the Spirit we become aware of our own unique gifts/charisms, and they are awakened through the Spirit (1 Cor 12). Thus, in these ways the "hypostasis" of the Spirit is in no way jeopardized by the Incarnation. The "indwellings" of Father, Son, and Spirit, and the definitive uniqueness of Jesus, are all to be kept in focus.[11]

Here might be the appropriate place for a footnote. Some have asked why the Incarnation cannot happen an indefinite number of times. And some might want to lodge an appeal to the Spirit as the basis for this: Why cannot the Spirit enable all of us to have the Logos dwell in us as it does in Jesus? Thinking along with the biblical texts, I am led to view this as a pre-personal way of thinking of revelation. If God fully personalizes the divine self, this self must enjoy the individuation and uniqueness of the fully personal. And, for the reasons given, it must be definitive as well. Thus it is that there can be only one Incarnation. The Spirit does not cause the Incarnation to repeat itself, but invites and enables all of us to share in this personalization in a manner appropriate to our own uniqueness. For the Spirit universalizes and particularizes in the senses above. In an economy of such a personal revelation, what seems required is not that all are equal in all respects, but that we all share in the benefits of the Incarnation in a way appropriate to our own unique potential.

Difficulties

An immediate argument against the above would be to say that the kind of love-differentiation that we have attributed to Jesus the Christ can be attributed to some strands of Hinduism (most especially the loving relationship between Arjuna and the "deity" Krishna in the Bhagavad Gita), and perhaps some strands of Mahayana Buddhism (one thinks especially of Pure Land Buddhism). I certainly think there are profound and distinct expressions of the nature of love in these traditions, as well as in some strands of Chinese thought, but I don't think they are exactly the same differentiation that we find in Jesus. I realize that these are turbulent waters, but it would seem that the sense of the "break" with intraworldly sacrality (again, what some anachronistically call "polytheism") is missing in these traditions, or at least still only incompletely differentiated. There just does not seem to be as differentiated a disclosure of divine transcendence as precisely uniquely distinct from the cosmos in these traditions. This is perhaps why Hindu avatars ("incarnations") are precisely not one-time events, or uniquely personal events, and why Mahayana Buddhism is a bewildering assortment of "deities" too. Again, the complex symbolisms of the Chinese "Tao" or the Confucian "Heaven" are rather more forms of intrawordly sacrality, it would seem. I simply am not aware of a struggle over idolatry in these traditions, or of a developed theology of adoration (the other side of the coin), both of which are something like "acid tests" of otherworldly transcendence, but especially as personalized in Jesus' incarnation. As we explained it earlier, with Walter Kasper's help, the personalization of God means that God is not an object to be judged by utility for us, but rather "a sovereign subject." And he continues: "The primary thing is not the significance of God for us, but the acknowledgement of the Godness of God and the adoration and praise of him."[12] Here the relevance of the theology and spirituality of adoration, so pronounced in the French School, peaks out at us. For Bérulle, we recall that adoration becomes perfectly possible only with Jesus' Incarnation.[13] And we should think of St. Ignatius Loyola's sense of adoring reverence too, so powerfully expressed at the beginning of his *Spiritual Exercises.*

Love, apparently, if we do our thinking with the differentiations disclosed in history, is not a univocal reality. It has differentiations, modulations. Jesus-like agape has about it an individuated quality that I don't think is paralleled or equalled in other traditions. Here I would point to a study by Henri de Lubac, which is a breakthrough for probing the subtleties of distinction between Buddhist charity and Christian charity. It can serve as a model of the kind of subtlety that is required in this delicate area of comparative thought. For example, Lubac says, persuasively, that Buddhism "is more concerned with suffering in general than with each suffering being in particular." Here we catch the difference in accents of the Buddhist and the Christian differentiations. The element of the personal is sharper, more defined, in the latter; we don't find "the penetrating analysis of love [in Buddhism] that we find... in St. Augustine, St. Bernard, Fénelon." The more "undifferentiated" (if I can put it that way) the charity, the more perfect it is for Buddhism. Hence, Lubac says, perhaps too negatively, "Now Buddhist tenderness,... even at its most sublime, never rises above pity," adding that the more "generalized" and "abstract" it is, the more truly Buddhist.[14]

Hinduism knows about the reality of love as well. What else can one make of Krishna's statement: "Only by love can man see me, and know me, and come unto me" (Bhagavad Gita 11:54; cf. 4:11, 35; 6:28–31; 7:17; 9:31; 12:12)? But we must remember that there does not seem to be that radical "break" with intramundane sacrality. Thus, Krishna says, immediately before the just quoted utterance: "Thou hast seen now face to face my form divine so hard to see: for even the gods in heaven ever long to see what thou hast seen" (11:52). Again, the Hindu avatars, so powerfully spoken of in the Gita's Book

10, for example, are not mediations of the world-transcendent God in the clearly differentiated sense.[15]

A further objection that comes to mind is the idea that it is impossible to arrive at judgments about the "definitive" nature of Jesus, given the limited nature of our knowing and the incompleteness of history. After all, something more "perfect" might come along later, so the view goes. So we must be willing to remain "open" and ready to change allegiances, if I understand this correctly. This reminds me of what Voegelin colorfully called the "sausage" view of history: just keep collecting data, but never arrive at any definitive truth.[16]

Here I would suggest keeping in mind the differences between the source, the justification, and the discovery of truth. Truth surely can come to us only through our history, which remains incomplete. History is our source. But does this mean that we cannot know truth in any final sense? Certainly theologians at least would want to claim that God's existence and absoluteness are definitive truths. But how can one know something definitive in the midst of undefinitive time? Apparently one can grasp what is logically implied in our experience. This is not a matter of surveying the total sweep of history, which would be impossible in any case. It is rather a matter of being able to think through the implications of our experience. But, of course, others do not seem to be able to do so. Or do it quite differently. Logically, then, we must distinguish truth's source and justification from the discovery of truth itself. Some final truths do seem available to us in our changing history, but not everyone is able to mount an equally convincing justification of those truths.

From our faith perspective, I think this view is deepened and further legitimated by our belief in God's Spirit guiding us into participation in the divine truth through the historical community of the church. If God is Word, then this Word should be audible for us, should it not? But let me underscore that I am not trying to present some kind of a priori proof for the Incarnation in the comments above. Rather I am simply trying to present a theological meditation on the historical reality of the Incarnation, probing its implications with respect to the issue of uniqueness. I trust that the Incarnation happened. The witnesses and texts are there. The symbolisms and narrative experiences are celebrated throughout the New Testament.

Intersections with Mariology and Adoration

Before moving further, let me indicate that this approach to Jesus by way of the "divinely personalized amorization" connects with the terrain of mariology, discussed in our previous chapter. There seems to be a very close connection between the two: if we take a clue from history itself, Mary is a route to a proper appropriation of the Incarnation. Again, according to the opening lines of the celebrated prayer of the French School, "O Jesus living in Mary, come and live in your servants. . . . ," through Jesus Mary somehow guides us to her Son. It was and is through her that God brings us to the Incarnation. Does this mean that where mariology is truncated, christology is too? I am inclined to think so.

Let us recall some basic notions. Mary as the model of the Christian disciple, of course, symbolizes the dimension of "participation" unleashed in Jesus through the Spirit. She is the new form of personalized participation in God (= "discipleship") now made possible in the economy of the Incarnation. Her participation is the first form, the "womb" or "matrix," of a new form of participating in God in history. I think, too, that the dimension of how our participation is one of "unique individuation," and not simply an amorphous and undifferentiated relationship with God, surfaces strikingly in the Marian mystery. Her so-called privileges (the immaculate conception, assumption, virginal conception of Jesus, etc.) symbolize, we suggested, this individuated (and thus privileged) manner of relating to God made possible with Jesus. None of us is a carbon copy, when we're speaking of a uniquely individuated and individuating God. There is perhaps more too, which has a special relevance in the context of this article about the Incarnation's definitive uniqueness. Again, I return to Voegelin's important Letter "On Christianity," in which, after speaking about how the Marian dogmas symbolize the creature's participation in God through Jesus (following up a comment by Karl Barth), he suggests:

> The fact that the creature is capable of participating does not mean that created everyday man can spit on his palms and take a hand in salvation as Christ's co-redemptor, with license to do all kinds of mischief in the process, as happened for example with the left wing of the Puritans. For human beings, participation remains within the boundaries set for them by their nature. Just as Christ marks the end of the gods, Mary marks the end of superhuman vessels of the divine. In both instances the symbolism restores the balance between man's splendor and possibilities and his limitations.[17]

I have already touched on the question of adoration as one of the acid tests for the awareness of the kind of differentiated revelation we have in the Incarnation. This, too, deserves much more pondering, and I am inclined to think that adoration represents an essential spiritual experience for those wanting to appropriate the Incarnation. In other words, where adoration weakens, so does incarnational faith. I have in mind our previous study of adoration as the experience and genre recognizing God as the "sovereign subject" who not only transcends all creaturely manipulation but is able to draw near to us in sovereignly personal freedom as the incarnate Word. God is the supremely beautiful One, apart from all human considerations: truly a *sovereign* subject. But as sovereign, also *free* to be incarnately personal for us. Where this adorational posture is missing, the deepest meaning of the "personal" is missing too. We remember that Bérulle, whose own spirituality is so thoroughly penetrated by this sense of adoration, also very interestingly sees that "servitude" (today we say "service") is adoration's other side. That is, adoration transcends the selfish tendency toward manipulation: one does not use, one reverences, "serves."[18] Many ambiguities still remain as a result of this analysis, given our current ecumenic horizon. Still, I think it a more sound procedure to move from what seems less obscure to the more obscure, rather than vice versa. Christian theologians would seem to be methodologically justified in beginning with what seem relatively more secure positions, rather than with grand and vague generalizations about the religions as a whole.

Further Questions

I am inclined toward thinking that the above position on the Incarnation is compatible with a more "inclusivistic" approach to the religions. I mean by the latter a view that considers Jesus the Christ to be the triune God's definitive revelation, yet considers it possible and perhaps probable that intimations of that revelation are found throughout humanity's and the universe's history. Jesus somehow "includes" all others. This is quite different from an exclusivism, which refuses to recognize any possible revelatory dimension outside the Christian orbit. It is also quite different from a relativism that wants to equalize all the religions but give up on finding truth in any, or from the kind of radical "pluralism" that wants to accord an equal revelatory value to all of them. Brian Hebblethwaite put it nicely and briefly: "The Incarnation provides a total interpretative key by which all other knowledge of God is to be finally illuminated and transformed, just because it is God's own particular act in time and for eternity." And he helpfully sees that "The unity of God and the uniqueness of the Incarnation lead Christianity to postulate and hope for the unification of humanity under God in Christ, whether here or in eternity."[19]

What seems essential is that this inclusivism be coherent; that is, that it cohere with reality. The other alternatives must be judged untenable because they do not so cohere. In a personalistic universe, under a personal God, Christians should not be surprised that there are different and unequal differentiations within reality, nor that God's uniquely personal revelation has about it a once-for-all, unrepeatable, definitive, and unsurpassable nature. If our inclusivism is so coherent, then it will not do an injustice to other experiences in history: it will cohere with them.

Interestingly, following up a clue from Thomas Merton, thinking of the non-Christian religions in this way seems to cohere with their own understanding of the matter too, at least in some instances. Speaking of his experience of Zen Buddhism, for example, he suggests that it "is not Kerygma but realization, not revelation but consciousness, not news from the Father who sends His Son into this world, but awareness of the ontological ground of our own being." Or, speaking of the Buddhist nirvana in general, he suggests that it is a "self-emptying and enlightenment" rather than a revelation. "The chief difference [between Buddhist nirvana and Christian revelation] is that the former is existential and ontological, the latter is theological and personal." Merton, who seems to regard nirvana as a transcendent experience in some sense (it transcends the usual ego experience of the self as separate from others, if you will) would seem to accord it some "revelatory" value, for he says that "all transcendent experience is for the Christian a participation in 'the mind of Christ.'"[20] In other words, Merton seems to be suggesting that while there are some revelatory aspects within Buddhism, it is not primarily a differentiation of revelation in the sense that we Christians understand that notion as a clarifying differentiation of God through God's own personal gift of Self.

If I might borrow some technical notions from Voegelin's helpful studies, Buddhism primarily seems to be a noetic rather than a pneumatic (= revelatory) differentiation. Human experiences are some kind of blend of noetic and pneumatic aspects, for humans and God are always interrelated. But both poles need not be equally differentiated, and we seem to have a greater differentiation of the noetic rather than the pneumatic in the Buddhist orbits. This is why, in a study of the religions written from a Voegelinian perspective, the traditions of the Far East are seen as emphasizing the role of the "sage" more than that of the "prophet."[21] This book by John Carmody and Denise Lardner Carmody suggests that what is true of Buddhism is true of the Far Eastern orbit in general: the sage is the key figure for Hinduism, Buddhism, and Confucianism-Taoism. This is why the first two especially, and the latter less fully, engage in enormously complex explorations of the strata of consciousness. Voegelin, of course, while seeing pneumatic dimensions in the Greek experiences, views them as mainly noetic too (Plato and Aristotle are maximal differentiations of the noetic for Voegelin).[22]

Judaism and Islam are difficult, from our inclusivist perspective, and they, like the other experiences touched on here, need and demand much more subtle treatment. Still, I would suggest that Islam, at least at its core in Mohammed, represents in some respects an intensified expression of the differentiation of the world-transcendent God already found in Israel, not a really new differentiation surpassing or necessarily equalling that. Israel, on the other hand, contains enormously subtle revelatory experiences, but I do not think it matches the personalization of God through Jesus in the Incarnation. But, and this is crucial, it does not claim to. In other words, our inclusivism would seem to cohere, not only with what we think is the case, but also with Israel's own understanding of the matter. Perhaps in some messianic strands of Judaism we might say there is a tradition of an "expectant messianism" that seems to "intimate" the Incarnation. But what Judaism, at least in some sectors, perhaps intimates, we Christians believe has come.[23] Obviously our inclusivism would cohere with oral religions and cultures, which, while arguing for the revelatory dimension of nature (God's immanence, we might say as Christians), do not claim to have differentiated the world-transcendent God, not to mention the God of the Incarnation.

The notion of revelation is, I know, troubling, and so far as I can see, confusing. Some prefer to limit it only to the Jewish-Christian sphere; all the rest is considered "natural" and "non-divine." This usage seems influenced by a kind of Enlightenment naturalism, which relegates the sphere of revelation to one completely outside of nature and normal human history. I think this is to give in too quickly to the worst strand of the Enlightenment. We Christians believe that God is present in this "graced" world, in varying manners, and thus in some sense this suggests that, to one properly disposed, intimations at any rate of revelation would be available here and there throughout the world. Let us recall here the work of the Holy Spirit, inviting all into the trinitarian family.

Others want to limit revelation to the differentiation of God's personal presence in history, without denying God's presence in a "non-personal" and "natural" form in the cosmos at large. Hence, revelation is again limited to the Jewish-Christian sphere for all practical purposes. This surely is an honorable tradition, seeking to express the element of the "personal" coming to expression in the Jewish and Christian orbits. But I think it's a usage that is imprecise. For revelation seems legitimately to be a notion wider than "personal" presence, and even the Jewish-Christian scriptures celebrate God's presence in nature. At the same time, it seems difficult to separate the "natural" from the "personal" God. They can be distinguished, surely, but not separated. It seems hard to imagine a purely "impersonal" differentiation of God. Even the ancient myths seem to be a mix of the cosmic and personal, neither clearly differentiated.[24]

A further difficult area for an inclusivistic approach to the religions is that of salvation/soteriology. In what sense can we speak of other contributions to salvation, in the light of 1 Timothy 2:5-6, for example, which speaks of the "one God" and "one mediator between God and the human race" who is Jesus? (See also Jn 14:6 and Acts 4:12) Inasmuch as salvation means the bridging and indeed restoration of a failed personal relationship with God, it would seem that it becomes finally possible only through the amorization event of Jesus. And I think that is finally what salvation must mean from a Christian perspective. Through God's personal love, we are united with God, forgiven our sins, and enabled to trust and love in a new and redeemed way.

Yet other traditions view themselves as in some sense soteriological. This is true of Buddhism, for example: think of its four noble truths, which are concerned with the origin of suffering and the therapy for its cure. Particularly striking in this regard is the Gautama Buddha's sermon on "questions not tending toward edification." Here the point is precisely to critique a fascination for spinning out dogmas that can blind us to our real plight of bondage.[25] There is a soteriological thrust in the Greek, classical orbit too. Plato, for example, was concerned with the therapy for right civil order and the diagnosis of disorder. Few traditions can match the classical philosophers' analysis of human soul-disorders, ranging from the tragedians, through Thucydides, Plato and Aristotle, and on through the Stoics. Augustine's famous analysis of human evil in Books 13 and 14 of the *City of God* would probably have been impossible without these classical thinkers.[26]

Coherence indicates, however, that we take the same view with respect to salvation that we took with respect to revelation. Inasmuch as salvation becomes possible only through the establishing of a truly personalized and so loving relationship with God, then salvation happens only through the God revealed in Jesus Christ. This God is certainly actively present throughout the cosmos, and we need not believe that only professing Christians experience it. Let us recall the "hypostasis" of the Holy Spirit, at work universalizing Jesus. At the same time, an inclusivistic vision would seem to indicate that God somehow works in and with other contributions to salvation, nurturing them when possible, completing them through personalization and amorization, and even correcting them where necessary. Again recall that the Holy Spirit also nourishes and protects our "particular" gifts, our unique qualities. This should include those beyond the explicitly Christian orbit. Christians would seem to witness explicitly to this work of salvation in history, of course. The afterlife would seem to have its essential role to play here too. Not only does a belief in it enable us to grasp a little more meaningfully how non-Christians might come to a fuller participation in Jesus. It is also in the afterlife that many Christians come to an appropriately deep relationship with Jesus through the Spirit.

Here I want to offer some comments on Jesus' maleness, an issue of some concern in women's theology. If we are correct in locating the core of the Incarnation's revelation in God's loving personalization as a human being, this would suggest that we view Jesus' maleness (sex and gender), along with his full humanity, as an aspect of the "scandal of particularity" involved in the Incarnation. This "scandal" may not be the story we would choose to narrate, but it is the story God told. God has not remained undefined, but *particularized* God's Self for us in Jesus. In this sense, the Incarnation is the "concrete Universal." It is not a "Christ idea" or "*Logos* idea," but the concretely particular God-man Jesus Christ whom we confess. Holding these two together — Jesus' human particularity (including his maleness and bodiliness) as well as his divine universality — is the challenge and blessing of the Incarnation. This rules out docetism of any kind: We cannot and should not think that Jesus' humanity (and maleness) is "insignificant," although there are seemingly varying degrees of significance among the aspects of his humanity. But this is really good news. For it is through this particularity that God has reached out to offer us communion and saving participation in the Trinity. A *Logos asarkos* approach to the Incarnation, which tries to detach Jesus' divinity from his particular humanity, in the end depersonalizes God and renders impossible the intimate and personal communion to which we are invited by the Spirit. If you will, through Jesus' particularity, all created and human particularity (men, women, and creation) is blessed. Take away his particularity, and no particularity has been "assumed" and so "healed" by God. As we share in communion with Jesus, we become "configured" to him, "images" of his saving presence (Rm 8:29). We are not called to become photocopies or duplicates: this erases Jesus' unique particularity. We are called to communion, which presupposes oneness and difference. This is sufficient to bring us all to salvation.[27]

In our own culture there are strong tendencies to level all differences, reducing all to a kind of shallow "equality" that abolishes all unique individuation. In this climate, the uniquely individuated and individuating love that is Jesus Christ has a special liberating quality about it. The kind of "equality" we seem to be promised by our faith is that of God's desire to love us all uniquely. In other words, the divine kenosis, fully revealed in Jesus, presents us with a highly personalistic "economy." This means there is room for difference, for uniqueness, for personality, etc.

This stress on "difference" does not mean there is nothing shared in common. We all surely "share" the same God. There is a oneness. But on Christian grounds it is a richly differentiated oneness, a unity in diversity, which reflects the one yet triune God we Christians confess. Here we seem to have a personalism that accords well with an "analogous" view of the religions and of reality in general. There are enormous varieties of the "unique" (against simple univocity). There is also genuine unity and communion (against simple equivocity). The "one" exists in and with the "other" (which is analogy). And we can plausibly say, with Barth and Balthasar, that in the case of Jesus' uniqueness we are dealing with what, at first, is without analogy, but itself gives birth to various analogies in history.[28]

The kenosis of Jesus is not just another example of the "same" (the univocal). But this makes room for truly appreciating the unique contributions of the other religions in history, without assimilating them into some monistic scheme (which is perhaps the scholar's great temptation). A personal God makes room for others, creating a space within which diversity can exist. Such a God even makes us open to the fact that not all "religions" seem concerned with, or equally concerned with, God's revelation. And this God creates a space for many things besides only revelation. We theologians need to be reminded of that. God does not just seem to be about the "business" of revealing the Divine Self. God is a God of the "space" within which we can and should pursue art, science, work, and the many other realities of life, even as we first pursue our personal union with the Lord.

CHAPTER NINE

The "Contemplation and Action" Question in Christology

In popular thought and discourse contemplation and action are frequently played off against each other, opposed, thought of as contraries. Thus, a "contemplative" style of theology is conceived of as more passive, receptive, meditative in a disengaged and reflective sort of way, "still." Or it is labeled as more "hellenistic," "Neoplatonic," and so more theoretical and distant from the realm of action, the realm of life's real dramas. A "practical" style of theology, on the other hand, strives to be more engaged, to involve itself in the lessons of people's living personal and social experience and struggles, not to stray off into "sublime abstractions" that can't be backed up in some way by practical experience. Here the weight and "primacy" goes to the practical, and the theoretical side of this style of theology is a "second" moment, properly flowing out of practical experience and always staying in tune with it and ready to "defend" itself at the bar, so to speak, of practice.

If the reader has a "sense" of suspicion about this book, with its heavy emphasis upon consulting spiritual/meditative traditions as a matrix for doing christology, he or she may be showing by that fact the influence of this "popular way" of thinking of the relationship between contemplation and action. This "popular" suspicion, of course, didn't just drop out of nowhere. Like many things "popular," it may represent a reaction to unhealthy tendencies slowly accumulating in intensity down through the ages. There is a sort of "living critical sense" among many people, a "common sense" coming from listening to the lessons of experience, and so the suspicions about a "contemplative" style of theologizing do deserve attention.[1]

This chapter doesn't intend to be a sort of "survey" of the various positions on this question of the relationship between contemplation and action and action in theology and christology. Suffice it to say that a number of factors have given rise to the observations to follow in this chapter. First, I do think there is something to the popular suspicion deserving of attention, although it's very hard to draw the most accurate conclusions from it. Secondly, I do want to engage, throughout this book, in a piece of critical theological reflection. And that means that I need to be willing to submit my views and preferences to a self-critique. Hopefully that has been sensed by the reader throughout, but this chapter represents a more sustained self-critique. Thirdly, some of the most important theological figures in my formation have practiced theology with a heavily "practical" intent, and that has created both a sensitivity in me that I welcome, and also something of a guilty conscience about possibly sliding into social and political amnesia.[2] Finally, there is an intense debate going on right now in theology and the churches about the relationship between theory and practice, ideas and the struggle for justice and peace, a debate intersecting that between modernity and postmodernity. I regard this debate as very important, an "intimation" of something critical for theology and christology, and therefore something that stimulates and helps me carry forward the observations to follow.[3] Perhaps, too, there is a bit of wisdom "encased" within the meditative traditions that just might cast some illumination upon the shadows of this important discussion and debate.

The "Practical" Dimension

Experience, human and Christian, is a complex, multi-layered reality, it seems. It knows many "modes." There is "sense" experience, the realm of the physical sensorium, which forms a basic substratum of all human experience. For some of a very narrowly empirical bent, this is the only kind of human experience there is. But for others of us, human experience embraces the full potential of the *humanum*, including the aesthetic (beauty), the moral (conscience, responsibility, guilt), the intellectual (insight, noetic analysis, symbolization, etc.), and the religious, not to mention other constitutive aspects, such as experience's symbolic-linguistic, narrative, and personal-social dimensions. And in a christic universe, "graced" by Jesus Christ, human experience becomes the medium of grace. The "practical" is a mode of human experience, too: it is human experience in the form of drama, activity, doing, transforming. Of course, what we discover is that not every "activity" or "doing" is necessarily "practical." Some "doing" just doesn't work, doesn't pay off. So the word "practical" injects a nuance into human activity. It means activity that has been reflected upon, learned from, refined.[4] The narrative/drama genre, we might

173

add, is a fine example of action-like experience that has been reflected upon that makes it very appropriate for addressing questions of action. We might say that "practice" ("Practice makes perfect!") makes activity human and humane, instead of the "doings" of a mere brute. If our activity is "refined" by becoming the true medium of Christian grace, then it becomes "Christian practice."

Now it is this Christian practice that we are especially interested in. And this is the primary concern of more practical styles of theology and christology. Speaking very broadly, contemporary sociopolitical theologies and feminist theologies are two of the major forms of this kind of theology with a heavy practical accent. Not all of these theologies necessarily agree on the precise relationship between theory and practice, some don't spend much time reflecting on the issue at all, some assign the "primacy" to practice rather than theory, others, the reverse, and so on. But all of them try to pay close attention to the lessons of human and Christian "activity," seeking out what is truly "practical" or "liberating" for humans and Christians, women as well as men, in the sociopolitical realm and personal realms.

Typically the "progression" goes like this: a willingness to stay attuned to the lessons of practical experience, a resulting "discovery" of what isn't "practical" or "liberating," a searching out of the causes for this in past and present, and the proposal of more "liberating-practical" alternatives on the basis of human and Christian sources, past and present. If we were to take the case of feminist theology, this would mean that an attentiveness to the "real" and "actual" situation of women on the level of practice reveals serious degrees of inequity and "sexist oppression," in various societies, and even in the Christian tradition. Somehow this just wasn't "noticed" before, at least in any sustained manner by Christian thinkers, until relatively recently. Not unlike the case of slavery in the United States, perhaps. Good "Christian" people just didn't notice that it was incompatible with the gospel. Somehow theologians and other Christians allowed themselves to be too distant, too removed, from this practical, day by day, experience of women to become sufficiently attuned to it and what it might mean.

I wouldn't want to deny that one could "reason" through to an awareness of the incompatibility of sexism and slavery to Christianity in a more theoretical manner. But generally speaking, attunement to practice and staying with it and working through it creates a sensitivity and awareness that normally won't come in any other way, except perhaps in great moments of creative imagination. In the area of feminist (perhaps better: woman's) theology, this has led to a search for the causes in the tradition, past and present, contributing to this, as well as to resources for a more liberating existence for women in church and society available in the same tradition. Of course, this is a matter of intense debate, and views span a wide variety. But at this point I'm more interested in the role of attunement to the practical as the basic teacher here.

A number of elements do, typically, seem to accompany this attunement to the practical. Perhaps there is an intrinsic logic to this, what can be called a *logique du coeur*. Not only is there the typical "progression" in the steps of analysis outlined above, but there is typically an uncovering of "layers" that seem to overlay one another. Persons are agents or actors in society, and so there are typically sociopolitical and economic dimensions influencing our practice. If one sticks with a "practical analysis" long enough, likely one will come across this more "hidden" and "anonymous" but still real social dimension. And because it is more anonymous, it seems harder to "own" in a personal way and harder to "change." And so a woman's theology becomes, at least in part, a sociopolitical theology and a socioecclesial one. Typically, too, the "hidden" nature of the evil one is discovering leads one to become suspicious, to recognize how hardened and blind "hearts" can really be, how "sincere" and yet "blind," and so one is led to a search for "methods" that are skilled at uncovering the deeply hidden, like forms of psychoanalysis and their equivalent on a political level. Typically we find a stress upon the dimension of the future, too, for practice surfaces the human ability to bring about the "more humanly new" through experimentation and discrimination. The process of moving from mere "activity" to "practice" illustrates this breaking out of the "fate" of meaningless doing and opening up a *novum*, a more humane set of possibilities. I believe that, painting with a rather broad brush, one can notice this constellation of characteristics in the styles of theology varyingly known as practical, political, liberation, etc.

The Contemplative Dimension

What role might our contemplative style of christology and theology have in this turn to the practical in theology? First of all, we should note that a truly practical theology needs its reflective, theoretical dimension. This is why we've tried to make the distinction between simple "activity" and "practice" (the tradition and scholars commonly make this distinction or ones that are structurally equivalent). It is not mere "doing," but humanly and Christianly meaningful doing (that is, "practice") that we are interested in. Human activity needs to be listened to attentively and with discrimination, it needs to be thought about and lessons need to be drawn from it — that is the role of the "theoretical" dimension in our experience. And so "practice" is human activity as reflected upon in theory. The kind of "theory" that listens to human activity and draws lessons from it can uncover patterns in our experience, search out its possible human meaning, make projections as to where our experience is heading, magnify dimensions for the sake of more careful analysis, etc. And all of this goes on in varying ways in the more practical and narrative/dramatic styles of theology today.[5]

Now the fact that theory and activity can coalesce in "practice" indicates that these are not fully separable in the human subject. At a deep-down level they are in union. Each can be refined and distinguished from the other. What is compactly one in an undifferentiated state can and will become differentiated through refinement and use. But they are united in a deeper oneness, or else we would fall into a final dualism in which theory could not refine activity, nor activity, theory. Now I would suggest that one of the ways of looking at contemplation is to see it as the effort, more or less disciplined, of keeping theory and activity in fruitful union and communion. Contemplation can do this because it "sublates" both, keeping theory attuned to practice and practice from degenerating into simple "activity."

If the reader will look back upon the earlier chapters in this book, he or she will notice a great effort to keep theological/philosophical "theory" rooted in spiritual and Christian experience-faith. The return of theory to living, spirituality-Christian experience is precisely what we mean by the turn to spirituality, mysticism, and the contemplative in theology and christology. I think, in the light of this, that we can say that a contemplative style of theology tries to keep our theoretical and intellectual operations rooted in the real *plenum* of human and Christian experience. Interestingly, we're saying that the thrust toward contemplation keeps our explanatory operations in theology attuned to practice, since this is an aspect of our living faith experience. The sensitivity to narrative, biography, etc., is of a piece with this. In other words, the link between theory and practice — the deep-down hinge — is the thrust toward the contemplative.

The contemplative thrust saves theory from mere abstractions. It also saves theory from illusion, which I take to be a form of "abstraction" whose "unreal" nature is more hidden and difficult to notice. Theologies that specialize in the manufacturing of ever finer "distinctions" that seem more and more to try to precise the necessarily "mysterious" regions of the supernatural might be considered excessively abstract. Or theologies that manifest a supine unconcern for ethics, spiritual life and liturgical life, and the problems of justice and peace could also be considered abstract. So, too, are theologies that try to wrap up revelation simply into propositions — a sort of conceptualism or "doctrinization" in Voegelin's pejorative sense.[6] We might say that excessively abstract theologies become illusionary when the factors causing them cannot be overcome through a simple intellectual process of ratiocination, but require a kind of moral and practical effort of resistance to forces, personal and/or social, blocking their uncovering. I would suggest that the ascetical traditions of moral purification and the discernment of spirits, and especially the deeply purifying dark nights of the mystics, are relevant here as appropriate ways of breaking through the illusionary.[7]

I think of how Karl Rahner's style of theology seems to illustrate this point of how contemplation keeps theological theory attuned to experience in all its modes, including the practical. One could not read him for long without noticing his extensive writings on spirituality, mysticism, pastoral theology, and eventually even on political theology. Here was a modern Catholic theologian who moved easily from prayer to analysis and back again, keeping each in a fruitful relation and even tension, without collapsing one into the other. There was also a marvelous openness in Rahner, a willingness to incorporate new dimensions (for example, the sociopolitical) that he may have overlooked earlier in his career. I think Rahner himself, both in theory and in practice, would agree that the contemplative thrust as the deep-down response to God's gracious self-communication is the key factor enabling him to unite all these factors. Thus it wasn't surprising for me to read, in one of his later interviews, that, for him "in comparison with other philosophy and theology that influenced me, Ignatian spirituality was indeed more significant and important." It was the "spirituality of Ignatius [Loyola] himself, which one learned through the practice of prayer and religious formation," that was "more significant for me," said Rahner, "than all learned philosophy and theology inside and outside the order." Thus he refused to practice a sort of "art for art's sake" theology "that was usual in scholarly theology" before his time. On the contrary, "compelled" by spirituality and pastoral work, he strove to build up his own style of theology in which "there is no exact boundary between...spiritual writings and...more systematic theology."[8]

There are many other examples — theological "greats" — who deserve mention: Newman and Hügel, in an earlier generation, and Balthasar from Rahner's own generation. The style of theology of the Eastern Orthodox, it needs no reminding, is typically stamped by the contemplative thrust. Like Rahner, much of their theology makes no clear separation between the spiritual and the theoretical, the needs of church and society and personal ethics, and theology.[9] Karl Barth is another "great" from the Protestant tradition who also moved easily between analysis and prayer, systematics and personal and social ethics (his *Church Dogmatics* always treats ethics with each of the great dogmatic themes). He, too, has that gift of openness and growth, the mark of the thinker attuned to grace. Think of the "developments" within the *Church Dogmatics*. Let these words of his serve as a testimonial from the Protestant tradition: "The first and basic act of theological work is *prayer*." It must surely, too, he went on to say, be "study" and "service," what I am referring to as theory and practice. But note that Barth places a certain primacy on prayer. "But theological work does not merely begin with prayer and is not merely accompanied by it; in its totality it is peculiar and characteristic of theology that it can be performed only in the act of prayer."[10]

It can work the other way too: Not only does contemplation keep theory rooted in practice, it also keeps practice rooted in theory. Here there is something to the common notion of contemplation as a kind of "slowing down," an entering into a clearing ground or space that promotes self-reflectivity, distance, "indifference" in Ignatius Loyola's sense of "the existential distance from things that is self-appropriated in such a way that it even frees the will to reject its own prejudices."[11] Through contemplation the "doer" or "activist" learns to "detach" the self from the intoxicating quality of acting, but to do it without completely breaking loose from action (which is perhaps the inner tendency of "theory" unmoored in contemplation). It is not flight but perspective and more freeing and meaningful practice that is the goal. Here we link up with the millennial teaching on asceticism as an intrinsic aspect of authentic contemplation. The latter strives to be a disciplined way of staying open, attuned to the lessons of experience and reality. And so contemplation will lead practice to the humility of undergoing criticism from theory. Yet it keeps theory humble too, preserving the edges of mystery.

As theory becomes too abstract when it is severed from practice, so practice becomes too concrete — merely unthinking activity — when it is likewise severed from theory. "Concrete" is not a bad image: hard, something that crushes and smothers, no open spaces for breathing, where all is thrown together and distinctions are collapsed. The intoxicating quality of action brings power, movement, an ecstasy of sorts, a Promethean feel. But this can blind and crush if it's not accompanied by self-reflective distance and a healthy measure of detachment. Contemplation, I am suggesting, promotes sufficient openness to theoretical critique, yet without lapsing into an intoxicating mental world of sociopolitical amnesia.

At the deepest level, our own contemplation is a participation in the "contemplation" of the trinitarian mystery revealed to us in Jesus Christ. The Father's own "self-reflectivity" is the Son. If you will, the Father expresses a healthy self-detachment in the Son. The Son's complete attunement to the Father enables him to be the Father's pure self-reflectivity. And the fertility of this mystery of mutual openness is the overflow of the Spirit. In the light of this, contemplation is a supremely trinitarian-christological reality. Strictly speaking, our own contemplation is made possible by that of the Trinity revealed through the God-Man. The Father brings about a contemplative self-reflective space through the Son, and enables us to participate in it through the Spirit. Jesus' own unique contemplation of his Father was the definitive earthly reflection of his trinitarian contemplation, and our own shares in this same mystery and is made possible through it.

Speaking reverently and analogously, we might consider Father, Son, and Spirit as the ground and enabler of Contemplation, Theory, and Practice. The Father's contemplation finds its expression in the reflectivity of the Son. If you will, the Son is the "exegesis" of the Father: "No one has ever seen God. The only Son, God, who is at the Father's side, has revealed [*exegesato*] him" (Jn 1:18).[12] This "exegesis" that the Son is constitutes the reality of "theory" in the trinitarian life, and makes it possible on our level. The Father's contemplation gives birth to theory, leads to it. But it also leads to practice: the Spirit. For the Father's contemplation in the Son is not sterile, but fecund: an unending source of life, of renewal, of transformation. Basil captured this in a compellingly metaphorical way: "The Spirit is ... from God ... not by way of generation like the Son, but as the breath coming from God's mouth."[13] The Spirit, as the principle of practice, is the "breath" of the Son, that which keeps his "exegesis" alive and flowing between Father and Son. Note, too, the role of the Father in uniting both theory and practice in contemplation. The Father keeps the two contemplatively in interrelation and union. Through the Father, theory also remains open to the Mystery and doesn't derail into rationalism. Practice, too, stays linked to contemplative theory, yet without losing its dynamic "energy." For the Spirit is "normed" by and leads to the Son, yet in a free and creative way. It is in this "contemplative" sense that we can understand the biblical notion that true knowing is doing, and true doing, knowing (Gn 4:1, Jer 22:16, Mt 1:25, Lk 1:34, 1 Jn 2:3, 4:8).

The Ultimacy of Doxology

It may sound strange in a chapter trying to show that a contemplative style of theology/christology is not insensitive to practice to say that theory and practice are both directed to the Father's glory. But that is what I am led to suggest by the biblical evidence. Contemplation inevitably leads to doxology. And if it is contemplation that grounds and unites theory and practice, then they too must result in doxology. Why? Because the movement of Son and Spirit is *toward the Father*.

179

This seems to be what Paul has in mind when he speaks of Jesus the Son handing all things over to the Father: "When everything is subjected to him [Jesus], then the Son himself will [also] be subjected to the one who subjected everything to him, so that God may be all in all" (1 Cor 15:28). Thus, drawing a pastoral lesson from this, Paul tells the Thessalonians to "conduct yourselves as worthy of the God who calls you into his kingdom and glory" (1 Thes 2:12). A passage that is particularly rich in its trinitarian resonance, and that brings out the doxological orientation of the Christian life, is found in 1 Peter: "Whoever preaches, let it be with the words of God; whoever serves, let it be with the strength that God supplies, so that in all things God may be glorified through Jesus Christ, to whom belong glory and dominion forever and ever. Amen" (1 Pt 4:11).

Doxology, the movement never without petition toward thanksgiving, then praise, and ultimately adoration, flows from the return of all things to the Father. The more we participate in that great movement, the more we become doxological. Here I would suggest that this doxological orientation keeps our theological theory open to the personal mystery of God. Theology as theory remains first a response to grace, a personal participation in God's self-communication, a gift. The ever-present temptation of theological theory to become mere information gathering, or conceptualism, or rationalism by whatever name is transcended in the doxological movement.[14]

The doxological movement also keeps our practice from degenerating into mere technological manipulating, a sort of technique fetishism, where we confuse means with ends, or reduce ends to means. Our doing is for the sake of the Father's glory; that is, it is a glad recognition of the sovereignty of Divine Love, the sheer breathtaking goodness of God's overflowing, non-manipulable, but "selfless" love. As we transcend our own egocentricity of "thought" and "action" in doxology we experience something of what this sovereignty means. Jesus' own return of all things to the Father (1 Cor 15:28), his abasement or kenosis, is his fullest sharing in glory precisely because it is his fullest self-emptying: "I am troubled now. Yet what should I say? 'Father, save me from this hour'? But it was for this purpose that I came to this hour. Father, glorify your name" (Jn 12:27–28).[15]

From Contemplative "Moments" to the Contemplative "State"

Here I would like to recall Bérulle's use of the term "state" in a somewhat technical sense as indicating something permanent, "deep" in the sense of what lasts after all the passing elements have gone. Thus, the "states" of Jesus are the ongoing, eternally effective aspects of the entire mystery of Jesus. In the tradition of the French School, then, to enter into a state is to enter into something very deep and permanent, something "eternally effective." The contemplative "state," in this sense, would be something like a permanent and deeply transformative regrounding of the Christian. This is not a bad definition of the "mystic" or "saint" (the canonized mystic), as distinct from the *potential* mystic/saint. But in any case, most of us have yet to experience the rather totalistic regrounding and transformation around the axis of Jesus and the Trinity. We can speak of "moments," more or less prolonged, on the way to a greater transformation. In a certain sense, this transformation is an eschatological reality.

In some ways, the tension between "theory-heavy" and "practice-heavy" christologies/theologies, of today and yesterday, reflects this ongoing passage from a theology simply experiencing "contemplative moments" to one becoming more deeply transformed into a "state" in which theory and practice, knowing and doing, find that *circulatio* most fully revealed in Jesus the incarnate God-Man and the trinitarian Life in which he fully shares. Sometimes theology/christology reflects too much "knowing" and not enough "doing." "Not everyone who says to me, 'Lord, Lord,' will enter into the kingdom of heaven, but only the one who does the will of my Father in heaven" (Mt 7:21). These words apply to the theologian, and not simply to the "non-doctored" Christians. Christologies that try to probe the contribution of Jesus to justice and peace are surely sensing contemplation's tug toward reappropriating the kind of "doing" Jesus calls us to. To write an entire christology and not note the universal, inclusivistic love to which Jesus calls us, all of which either explicitly calls for a new posture to society's alienated, or at least implies it — to not see this is surely to fall victim to theological "conceptualism."

But sometimes our christology reflects too much "doing" and not enough "knowing." Note how, at least in Luke's form of the "hard" saying of Jesus to his family, the Lord calls for both knowing (="hearing") as well as doing: "My mother and brothers are those who hear the word of God and act on it" (Lk 8:21). Christology must make a genuine effort to "hear" God's word, and this demands the asceticism of the mind and a willingness to submit to some effort of theoretical appropriation and critique. Christologies with an accent on justice and peace do little good if they base themselves on political agenda that are incompatible with the gospel, or not the "best" option available. Something has to widen our knowing into more attentive doing, or our doing into more attentive knowing. And I am suggesting that it is the primacy of the contemplative thrust in christology that has to be the key. For it helps move us beyond our self-interest, of either an intellectual or a more "practical" sort, toward the kingdom of kenotic love proclaimed by Jesus and found in its perfect form in the kingdom of Father, Son, and Holy Spirit.

The "Struggle for Order" and Trinitarian Christocentrism

The "practical" dimension in a contemplative style of christology inevitably means that christology must intersect with the terrains of political theory and political theology if it is to be faithful to its own intrinsic dynamism. As Eric Voegelin has repeatedly sought to remind us, the great project of humanity down through the ages has been that of the struggle for "true order." As he put it at the beginning of his great work *Order and History:* "Every society is burdened with the task, under its concrete conditions, of creating an order that will endow the fact of its existence with meaning in terms of ends divine and human."[16] In some sense, practical and political theologies are simply an attempt to participate in this struggle in a Christian way.

I, like Wolfhart Pannenberg, am rather fond of Voegelin's understanding as expressed here, because it brings out the societal nature of the search for order, without necessarily denigrating the place of the individual person. The relative place of the latter will depend upon the nature of the "order" conceived and symbolized by the particular people under consideration. As Pannenberg puts it, "It was not until the modern period that the principle of individual freedom was made the criterion for the true order of society."[17] I also appreciate the focus on "struggle," because it highlights the non-utopian, modest nature of our varied attempts at true order. Over and over again the lessons of history are that utopian dream worlds are straitjackets rather than liberators. Voegelin also speaks of "true" order, for he was painfully made aware, through the Nazi horrors, of the lack of attunement to order and its devastating effects. An urgent task of political philosophy and theology is a "science" of disorder, a science to which Voegelin has made great contributions.

In any case, the irruption of Jesus Christ and the "formation" of the Christian tradition eventually resulted in a modulation of the meaning and symbols of societal order for Christians, a "reformulation" that I think was completed in principle with the great christological and trinitarian councils, although probing their political significance is a task forever imposed upon us. If we follow Voegelin's general typology of orders, the Christian symbolism of order no longer simply conceives of society as a "microcosm" of the cosmic "macrocosm," a sort of "representative of cosmic order," as was typical of cultures before the awareness of a transcendent God. Nor, as both Voegelin and Pannenberg indicate, can the Christian view of order be simply imposed through a sort of "positive law," as if people can magically break through to a differentiated faith and understanding. Although this doesn't mean that "law" has no place. The Christian "order" takes its substance from both Christ and the Trinity, and this is why I would prefer to speak of it as an order inspired by christocentric trinitarianism. And the Jewish tradition, with its revelatory breakthrough of a world-transcendent God, is the necessary presupposition for the Christian tradition of order.

Pannenberg's own way of putting it is to suggest that "in Christian history the social system has been conceived of... as anticipating the eschatological Kingdom of God which is to transform this present world." This makes sense, for it recognizes the ultimacy of Jesus whose own mission was that of the inauguration of his Father's kingdom. I would prefer to speak of the Christian "order" in more explicitly christological and trinitarian symbols. For example, Christian society anticipates our final participation in the trinitarian community made available to us in at least an anticipatory way through Jesus Christ. This is our Christian "substance," if you will. It is what the real struggle is all about as far as we are concerned.

Pannenberg helpfully indicates that "Christian history is characterized by an institutional distinction" as a result of its newly conceived order. On the one hand there is the realm of "political order," which concerns itself with how to represent the kingdom "under the present conditions of the social system." On the other hand, the church becomes the witness to the eschatological kingdom, reminding "the political order of its provisional nature."[18] If I read him correctly, he is suggesting that Christian *society* is made up of "state" and "church," and in this sense it is a differentiated unity. Both are engaged in the "struggle" for the kingdom — or participation in the trinitarian community — but in a differentiated manner. Hence the "twofold symbolism" of Christian order arising from our "election" as witnesses to the kingdom: "that exhibited within the life of the church; and that which emerges from the transformation of society into a provisional symbol of God's Kingdom to come through Christian criticism of the social structures in their self-affirming form."[19]

Historically there has been a tension between these two "institutions." And that tension would seem to indicate the crucial necessity of maintaining the differentiated nature of the Christian social order. One option is to tend toward smothering the church by virtually controlling it. This seems to have been one of the great struggles in the church's earliest period, from Constantine on. And occasionally, in Christian countries, it still can be a danger. One could call this "Christian empire over church." Clearly this entails the danger of state absolutism, whereby it tends to forget its provisional nature, becoming a sort of substitute gospel. On the other hand, the church can tend toward smothering the state, which may have been the danger in the Western medieval period. Here the church runs the danger of losing its eschatological witness and turning itself into a simply this-worldly, immanent reality. "Church smothering state" means a loss of the distinction between eternity and time, transcendence and imma-nence, the Trinity as our true homeland and the fragmentary attempts at communion now. We are perhaps inclined to think that this temp-tation no longer exists, because the church would seem to lack the necessary political power. Still, wherever the church effectively be-comes a "surrogate" political government — perhaps in states whose imposed governments are very unpopular, and the church functions to some extent as the symbol of the country's one-time freedom — this "theocratic" temptation exists. Pannenberg is inclined to believe that the division of the churches is God's "judgment" against the intolerable theocracy of the medieval period.[20]

In the contemporary West, we are now in a period of the "legal" separation of church and state for the most part, a period in which the state is increasingly influenced by non-Christian conceptions of social order. The church is still called to struggle for a Christian order, but under new conditions to some extent. I do not pretend to understand all the complexities of the situation imposed upon us Christians by our present period. Here I am intersecting with the concerns of prac-tical/political theologians and specialists, and I will gladly yield to their greater wisdom. Let me just offer a few observations based on my christological concerns.

First, there is the danger of a new, secularized form of state impe-rialism — the old state over church problem. Perhaps now it is not the former "Christian state" that is in danger of smothering the church and its eschatological witness, but a more amorphous, somewhat secu-larized, somewhat Christian state. The danger is again a form of state absolutism (the demonic nationalism partly represented by the Nazis, for example), or a kind of empty tolerance for anything in a pluralistic state, which fosters a sense of the loss of meaning and destiny. Such is not "order" in Voegelin's sense, but a deep spiritual "disorder" patched up in varying ways by laws and structures, and especially by the many *divertissements* of the luxury and pleasure seekers.

Secondly, there is the problem of how the church will respond. There is the possibility of the church smothering the state. Perhaps not in the older medieval sense, when the church effectively func-tioned as a political lord. But perhaps in a more "sectarian" sense of withdrawal from political concerns, and viewing the church as separate from the *polis*. This could be accompanied by a form of "privatism," too, in which religion becomes increasingly a private

184

matter, of relatively little concern to matters political. And, of course, this will foster a desire for more communitarian forms of participation as a compensation. All of these are tendencies in the modern Western democracies.

In any case, it does seem important to recognize that we Christians are involved in a genuine "struggle for order" in a new and not fully understood way today. And we do have lessons to learn from our past history, with its "judgments," to use Pannenberg's term. Any "true" Christian order needs to learn from these "judgments" while trying to remain committed to real Christian substance. Interestingly, something that does emerge from this brief narrative is the "practical" significance of christocentric trinitarianism as the substance of Christian social order. The mission of Jesus as the revelation and invitation to participate in the trinitarian family keeps us Christians focused on the "true" nature of community as a differentiated unity in plurality, a oneness in diversity, in which mutuality should not smother uniqueness but enrich it. And yet uniqueness should not lead to exclusivism, but genuine participation. To the extent that we witness to this, we will not retreat into a sectarian ghetto, nor into a narcissistic privatism, nor into a collectivistic smothering of individuality. At the same time we recognize Jesus as the definitive embodiment of this new order in his own life. His own life becomes a prefigurement of the trinitarian family to which we are invited. The victory of his resurrection assures us of the truth of our calling, but his ministry and especially his death on the cross symbolize for us the "struggle" that is involved, the unfinished nature of our present participation in the kingdom.

Just how this can be effectively done is a matter of "practical" wisdom in the contemplative sense indicated above. I have tried to indicate some of the "theoretical" dimensions involved, especially that concerning our christocentric trinitarian "substance," but the theoretical elements need to be brought into creative relation with our new practical situation in a way which maximalizes the chances for the struggle for a Christian social order succeeding. But in the end there is doxology: petition, thanksgiving, praise, adoration. The "excess" of the Father's love for the Son in the Spirit, revealed in the "excessive" love of Jesus' life, cross, and resurrection, stirs us with an adoring wonderment even as it helps us move beyond the kind of manipulation of persons that is the loss of "true Christian order."

Postlude

As I conceive it, a "christologian" is someone who tries to participate in the *logos*, the "conversation," about the *Christos*, about Jesus
the Christ. And the christologian is a "theologian" as well: someone
trying to participate in the *logos*/conversation about God. But the
christologian concentrates upon Jesus the God-Man as the definitive
mediation of this divine conversation with humanity, the "Word" enabling our many "words" to take place. There are many conversations
going on in "reality," surely, and many other conversations either
waiting to happen or waiting to resume anew. But the christologian
is primarily interested in the trinitarian conversation opened up to
us in Jesus through the Spirit. Jesus, the christologian believes, is *as
human* the "word" of the "Word" of God. His invitation to dialogue
and intercommunication, which simply constitutes his humanity, is
the expression of the Word being uttered in the trinitarian mystery,
the expression of the Great Dialogue that Father and Son are in the
Spirit.

As far as the christologian is concerned, this "christological" conversation is the primary conversation, the deepest reality of all, to
which she or he wants to be committed and dedicated. There are
many other "secondary conversations" going on, and in fact the christologian is convinced that the Mystery of the Trinity as conversation
revealed through Jesus helps us understand why humans long to dialogue and can do so. But the christologian knows that these many
other conversations in our modern and postmodern world, while
possessing their relative validity, must not be allowed to drown out
the centrality and primacy of the Christ-conversation. Witnessing to
this centrality and primacy becomes, in effect, the key service of the
christologian, as I am coming to understand it.[1]

But how can this be done? How can the theologian and christologian — and all Christians are called to be such in a living, realistic
sense — remain in touch with the "reality" of Jesus Christ? How can
we "insure" that we not "eclipse" this reality, but unveil it? "Insure"
is a bad word, for it gives the impression of a kind of magical recipe
waiting around somewhere that we can find and secure for ourselves.

But if the "clues" presented in this book are any indication, no such magical techniques exist. Conversation is not magic: it requires participation, commitment, faith, obedience, discipline, a willingness to correct and allow the truth the primacy, and so on.

We Christians do believe that we are "invited" into the primary conversation with Jesus the Word: the Spirit is the overflow of Father and Son to us (their bond and our bond to them), and through the Spirit Jesus happens and our participation with Jesus happens too. The Spirit means that the Father's dialogue with the Son is kept open, and that means it can be revealed in history to us in the Incarnation and that we can share in it. The Spirit invites and enables our participation in the Christ-conversation, and this should promote in us a "deep down" fundamental trust and "security" liberating us from the kind of *Angst* that is symptomatic of those who don't believe that the deepest nature of reality is the "dialogue."[2] But the Spirit's aid does not take away our freedom, our response, our ability to misuse our freedom. Alas, the Spirit does not magically liberate us from our sinful failure to engage in the great conversation. But the Spirit does prompt and lead us toward those commitments most calculated to help us resume the conversation anew.

The Spirit of Christ leads us to "reality," in other words. To the "reality" of Jesus the Christ. But again, not by magic, but by grace, a graceful enabling of our freedom. Such is the nature of dialogue, especially God's dialogue, as distinct from the "oration" of the sophist that demolishes freedom.[3] In this work, however, I've tried to push a little beyond vague generalities and explore how this participation in the Christ-conversation might actually occur. Let me rehearse the key aspects of the proposals put forth.

First of all, I've suggested that the "turn to spirituality" be our guiding thrust. For some, right off this wouldn't seem to be a very promising way to remain in touch with reality, however conceived. Reality is surely much more "solid" and reliable than something as vague and misty as the "spiritual" and the "mystical," or the "pious" as the Reformed might put it. Given this alleged vagueness, then, it's apparent why some would prefer to move down other paths. "Reason" in its critical use is preferable, say some, even some Christian theologians. But reason, I suggest, is only helpful to the extent that it stays close to the fullness of experience, promoting moments of luminosity and serving such luminosity. Detach reason from its experiential manifold (including its historical, practical, and narrative aspects) — fail to view it as a noetic moment of differentiation within the rich manifold of experience — and it becomes the kind of theological conceptualism and rationalism that gets lost in empty abstractions unrelated to or only slightly related to reality. On the ecclesial level, this kind of "detached conceptualism" often takes the form of doctrine-memorizing or simplistic appeals to doctrines, uprooted from their narrative-experiential matrix. The turn to spirituality in Christian theology is meant to be a turn to the fullness of Christian experience, to the rich manifold of the Christian experience. Reason and doctrine have their role as one of service to this manifold, as a way in which our faith-consciousness can achieve a certain measure of luminosity in a refined and church-enriched manner. But detach them from the manifold of experience, and they tend to "create" illusionary realities — what Voegelin calls "second realities."[4]

Thus, my tendency is not first toward the "rational" dimension of theology. To move to this too quickly, without the properly meditative safeguards of attempting to remain anchored in the richness of Christian experience, is dangerous. In ancient times this might be called a form of "gnosticism" in the sense that it tries to substitute *gnosis* for faith. "Gnostic christologies" tend to fashion Jesus in ways that are congenial to the reigning intellectual "schools," and not in ways that are congenial to the "miracle" of the Incarnation. The turn to spirituality, in its Christian form, reminds the theologian who is more prone to take up the causes of critical reason to view "truths, realities," as we saw Hügel's spiritual director advise him, "as *intensely luminous centres*, with a semi-illuminated outer margin, and then another and another, till all shades off into utter darkness."[5]

My own view is that Arius represents the "gnostic tendency" in the history of christology in something of a paradigmatic sense, and that is why it is so important for contemporary christologians to struggle with him and his "school" still today. The *Logos* of Jesus, he thought, could not be God in the "fullest" sense of that term — such "contradicted" the inherited "subordinationism" of the epoch: the "further" removed from the Divine Sphere one becomes, the "less divine" the "word/*logos*" emanating therefrom becomes. The "reasonable" view was to opt for subordinationism, not for the much more "unexpected" view that God is the God of the "dialogue," whose "Word" is truly God. To "hear" this Word, reason must be open to what the Word says, not simply to what it wants to hear. It must be anchored in the rich narrative manifold of faith experience.[6]

Instead of moving first to the "theoretical" (to "reason") as the critical safeguard by which to stay in touch with reality, others are inclined first toward some form of "action" as the appropriate strategy for today's theology and christology. A kind of partisanship of an active kind for and with causes understood to be in the best interests of the gospel is the way to keep our theology and christology "real." And surely this must be an essential component of any valid theology, as we sought to show in our last chapter on the relationship between contemplation and action. But again the thrust of this book is to argue that we shouldn't move too quickly into "action." That action can be "dumb," not thought through, blind, dead end-like. And hence the crucial distinction between "activity" and "practice" (between "activity" and "action"), meaning by this latter an appropriate kind of action that seems genuinely expressive of the gospel. Simplistic moves to "action" can mask an appreciation of the role of reflectivity in church and theology, a "failing" that is committed by "doing-oriented" types, in the academy, in the lay apostolates, and in the strata of the church's magisterium too.

Again, I suggested that the turn to Christian spirituality or Christian "living" can be of help here. For our faith-inspired, contemplative openness to the Word is the matrix, the ground, out of which both reason and action emerge, sublating both and keeping both in that fruitful tension that maximizes the benefits of both. The contemplative *indiferencia* helps us "distance" ourselves creatively from our activity, so that we can place it in the perspective of the Word and keep it attuned to the Word. Contemplation helps us transform activity into practice, mere doing into truly appropriate action. "Take care, then, how you hear," Jesus says in Luke (8:18). And a little later we hear Jesus say: "My mother and my brothers are those who *hear* the word of God and *act* on it" (8:21). It is not simply doing, nor simply hearing, but both in that rich unity we are naming the contemplative matrix that Jesus seems to have in mind.

What I am suggesting is that we meditatively — "piously," in the rich sense of Calvin — move into reason and action. The turn to Christian spirituality seems to offer us the best chance of keeping our reason "critical" and our activity "practical." The turn to spirituality, under scripture's guidance, is the turn to the fullness of Christian experience/narrative: a contemplative attunement to the Word as mysteriously but really disclosing the Divine Self to us in the unfolding narrative of our thought and action. This inevitably means a turn to the Christian experience of the Trinity, a discovery that the early church made, and a discovery that we must repeat if we are to "appropriate anew" the basic depths of the Christian experience and narrative. For the Word that is Jesus "points" us to a God/Father in uttermost personal communication with us as Word/Son, but a communication inviting and enabling us to participate as Spirit. But again, not as if "by magic." As we recall from this book's beginning, the turn to spirituality is the turn to a form of experience that has undergone the "test" of asceticism and discernment (recall that the word for "experience" and for "testing" derive from the same root in the Greek). It is the turn to an experience "shaped" into a narrative echoing the narrative of Jesus and the Trinity that is at issue here.

Sharing in the trinitarian conversation through the Word Jesus, in the Spirit, is a discipline of faithful attunement that can reach heroic depths and heights. The saints and mystic witnesses know this and attest to it, and whoever would try to keep her or his theology as closely linked to spirituality as possible, so that theology becomes a form of spirituality, will learn this lesson too. There are "stigmata" of the intellect that all who are committed to theology are called to undergo, if they will truly be in service to the definitive stigmatic, Jesus.

But what I would like to stress now is that christology lights up for us a special joy and happiness that we should sense. True, the Word that is Jesus is the revelation to us, through the Spirit, of an "excess" of love in God that inevitably makes all theology "eschatological," a sort of unending amazement on our part of the loving depths that God is. Quite properly, then, we should sense the inadequacy of what we have done so far, and we should be stimulated to think about the kind of "theology" that awaits us in a future life. If you will, a theology with a heavily doxological accent ought to have an eschatological cast to it, stimulating us to a longing for participation in a hoped-for future of praise and glory. But at the same time christology studies a God who has become Word for us in the Spirit. We aren't simply wandering around aimlessly in the dark. There is, at the bottom of it all, ultimate meaning and truth (the Word Jesus), and in the Spirit we can trust that we are both invited and enabled to participate in it.

That sense of trust in Jesus is what led Karl Barth to suggest that our participative "knowledge" of God "cannot take place except in joyfulness." For we "know" God because God gifts us with that "knowledge": "the subjectivity of our acknowledgement of His revelation means our elevation above ourselves." And it is this "elevating" that fills us with thanksgiving, a glad sense of humor, and joy. Note here how Barth links "knowledge" with "acknowledge": As we first acknowledge the gift of being elevated to God's revelation, we gain "knowledge." True knowing is a response to a gift, and so it is glad, joyful, or what Barth likes to call a "sober exuberance." When we say glad, we mean, says Barth, "the joy of the elevating" above the self, or the "exuberance of the movement" to God. "In this exuberance, which has nothing to do with conceit and presumption, in the exuberance of the worship of God in the heart and mouth of the sinful creature, human knowledge of God is an act of gratitude and therefore partakes of the veracity of the revelation of God."[7]

It is my hope that this book will offer a little "sober exuberance" to the church, the academy, and society as well.

Notes

Chapter 1:
Theology, Christology and Spirituality: Intersections

1. Sandra M. Schneiders, "Spirituality in the Academy," *Theological Studies* 50 (1989): 676–97. Something of the "ecumenical" nature of the academic interest in spirituality can be seen from the following: Cheslyn Jones, Geoffrey Wainwright, and Edward Yarnold, eds., *The Study of Spirituality* (New York: Oxford University Press, 1986); Frank C. Senn, ed., *Protestant Spiritual Traditions* (New York: Paulist Press, 1986); Louis Dupré and Don E. Saliers, eds., *Christian Spirituality: Post-Reformation and Modern*, World Spirituality, vol. 18 (New York: Crossroad, 1989).

2. Joseph A. Tetlow, "Spirituality: An American Sampler," *America* 153 (1985): 261–67, cited by Schneiders, ibid., 676 n. 1. On the "postmodern" phenomenon, and its range of interpretations (radically secular and radically Christian), see "Christianity and the Question of Postmodernity," *Communio* 17/2 (1990).

3. "Some Aspects of Christian Meditation," no. 1, *Origins* 19 (1989): 492; cf. 492–98.

4. The precise source is *The Interior Castle*: 4, 3, 10. In Spanish one can sense the pun with the words, as indicated in the edition of the Classics of Western Spirituality, trans. Kieran Kavanaugh and Otilio Rodriguez (New York: Paulist Press, 1979), 83 (the citation) and 205 n. 13.

5. See "Some Aspects of Christian Meditation," nos. 8–10, 494. Since the reader may not be familiar with Messalianism, about which it seems difficult to obtain information, here is what the Vatican text says about its adherents: "These false fourth-century charismatics identified the grace of the Holy Spirit with the psychological experience of his presence in the soul." And experiences of affliction or desolation "are not necessarily a sign that the Spirit has abandoned a soul" (no. 9, 494).

6. Bernard is hardly a good example, even to a fictional rationalist!

7. Baron Friedrich von Hügel, *The Mystical Element of Religion as Studied in Saint Catherine of Genoa and Her Friends*, 2d ed., vol. 1 (London: J. M. Dent & Sons, 1923; London: James Clarke & Co., 1961), 7. Of course, the Baron is trying to make the case for the legitimacy of the "mystical" element to the "rationalist."

8. *The Mystical Element*, vol. 2, 340; cf. 290–91.

9. Evelyn Underhill, *Mysticism: A Study in the Nature and Development of Man's Spiritual Consciousness* (New York: World Publishing, 1955), 453–54. An analogous interpretation of the mystics can be found in Henri Bergson, *The Two Sources of Morality and Religion*, trans. R. Ashley Audra and Cloudesley Brereton, with assistance from W. Horsfall Carter (Notre Dame: University of Notre Dame Press, 1977).

10. Although a certain amount of *abobamiento* may be the "necessary" price to be paid, under the contingent conditions of history, for the flowering of *arrobamiento*. And the verdict is still out on whether Underhill's historical thesis is correct, for it may well be that the centuries she mentions were great flowerings, even if some derailments occurred.

11. See Schneiders, "Spirituality in the Academy," for the history and meanings of "spirituality," with extensive bibliography.

12. It goes without saying that one might employ equivalent terms for what many of us call a "mystic"; viz., the "sanctified" or "deified," or the great Christian "witnesses," etc.

13. See the suggestive writings of Harvey D. Egan, especially *Christian Mysticism: The Future of a Tradition* (New York: Pueblo Publishing Company, 1984), 1–29, 303–83; "The Mysticism of Everyday Life," *Studies in Formative Spirituality* 10 (1989): 7–26, where he offers a very suggestive overview of the various meanings of "mysticism," using Karl Rahner as his conversation partner; and his *Ignatius Loyola the Mystic*, The Way of the Christian Mystics 5 (Wilmington, DE: Michael Glazier, 1987), which is especially helpful on the trinitarian dimensions of Loyola's mysticism, as well as on extraordinary mystical phenomena, both in general and in Loyola in particular.

14. Not all mystics would seem to provide us with examples of what I am calling "mysticisms of theology." But surely one would seem to have to be a mystic to be able to provide us with a mysticism of theology.

15. That is, because Christianity dominates a culture, one absorbs the Christian tradition much as one absorbs culture in general.

16. Karl Rahner, "Christian Living Formerly and Today," *Theological Investigations*, vol. 7, trans. David Bourke (New York: Herder and Herder/Crossroad, 1971), 15; see 3–24.

17. See Schneiders, "Spirituality in the Academy," for bibliographical references linking spirituality with the turn to "experience." Particularly helpful here is Ewert H. Cousins, "Spirituality: A Resource for Theology," *Catholic Theological Society of America Proceedings* 35 (1980): 124–37. A rather recent example of this attempt to link up with the fuller texture of Christian experience chiefly through the metaphor of the "heart" is Annice Callahan, ed., *Spiritualities of the Heart: Approaches to Personal Wholeness in Christian Tradition* (New York: Paulist Press, 1990).

18. Very helpful here is Nicholas Lash, *Easter in Ordinary: Reflections on Human Experience and the Knowledge of God* (Charlottesville: University Press of Virginia, 1986). We might say with Eric Voegelin, if we properly understand it, that we aim to be "empirical — in the pregnant sense" when

we turn to Christian experience in theology: cf. his "Consciousness and Order: 'Foreword' to *Anamnesis* (1966)," *Logos* 4 (1983): 18.

19. For some helpful insights into the use of the term in the Christian tradition see Hans Urs von Balthasar, "Experience God?," *New Elucidations*, trans. Mary Theresilde Skerry (San Francisco: Ignatius Press, 1986), 20–45.

20. A good entry into the complex world of narrative theory is Stanley Hauerwas and L. Gregory Jones, eds., *Why Narrative? Readings in Narrative Theology* (Grand Rapids: William B. Eerdmans, 1989). Robert A. Krieg, *Story-Shaped Christology: The Role of Narratives in Identifying Jesus Christ*, Theological Inquiries (New York: Paulist Press, 1988), thoughtfully extends the discussion of narratives into the terrain of christology.

21. The bishops' address to the 1894 General Conference of the Methodist Episcopal Church South, as cited in Senn, *Protestant Spiritual Traditions*, 272 n. 99.

22. See my *Fire and Light: The Saints and Theology* (New York: Paulist Press, 1987), 80–82, 122–25, for some further observations on poem and commentary in John of the Cross, with bibliography, as well as *The Poems of St. John of the Cross*, trans. John Frederick Nims (Chicago: University of Chicago Press, 1979), 123–51, and *The Poems of Saint John of the Cross*, trans. Willis Barnstone (Bloomington: Indiana University Press, 1968), 18–36.

23. Hans-Georg Gadamer, *Truth and Method*, 2d ed., trans. rev. Joel Weinsheimer and Donald G. Marshall (New York: Crossroad, 1989), 355.

24. "Christian experience" seems to embrace something of a combination between the "uniquely Christian" and the more "general" aspects of human experience (understood as below). Jesus, for example, is unique, yet he shares much in common with other humans and with the heritage of his time. So, too, the ongoing Christian narrative and experience. The special (uniquely Christian) and the general remain in union, but the general is in the service of the special and under its primacy. Expressed otherwise, the analogy of "being" (general experience, viewed as not autonomous, but dynamically in relation to God) is, in a graced universe, in the service of, and grounded upon, the analogy of faith (special Christian experience).

25. A. Walde, *Lateinisches Etymologisches Wörterbuch*, rev. ed. J. B. Hofmann, vol. 2 (Heidelberg: Carl Winter, 1954), s.v. *"periculum,"* 288–89.

26. Here one might think of Gadamer's book *Truth and Method*, which can be seen as an attempt to transpose these ideas, well known in the area of Christian spirituality, into hermeneutical terms.

27. "Some Aspects of Christian Meditation," no. 31, 497.

28. *La vie et le royaume de Jésus dans les âmes chrétiennes* 6, 18 (*Oeuvres complètes*, vol. 1, intro. and notes by Joseph Dauphin and Charles Lebrun [Vannes or Paris: P. Lethielleux, 1905], 542), my translation.

29. John Macquarrie, "Prayer and Theological Reflection," in *The Study of Spirituality*, ed. Jones, Wainwright, and Yarnold, 587.

30. See William M. Thompson, ed., *Bérulle and the French School: Selected Writings*, Classics of Western Spirituality, trans. Lowell M. Glendon (New York: Paulist Press, 1989), 77–96, for the French School's influence

on Balthasar and Rahner, and our chapter 5 for its influence on Hügel. For the influence upon Thérèse, see Ida Friederike Görres, *The Hidden Face: A Study of St. Thérèse of Lisieux*, trans. Richard and Clara Winston (New York: Pantheon, 1959), 344–48. See, too, Pierre Descouvemont, *Sainte Thérèse de l'enfant Jésus et son prochain* (Paris: P. Lethielleux, 1962), who shows that Olier's life was read about and known: see especially 249. For the influence upon Wesley see Jean Orcibal, "The Theological Originality of John Wesley and Continental Spirituality," trans. R. J. A. Sharp, in *A History of the Methodist Church in Great Britain*, vol. 1, ed. Rupert Davies and Gordon Rupp (London: Epworth Press, 1965), 83–111.

31. See my "Christologies from Above and Below," *Chicago Studies* 26 (1987): 300–314, for an earlier study of this issue.

32. Some of this material, in an earlier version, was presented to the "Working Group on Roman Catholic Modernism" (using "modernism" in a very extended sense now, not only in its Vatican and "condemned" sense) at the 1989 American Academy of Religion convention.

33. As the reader will see, Hügel leaves the trinitarian dimensions of the divine "personality" somewhat sketchy, although suggestive. We have tried to supplement him.

34. See my "The 'Theological Attraction' of Saints and Mystics," *Bulletin de Saint-Sulpice* 16 (1990): 104–16, for an earlier study.

35. Hügel, *The Mystical Element of Religion*, vol. 1, ix.

36. Only three volumes of this remarkable eleven-volume work appeared in English: *A Literary History of Religious Thought in France from the Wars of Religion Down to Our Own Times*, 3 vols., trans. K. L. Montgomery (London: SPCK, 1928–36). With my good friend Raymond Deville, I wonder why the word *sentiment* was translated as "thought" in the title? Is this an indication of the very rationalism Bremond was opposing? A helpful introduction to Bremond, who deserves to be much more known in this country, is Henry Hogarth, *Henri Bremond: The Life and Work of a Devout Humanist* (London: SPCK, 1950). One will find here a good overview of the major writings, but see, for a more scholarly appraisal, Émile Goichot, "Du 'siècle classique' au 'siècle mystique': l'apport historique de l'abbé Bremond," *La vie spirituelle* 142 (1988): 433–50.

37. A number of people were kind enough to send me substantial comments on this piece in one or another of its varied versions, and I am most thankful for this. An earlier, published version appeared as "Jesus' Unsurpassable Uniqueness: A Theological Note," which included responses from Leonard Swidler and John Hick, and a final response from myself: *Horizons* 16 (1989): 101–30. Readers will note that I have emphasized the "unequalled"/"definitive" nature of Jesus as well as his unsurpassable nature, in the senses indicated, in my reworking of this study.

38. Jürgen Moltmann, *The Trinity and the Kingdom: The Doctrine of God*, trans. Margaret Kohl (San Francisco: Harper & Row, 1981), 152.

39. Karl Barth, *Church Dogmatics*, 4 vols., ed. G. W. Bromiley and T. F. Torrance, trans. G. W. Bromiley et al. (Edinburgh: T. & T. Clark, 1936–77), 2:1, 219; references to 1:1 will always be to the 1975 2d ed.

Chapter 2:
Conversation, Narrative, and Contemplation

1. Gadamer, *Truth and Method*, 2d ed., trans. rev. Joel Weinsheimer and Donald G. Marshall (New York: Crossroad, 1989), 369. For the reference to Paul Ricoeur, see his *The Conflict of Interpretations*, ed. Don Ihde (Evanston: Northwestern University Press, 1974).

2. Eric Voegelin, *Order and History*, vol. 3, *Plato and Aristotle* (Baton Rouge: Louisiana State University Press, 1957), 10–12. Voegelin points to Paul Friedländer, *Plato*, vol. 1, *An Introduction*, 2d ed., Bollingen Series 59, trans. Hans Meyerhoff (Princeton, NJ: Princeton University Press, 1969), 154–70, as an important source. For Voegelin, I recommend Eugene Webb, "In Memoriam: Politics and the Problem of a Philosophical Rhetoric in the Thought of Eric Voegelin," *Journal of Politics* 48 (1986): 260–73.

3. Hans-Georg Gadamer, *Reason in the Age of Science*, trans. Frederick G. Lawrence (Cambridge, MA: MIT Press, 1986), "Translator's Introduction," xix; see ix–xxxiii.

4. Eric Voegelin, *Order and History*, vol. 4, *The Ecumenic Age* (Baton Rouge: Louisiana State University Press, 1974), 186; see 178–92, on "The Dialogue of Mankind."

5. Gadamer, *Truth and Method*, 270.

6. Ibid., 304, 306. For the critical element in Gadamer: "...we are continually having to test all our prejudices" (306). Helpful on this issue of the critical in Gadamer is Richard J. Bernstein, *Beyond Objectivism and Relativism* (Philadelphia: University of Pennsylvania Press, 1983), 109–69.

7. This is by no means a fully adequate formulation of the thorny issue of scripture and tradition among the various churches. I am simply trying to restate the issue along Gadamerian-inspired lines. Could we consider scripture, in its oral phase, as tradition in the oral sense? Christian tradition that is authentic would always be "implicitly" scriptural and normed by scripture as the primal, unnormed witness to the primal, unnormed revelation of the triune God of Jesus, the former "reflecting" and safeguarding the latter. See our note 46 in this chapter. Here I would especially recommend Yves Congar, *The Meaning of Tradition*, Twentieth Century Encyclopedia of Catholicism 3, trans. A. N. Woodrow (New York: Hawthorn Books, 1964), his more ample *Tradition and Traditions: An Historical and a Theological Essay*, trans. Michael Naseby and Thomas Rainborough (New York: Macmillan, 1967), and Gerald O'Collins, *Fundamental Theology* (New York: Paulist Press, 1981), 192–224.

8. Gadamer, *Truth and Method*, 367.

9. Ibid.

10. Voegelin, *The Ecumenic Age*, 330; for his analysis of *doxa* in Plato, see *Plato and Aristotle*, 73–81. See Gadamer, *Truth and Method*, 362–79. Friedländer, *Plato*, 168, is helpful on the ascesis involved: "One of the basic principles of the Socratic conversation was to destroy in the pupil his belief that he had knowledge or to awaken him to the realization that he had none — not, by any means, in order to conclude with a skeptical position, but in order to stimulate a continuous mutual quest for the truth."

11. Gadamer, *Truth and Method*, 395, is referring to the written text when he argues that the focus is not the author's intention, but the subject matter. In a face to face conversation one can try to bring forth the relevant intentions into speech, but even here it is not every intention, but those which form the subject matter, which are relevant. In the case of the written text, we might say that the author's intentions, inasmuch as they find inscription in the text, form part of the subject matter. This is why Paul Ricoeur likes to speak of what the text "opens up in front of itself," rather than of an "intention...hidden behind the text": *Interpretation Theory: Discourse and the Surplus of Meaning* (Fort Worth: Texas Christian University Press, 1976), 94.

12. David Tracy, *Plurality and Ambiguity: Hermeneutics, Religion, Hope* (San Francisco: Harper & Row, 1987), 19, basing himself "broadly" on Aristotle's *Nichomachean Ethics*, books 8 and 9.

13. Gadamer, *Truth and Method*, 276-77.

14. Eric Voegelin, *Autobiographical Reflections*, ed. Ellis Sandoz (Baton Rouge: Louisiana State University Press, 1989), 95.

15. See David Tracy, *The Analogical Imagination: Christian Theology and the Culture of Pluralism* (New York: Crossroad, 1981), 115-24, as well as all of his *Plurality and Ambiguity*. For Paul Ricoeur, I recommend, for a first look, *Interpretation Theory: Discourse and the Surplus of Meaning* and *Hermeneutics and the Human Sciences*, ed. and trans. John B. Thompson (Cambridge: Cambridge University Press, 1981). See Stanley Hauerwas and L. Gregory Jones, eds., *Why Narrative? Readings in Narrative Theology* (Grand Rapids: William B. Eerdmans, 1989), passim, for the discussion about whether "explanation" or "description"/"displaying" is a better way to speak of the argumentative moment in theology.

16. If I might paraphrase and build on Eric Voegelin's principle that "a theory of human existence in society must operate within the medium of experiences which have differentiated historically." Thus he formulates his view that there must be a "correlation between theory and the maximal experiential differentiation" (*The New Science of Politics: An Introduction* [Chicago: University of Chicago Press, 1952], 79, 80).

17. Eric Voegelin, *Order and History*, vol. 1, *Israel and Revelation* (Baton Rouge: Louisiana State University Press, 1956), 1. Cf. Friedländer, *Plato*, vol. 1, 41-43; Gadamer, *Truth and Method*, 295; Voegelin, *The Ecumenic Age*, 183-92 (for his notion of the "in-between," basing himself on Plato's symbolism of the *"metaxy"* in the *Philebus* 16c-17a and the *Symposium* 202a-203a). Most recently, William C. Placher has emphasized this feature of the conversation in his *Unapologetic Theology: A Christian Voice in a Pluralistic Conversation* (Louisville: Westminster/John Knox Press, 1989). See Augustine's *Confessions* 11, 20, for the notion of a present of past and future, made so much of by Paul Ricoeur in his *Time and Narrative*, 3 vols., trans. Kathleen McLaughlin (Blamey) and David Pellauer (Chicago: University of Chicago Press, 1984-88).

18. Voegelin, *Autobiographical Reflections*, 73; he continues: "The term *luminosity of consciousness*, which I am increasingly using, tries to stress this

In-Between character of the experience as against the immanentizing language of a human consciousness, which, as a subject, is opposed to an object of experience." And, to ward off accusations of subjectivism: this is "the luminosity not of a subjective consciousness but of the reality that enters into the experience from both sides" (73–74).

19. For Plato, see Voegelin, *The Ecumenic Age*, 300ff., 312, 315, 321ff., and Friedländer, *Plato*, 221–29 (on Heidegger's views in comparison with Plato); for Tracy, see *Plurality and Ambiguity*, 28ff. Also see Martin Heidegger, "On the Essence of Truth," trans. R. F. C. Hull and Alan Crick, in *Existence and Being* (Chicago: Henry Regnery, Gateway Edition, 1970), 292–324.

20. Voegelin is able to subsume the phenomenon of "objectifying" language (knowledge viewed as the intending of objects) within the larger phenomenon of human experience-consciousness. The concrete embodiment of consciousness (its somatic basis) causes us to imagine ourselves as over-against other embodied "objects." "In relation to this concretely embodied consciousness, reality assumes the position of an object intended. Moreover, by its position as an object intended by a consciousness that is bodily located, reality itself acquires a metaphorical touch of external thingness." But in a more comprehensive sense, "reality is not an object of consciousness but the something in which consciousness occurs as an event of participation between partners in the community of being." See his *Order and History*, vol. 5, *In Search of Order* (Baton Rouge: Louisiana State University Press, 1987), passim, especially 15, from which these citations come, for his final treatment of a philosophy of experience, consciousness, and symbolization. One can readily see how the language of myth tends to fall back upon the "objectifying" mode, and modern science perhaps has a tendency to move in this direction too. In the pregnant sense of "experience," I might add, one could argue that the term itself embraces and implies its linguistic, imaginative, consciousness-grounded dimensions, and whatever else makes up the human. But Voegelin, and I follow him here, tends to add those adjectives to "experience" as qualifiers, to bring out how human reality embraces these multiple dimensions.

21. Placher is helpful on foundationalism and relativism throughout his *Unapologetic Theology;* see also Francis Schüssler Fiorenza, *Foundational Theology: Jesus and the Church* (New York: Crossroad, 1984), 285–89. There is a curious lack of interest in the philosophy of consciousness (to which Voegelin always adds symbolization), which may have something to do with foundationalism and relativism. The thingifying, sense model approach to reality underlying both postures would not be congenial to a philosophy of consciousness, the latter perhaps being viewed as too "subjective" and "interior." The relative lack of interest in consciousness in philosophy and theology is unfortunate, for it means that interest in it migrates to various esoteric schools in psychology that often are quite unable to negotiate the difficult philosophical issues involved. And then consciousness becomes even more subjectivistic. See Eugene Webb, *Philosophers of Consciousness* (Seattle: University of Washington Press, 1988), for a helpful introduction to the issue in Polanyi, Lonergan, Voegelin, Ricoeur, Girard, and Kierkegaard. The current theological interest in imagination is, in part, a way back to

the theme of consciousness. Voegelin, I think, has always stressed the role of symbolization in consciousness (avoiding a "pure consciousness" theory), and in his *In Search of Order* has added a study of the role of imagination in consciousness (especially 37–39). This rooting of imagination in consciousness-symbolization enables Voegelin to develop a theory of how consciousness "governs" imagination. Thus, imagination can derail, as it clearly does in extreme gnostic texts, for example, and Voegelin is able to suggest that this derailment comes from inadequacies of consciousness and its differentiation. Some such "critical" theory of imagination seems called for. See Edward L. Murray, *Imaginative Thinking and Human Existence* (Pittsburgh: Duquesne University Press, 1986), for a helpful existential-phenomenological approach, rooting imagination in consciousness likewise. Philip S. Keane, *Christian Ethics and Imagination: A Theological Inquiry* (New York: Paulist Press, 1984), and Garrett Green, *Imagining God: Theology and the Religious Imagination* (San Francisco: Harper & Row, 1989), are very helpful here as well, and all these authors helpfully relate imagination to narrative and/or story.

22. See Tracy, *The Analogical Imagination*, especially 293–94 n. 57; John W. Van den Hengel, *The Home of Meaning: The Hermeneutics of the Subject of Paul Ricoeur* (Washington, DC: University Press of America, 1982); Eugene Webb, *Eric Voegelin: Philosopher of History* (Seattle: University of Washington Press, 1981), 52–88; Balthasar, *Theo-Drama: Theological Dramatic Theory*, trans. Graham Harrison, 2 vols. thus far in English (San Francisco: Ignatius Press, 1988–); David Ford, *Barth and God's Story: Biblical Narrative and the Theological Method of Karl Barth in the 'Church Dogmatics,'* Studies in the Intercultural History of Christianity, 27 (Frankfurt am Main: Verlag Peter Lang, 1985); Robert A. Krieg, "The Theologian as Narrator: A Study of Karl Barth on the Divine Perfections" (Ph.D. diss., University of Notre Dame, 1976); Karl Rahner, "Priest and Poet" and " 'Behold This Heart!': Preliminaries to a Theology of Devotion to the Sacred Heart," *Theological Investigations*, vol. 3, trans. Karl-H. and Boniface Kruger (Baltimore: Helicon/New York: Crossroad, 1967), 294–330. For one of my own attempts at the rehabilitation of the "originary," see my *Fire and Light*, 80–82, 122–25. John of the Cross sets a fine standard for the theologian in his to-and-fro movement between poem and commentary, with the former accorded the primacy; see, besides chapter 1, n. 22, this "close" study: Colin P. Thompson, *The Poet and the Mystic: A Study of the Cantico Espiritual of San Juan de la Cruz* (Oxford: Oxford University Press, 1977), especially 60–145.

23. Eric Voegelin, *In Search of Order*, 26, 24.

24. Stanley Hauerwas and David Burrell, "From System to Story: An Alternative Pattern for Rationality in Ethics," in Hauerwas and Jones, *Why Narrative?*, 177–78.

25. Paul Ricoeur, *Time and Narrative*, has been extraordinarily helpful to me. Also helpful here was Stephen D. Moore, *Literary Criticism and the Gospels: The Theoretical Challenge* (New Haven: Yale University Press, 1989), who has aided me with my summary of the rhetorical elements involved in narrative. But his work extends far beyond that. Hans Frei, *The*

Eclipse of Biblical Narrative: A Study in Eighteenth and Nineteenth Century Hermeneutics (New Haven: Yale University Press, 1974), has been most challenging, along with Ronald F. Thiemann, *Revelation and Theology: The Gospel as Narrated Promise* (Notre Dame: University of Notre Dame Press, 1985), George A. Lindbeck, *The Nature of Doctrine: Religion and Theology in a Postliberal Age* (Philadelphia: Westminster Press, 1984), and David Tracy, "Lindbeck's New Program for Theology: A Reflection," *The Thomist* 49 (1985): 460–72.

26. See Alasdair MacIntyre, *After Virtue: A Study in Moral Theory* (Notre Dame: University of Notre Dame Press, 1981), especially 196–97, for some provocative comments on conversation's relation to narrative. See also Tullio Maranhao, ed., *The Interpretation of Dialogue* (Chicago: University of Chicago Press, 1990).

27. "Well, thinking and discourse are the same thing, except that what we call thinking is, precisely, the inward dialogue carried on by the mind with itself without spoken word," says the Stranger to Theaetetus in *Sophist* 263e (Edith Hamilton and Huntington Cairns, eds., *The Collected Dialogues of Plato*, Bollingen Series 71 [Princeton: Princeton University Press, 1982], 1011).

28. Other candidates are, surely, Ricoeur's appeal to the insights coming from "methods of explanation" that can serve at least a subordinate role; Tracy's use of the same, but in his own special way (in *Plurality and Ambiguity* he appeals to "recognition" too: 22); etc. Again, the dialogue's "art of strengthening" is what we're living out when we make these appeals to various criteria or warrants. For my use of Voegelin, see his *In Search of Order*, especially 40ff., for his retrieval of anamnesis, and his tracing it through Hegel, Hesiod, and Plato. An earlier, very helpful study by him of anamnesis is his *Vorwort* to the German edition of his *Anamnesis: Zur Theorie der Geschichte und Politik* (Munich: R. Piper & Co., 1966), translated into English by Voegelin himself: "Consciousness and Order: 'Foreword' to *Anamnesis* (1966)." For the theme of recognition in Gadamer, *Truth and Method*, see 376. Also see Diana Culbertson, *The Poetics of Revelation: Recognition and the Narrative Tradition*, Studies in American Biblical Hermeneutics 4 (Macon, GA: Mercer University Press, 1989).

29. Yves M.-J. Congar tells us that Plato was the first to use the word *theologia* (*A History of Theology*, trans. and ed. Hunter Guthrie [Garden City, NY: Doubleday & Co., 1968], 26). Congar refers to the *Republic* 379a, and Paul Shorey's translation of this text brings out the dialogue nature of theology perfectly: "right speech about the gods" (Hamilton and Cairns, *The Collected Dialogues of Plato*, 625).

30. Voegelin, *The Ecumenic Age*, 192; see also, for the other citations, 186. Gadamer tends to leave the religious dimension rather "dim," but see his "Articulating Transcendence," in Fred Lawrence, ed., *The Beginning and the Beyond: Papers from the Gadamer and Voegelin Conferences*, Supplementary Issue of *Lonergan Workshop*, vol. 4 (Chico, CA: Scholars Press, 1984), 1–9, 9–12 (discussion).

31. Voegelin, *The Ecumenic Age*, 186. The notion of "belonging" in

Gadamer is a way of speaking about the universal supporting environment of the conversation of history; see s.v. in the index, *Truth and Method*, 581.

32. Dumitru Staniloae, *Theology and the Church*, trans. Robert Barringer (Crestwood, NY: St. Vladimir's Seminary Press, 1980), 93; see the entire essay, "The Holy Trinity: Structure of Supreme Love," 73–108. See any edition of the following: Augustine, *The Trinity* 8/10; Richard of St. Victor, *The Trinity* 3. Here is Walter Kasper's helpful formulation: "The divine persons are not only in dialogue, they *are* dialogue. The Father is a pure self-enunciation and address to the Son as his Word; the Son is a pure hearing and heeding of the Father and therefore pure fulfillment of his mission; the Holy Spirit is pure reception, pure gift" (*The God of Jesus Christ*, trans. Matthew J. O'Connell [New York: Crossroad, 1986], 290). I am not being trendy in using the symbolism of "Mother" for God; it is a traditional symbol, with a pedigree extending into the scriptures themselves. On this, see the helpful essays assembled in Joann Wolski Conn, ed., *Women's Spirituality: Resources for Christian Development* (New York: Paulist Press, 1986). Surely the rehabilitation of dialogue in contemporary theology owes much to women's critical reflections.

Clearly this area of trinitarian theology is most complex, particularly the issues of (1) the nature of God's oneness, given the triune relations, and (2) the respective emphases of Eastern and Western theology. The notion of "interpersonal Subjectivity" may be helpful with respect to the first. As regards the second, Kasper, *The God of Jesus Christ*, passim, is helpful, indicating that this is a matter of emphases, and that strains of each tradition show up in both East and West. But there are shades of accent that seem important, and in a fuller study these would need to be pursued. For example, the *Filioque* tends to bring out how the Spirit is "normed" by the Son, and so Spirit-inspired creativity is not a wild and "unformed" reality, but a creativity leading to the resurrection through the cross. The stress on "form" and incarnational mediation, highlighted by the *Filioque*, helps us understand the western stress on church structures, authority, ministry. The stress on the Spirit as equal to the Son, emphasized by the East, perhaps intensifies the dimension of collegiality, communion, unique charisms, and creative openness. Suggestive in this regard, building on Barth, Rahner, and Balthasar, is John J. O'Donnell, *The Mystery of the Trinity* (New York: Paulist Press, 1989), especially 75–99. Apply this to "dialogue/conversation": the *Filioque* might stress how conversation needs warrants, looks to a norming truth, and demands the *via crucis* of our pet theories; the pneumatology dimension perhaps stresses plurality, openness, change, communion, etc. The first is more *erklären* oriented; the latter, *verstehen*-oriented.

33. The authors referred to throughout these pages have influenced these thoughts; readers might fruitfully consult Amos N. Wilder, *Early Christian Rhetoric: The Language of the Gospel* (Cambridge: Harvard University Press, 1971), and Robert Alter and Frank Kermode, eds., *The Literary Guide to the Bible* (Cambridge: Harvard University Press, 1987).

34. Jean-Jacques Olier, *Catéchisme chrétien pour la vie intérieure et la Journée chrétienne*, ed. François Amiot (Paris: Le Rameau, 1954), 206, 208

(from the *Journée*). The exact text about Jesus' conversation with the disciples, which I only paraphrased: "I adore the conversation of Jesus Christ Our Lord with his disciples, which he filled with himself, as he had beforehand been filled with the abundance of his Father in conversation with himself."

35. Voegelin, *The Ecumenic Age*, 56.

36. *Dictionnaire de spiritualité* 10 and 2/2, s.vv. "Meditation" and "Contemplation," ed. M. Viller (Paris: Beauchesne, 1980 and 1953), cols. 906–34 at 907 and 1643–2193 at 1717–18, and Johannes B. Bauer, "Meditation," *Sacramentum Verbi: An Encyclopedia of Biblical Theology*, vol. 2, ed. Johannes B. Bauer (New York: Herder & Herder, 1979), 573.

37. Voegelin, *Israel and Revelation*, 1. The relation between God and humans in which God holds the primacy is not best viewed as an "Object-subject" relation; or if we do, we must take steps to avoid thingifying it. Speaking of God's primacy is equivalent to what some might call accenting and according the primacy to the "objective" pole of revelation, however.

38. John Macquarrie, "Prayer and Theological Reflection," in Jones, Wainwright, and Arnold, *The Study of Spirituality*, 586.

39. We never bypass the mediation of Jesus Christ in our relationship with God. However, its mode varies, from the apophatic ("transanalytic") to the kataphatic (more "thematic"). Here I clearly side with St. Teresa of Avila, who knows that contemplatives at times move into wordless/imageless prayer, but that this prayer is not a bypassing of Jesus but a non-discursive mode of his (risen) presence: "But such a person walks continually in an admirable way with Christ, our Lord, in whom the divine and the human are joined and who is always that person's companion" (*The Interior Castle* 6:7:9, in *The Collected Works of St. Teresa of Avila*, 3 vols., trans. Otilio Rodriguez and Kieran Kavanaugh [Washington, DC: Institute of Carmelite Studies, 1976–85], vol. 2, 401). Drawing upon the French School (see below), we can refer to Mother Madeleine de Saint-Joseph's "Letter 49": "Now I know that everyone cannot apply themselves to [Jesus'] mysteries in a discursive way; I am not speaking about this. . . . I am speaking of an adherence of will, either simple or strong, depending upon one's facility, God's gift, and the spirit's freedom; I am speaking of an adherence of the whole self to the Son of God . . . and of a permanent and continual homage . . ." (*Lettres spirituelles de Madeleine de Saint-Joseph*, ed. Pierre Serouet [Paris: Desclée de Brouwer, 1965], 58). See Karl Rahner, "The Eternal Significance of the Humanity of Jesus for Our Relationship with God," *Theological Investigations*, vol. 3, 35–46.

40. Hügel, *The Mystical Element*, vol. 2, 338.

41. See Eric Voegelin, "The Meditative Origin of the Philosophical Knowledge of Order," in Lawrence, *The Beginning and the Beyond*, 43–51.

42. This is what leads Hans Urs von Balthasar to see dialogue as one, albeit critical, element in the larger divine-human relationship, which he likes to think of in terms of the analogy of "drama": see his *Theo-Drama: Theological Dramatic Theory*, vol. 1, *Prolegomena*, 34–37. I, too, by showing how dialogue relates to narrative and the larger human drama, as well as to con-

templation, have tried to do the same. Tracy, *Plurality and Ambiguity*, 66–81, is very helpful on the breakdown of conversation, at least from our human side.

43. See Philip J. Rosato, *The Spirit as Lord: The Pneumatology of Karl Barth* (Edinburgh: T. & T. Clark, 1981), for very suggestive (if not always persuasive, for me personally) considerations along these lines. I have found Barth very helpful for both my own studies of the Trinity, and for narrative considerations. See his *Church Dogmatics*, 1:1 and 1:2; cf. 4:2, 43–44, on the theme of why it belongs only to the Logos to become incarnate. Cf. Yves Congar, *I Believe in the Holy Spirit*, vol. 2, *"He Is Lord and Giver of Life,"* trans. David Smith (New York: Seabury Press, 1983), 79–99, for important observations on the unity of action and diversity of persons in the Trinity. For the debate over whether and how (including what categories to use) it belongs only to the Logos to become incarnate, see Karl Rahner, *The Trinity*, trans. Joseph Donceel (New York: Herder and Herder, 1970), especially 11ff., 24ff., 73ff., and 103ff. Of course, all three persons are active in the Incarnation, but in a manner proper and appropriate to each.

44. For further insight into the notion of the "formative," I recommend Adrian van Kaam, *Formative Spirituality*, 4 vols. to date (New York: Crossroad, 1983–87).

45. A word I gladly borrow from Gadamer, *Truth and Method*, 576. Avery Dulles, *Models of Revelation* (Garden City, NY: Doubleday & Co., 1983), is very helpful on the role of the church community (211–27), as well as on symbol (language) and revelation in general.

46. I by no means intend to "reduce" the normativity of the scriptures simply to these hermeneutical observations. Clearly their theologically normative role stems from their being the inspired witness to Jesus Christ. But there seems to be a fit between hermeneutics and theology here, not unlike the "fit" (or "fusion") between form and content.

47. Congar, *Tradition and Traditions*, 446; see 435–50, and his *The Meaning of Tradition*, 133. The dogmatic, and not simply chronological, nature of the category of the *patres* and *matres* interestingly leaves open the question as to whether we should not "make room" for women writers (and others) of a period later than that normally given to the fathers. Perhaps the "full" and mutually equal role of women "ecclesiastical mothers" is one of those "fundamental traits" belonging to the mission of the *patres/matres*. Helpful also is Joseph Cardinal Ratzinger, *Principles of Catholic Theology: Building Stones for a Fundamental Theology*, trans. Mary Frances McCarthy (San Francisco: Ignatius Press, 1987), 133–52.

48. Congar, *Tradition and Traditions*, 444–45, shows the link between doctrine, canons, and liturgy.

49. See, for example, Geoffrey Wainwright, *Doxology: The Praise of God in Worship, Doctrine, and Life* (New York: Oxford University Press, 1980), and George S. Worgul, Jr., "Ritual as the Interpreter of Tradition," *Louvain Studies* 10 (1984): 141–50.

50. Plato's negative use of the term as mere "opinions" ungrounded in experience points to the negative counterfeit of legitimate "doxa."

51. Here one could fruitfully consult the work of Hans Urs von Balthasar on the divine glory: *The Glory of the Lord: A Theological Aesthetics*, vols. 1–7, ed. Joseph Fessio and John Riches (San Francisco: Ignatius Press, 1982–91). Geoffrey Wainwright broke new ground as he developed a systematics rooted in liturgical experience: see his *Doxology*. Daniel W. Hardy and David F. Ford developed an overview of the epistemological and thematic dimensions of theology in the light of doxology in their *Praising and Knowing God* (Philadelphia: Westminster, 1985), and building on Hardy and Ford, but adding their own nuances, Catherine Mowry LaCugna and Kilian McDonnell sketch out a doxological approach to trinitarian theology in their "Returning from 'The Far Country': Theses for a Contemporary Trinitarian Theology," *Scottish Journal of Theology* 41 (1988): 191–215. See, from a Catholic side, Frans Jozef van Beeck, *God Encountered: A Contemporary Catholic Systematic Theology*, vol. 1 (San Francisco: Harper & Row, 1989). The doxological dimension of theological hermeneutics is nicely developed, from an Eastern Orthodox perspective, in John Breck, *The Power of the Word in the Worshiping Church* (Crestwood, NY: St. Vladimir's Seminary Press, 1986).

Chapter 3: The Christologian and "Participating" in Jesus' Mysteries

1. Here I am inspired by the cardinal's attempt to relink "authority, holiness and light: three beautiful jewels in the priestly crown," albeit not limiting these "jewels" to the presbyterate in exactly the same was he does. For the source see his *"Pièce 891: A Letter on the Priesthood,"* in Thompson, *Bérulle and the French School*, 184. I will refer to this work — an extensive anthology, albeit incomplete — for my selections from the French School whenever possible, since it is the only major source available in English. When necessary, I will refer to the French editions I will need to work from (or translate).

2. "Science of the saints" is from Bérulle's *Mémorial* 11 (*Oeuvres complètes*, vol. 1, ed. François Bourgoing [Montsoult Seine-et-Oise: Maison d'Institution de l'Oratoire, 1960], 624–25).

3. *Discourse on the State and Grandeurs of Jesus* (hereafter referred to as *Grandeurs*) 5, 9 and 2, 2, 138, 115. This reference means, for example, "Discourse 5, Section 9" and "Discourse 2, Section 2," respectively, in the English translation by Glendon, noted above.

4. *Grandeurs* 6, 4, 140; 1, 6, 113; cf. 1, 6, 111; 8, 11, 147.

5. *Oeuvres de piété*, 77, 1 (*Les oeuvres de l'eminentissime et reverendissime Pierre cardinal de Bérulle*, ed. J.-P. Migne [Paris: Ateliers catholiques, 1856]), cols. 1052–53. The collection in Migne of the *Oeuvres de piété* is larger than that found in the Montsoult edition, hence my choice of citation, although it is best to check Migne against Montsoult, which is the *editio princeps*. Note that the numbering in the two editions doesn't always correspond.

6. For the reference to Bérulle, see *Oeuvres de piété* 17, col. 940; for Olier,

Mémoires 4:216–17, as translated by Lowell M. Glendon, "Jean-Jacques Olier's View of the Spiritual Potential of Human Nature: A Presentation and an Evaluation" (Ph.D. diss., Fordham University, 1983), 128. The *Mémoires*, covering 1642–52, span over three thousand pages.

7. "Q. What are the principal mysteries in which the soul can participate? A. It ought to participate in all, but principally in six, which are: the Incarnation, Crucifixion, Death, Burial, Resurrection, and Ascension of our Lord" (J.J. Olier, *Catechism of an Interior Life*, trans. M. Edward Knight [Baltimore: John Murphy & Co., 1855], 120).

8. *Grandeurs* 2, 1, 114–15. See 97–101, as well as Émile Bertaud, "Élévations spirituelles," *Dictionnaire de spiritualité* 4/1 (1960), cols. 553–58.

9. *Introduction to the Christian Life and Virtues*, chapter 4, in Thompson, *Bérulle and the French School*, 228–30 (unless otherwise noted, all subsequent references are to this); for *fond*, see the French edition, *Introduction à la vie et aux vertus chrétiennes*, ed. François Amiot (Paris: Le Rameau, 1954), 23.

10. *Grandeurs* 1, 2, 109–10. See Olier, *Catéchisme chrétien pour la vie intérieure et la Journée chrétienne*, 156 (from the *Journée*): "What an adorable mystery of a God adored and a God adoring in his Son!... what must be our joy is to know that in Jesus Christ God finally has the adorer he wishes...." Fernando Guillén Preckler, in his various studies, has been especially helpful on the centrality of adoration and service in Bérulle: *"État" chez le cardinal de Bérulle: théologie et spiritualité des "états" bérulliens*, Analecta Gregoriana 197 (Rome: Gregorian University, 1974) and *Bérulle aujourd'hui 1575–1975: pour une spiritualité de l'humanité du Christ*, Le point théologique 25 (Paris: Beauchesne, 1978).

11. *Grandeurs* 2, 13, 126.

12. Ibid., 11, 6, 153–54; *Oeuvres de piété* 87, cols. 1071–72. See Guillén Preckler, *"État" chez le cardinal de Bérulle*, 70–71, 129, for some of the sources in theology for the cardinal's thought. Suarez speaks of Jesus the man rendering a perfect adoration to the Father in *In IIIam part.*, q. 21, a. 4, disp. 45 (*Opera omnia*, ed. Vives [Paris: 1856f.], 18:435–36). Also see n. 75 in this chapter. Balthasar and his mystic companion Adrienne von Speyr are rather like the French School in seeking analogies between the Incarnation's mysteries and the Trinity. See Hans Urs von Balthasar, *Mysterium Paschale: The Mystery of Easter*, trans. Aidan Nichols (Edinburgh: T. & T. Clark, 1990), where Balthasar manifests a fair knowledge of the French School, although he misses its trinitarian exemplarism, and John Saward, *The Mysteries of March: Hans Urs von Balthasar on the Incarnation and Easter* (Washington, DC: Catholic University of America Press, 1990). As is well known, Karl Barth also commonly seeks out the analogies between Trinity and Incarnation throughout the *Church Dogmatics;* see John Thompson, *Christ in Perspective: Christological Perspectives in the Theology of Karl Barth* (Grand Rapids: William B. Eerdmans, 1978).

13. *Grandeurs* 5, 10 (*Oeuvres complètes*, 141). "Service" is Guillén Preckler's suggested contemporary rendering of Bérulle's "servitude": *Bérulle aujourd'hui*, 64–65 n. 39.

14. See Thompson, *Bérulle and the French School*, 14–16. It was partly a

matter of confusing this "vow" with another canonical vow, instead of seeing it as a reaffirmation of our baptismal commitment. But political animosities against the cardinal seem involved as well.

15. *Grandeurs* 2, 10, 122–24; cf. 36ff.

16. Ibid., 2, 10, 124–26, 187 n. 11. Bérulle is possibly referring to the *Timaeus* 90b.

17. *Catechism of an Interior Life*, 125. The English reader will find an extensive introduction to Condren in Bremond, *A Literary History of Religious Thought in France*, vol. 3, *The Triumph of Mysticism*, 243–358. The recent study of Raymond Deville, *L'école française de spiritualité*, Bibliothèque d'histoire du christianisme 11 (Paris: Desclée, 1987), 49–62, will bring the reader up to date on Condrennian scholarship. For the references to Paul's writings in Bérulle, see, for example, *Grandeurs* 2, 10, 123.

18. "Letter 144," in Thompson, *Bérulle and the French School*, 200, 202 (subsequent references to Madeleine will be to this edition, unless otherwise noted). The French School is particularly sensitive to deception in the spiritual life, perhaps especially there, regions which are supposedly "pure." M. Olier, for example: "Our pride is so subtle that when we close one door to it, it opens another one for itself." We no sooner renounce "worldly" greatness (in the prideful sense) than we seek "to be great and outstanding in grace." Perhaps must subtly: "... we can even love littleness on earth through proud desire, hoping, by this means, for greatness in paradise" (*Introduction to the Christian Life and Virtues*, 241). St. John Eudes, Bérulle's disciple, also counsels "perfect detachment," which is learning "to be detached even from God in a certain fashion," at least in the sense of overcoming our (inordinate) attachments to "the delights and consolations that ordinarily accompany the grace and love of God; ... from our desires for greater perfection," etc. (*The Life and Kingdom of Jesus in Christian Souls* 2, 10, in Thompson, *Bérulle and the French School*, 310).

19. *Grandeurs* 3, 8, 127–28. It is in this text (129) that Bérulle mentions his celebrated "two Trinities": that of "subsistence in a unity of essence" (i.e., Father, Son, and Spirit), and that of "essence in a unity of subsistence" (i.e., Jesus' body, soul, and divinity in the unity of his divine "person/hypostasis"). Bérulle loved imaginatively to explore what he thought must be correspondences between the trinitarian Mystery and its revelation in history in the Incarnation.

20. Jean Dagens, ed., *Correspondance du Bérulle*, 3 (Paris: Desclée de Brouwer, 1939), 836, 561; *Collationes* 1614, 199 (as cited by Guillén Preckler, *"État" chez le cardinal de Bérulle*, 167 n. 79); *Grandeurs* 8, 10, 144. See the compact text in Olier's *Journée*, 154: "Our Lord living on earth was simultaneously comprehensor and voyager. He was comprehensor in a portion of himself, and as Son he enjoyed the glory of God; and in the other portion he experienced privation, and lived as the faithful servant of his Father." The classic text in Aquinas is *Summa theologiae* 3, 15, 10.

21. *Grandeurs* 8, 11, 146–47. Throughout the various meditations of the French School on Jesus' infancy, there are many forms that our participation in this mystery takes, "reproducing" the forms it takes in Jesus to some extent.

Here is an example, from a letter of M. Olier to Sister Marguerite du Saint-Sacrement (herself an important conduit of the infancy devotion): "Can one believe that Jesus Christ has become an infant; that he comes to reside in a heart which he consecrates to his nativity, that he regards it as his crib, and that he gives entry to someone in order to be continually adored, and to fill it with his divine life and anoint it with perfumes, by the same oil with which he enlivens souls?" (É. Levesque, ed., *Lettres de M. Olier* [Paris: J. de Gigord, 1935], vol. 1, no. 141, 346).

22. *Grandeurs* 11, 6, 154. The last three discourses of the *Grandeurs* (10–12) are a "celebrated" meditation-elevation upon Jesus' three births: in eternity, in time, and into immortality-resurrection.

23. All citations from *The Life of Jesus* are from Thompson, *Bérulle and the French School*, in this order (hereafter references to the *Life* are followed by the chapter and section number, and then the page in the Glendon translation, ibid.): *Life* 6, 1, 159; 28, 1, 160; 29, 1, 167; 29, 2, 168–71. As I indicated, Bérulle goes far, but then keeps his balance in the end: Mary attains "the very boundaries of the Godhead" (*Life* 28, 1, 163); "in a way, she lost her own life and personal subsistence in order to live in him who is life itself and her life as well" (*Life* 29, 1, 166).

24. *Life* 6, 1, 159.

25. See the introduction of Joseph Beaude in his edition of Bérulle's *La vie de Jésus*, Foi vivante 236 (Paris: Cerf, 1989), 20–29. Beaude stresses how often "instant" and "moment" surface in the *Life* (23). As Bérulle puts it, to use one example, "For it is in Nazareth, in this birth of Jesus in her, *in this moment* that these things are accomplished" (*Life* 29, 2, 171 [my italics]). Guillén Preckler stresses the Bérullian notion of the "first instant" of the Incarnation in a way analogous to Beaude, seeing it as a kind of "solemn profession" by Jesus (*Bérulle aujourd'hui*, 77–82). Is this an equivalent to Ignatius of Antioch's suggestion that Mary's virginity and child-bearing (and Jesus' death is included by Ignatius) occurred in God's silence (*Ephesians* 19, in *Early Christian Writings*, Penguin Classics, trans. Maxwell Staniforth, intro. and ed. Andrew Louth [Harmondsworth: Penguin Books, 1968], 66)? Perhaps, if with Saward, *The Mysteries of March*, 36, we see this "silence" as a metaphor for the transcendent origins of the Incarnation. Readers wanting further information on the infancy theme can consult Irénée Noye, "Enfance de Jésus (dévotion à l')," *Dictionnaire de spiritualité* 4/1, cols. 652–82. Two suggestive contemporary interpretations: Karl Rahner, "Ideas for a Theology of Childhood," *Theological Investigations*, vol. 8, trans. David Bourke (New York: Herder and Herder/Crossroad, 1971), 33–50, and John Saward, "Faithful to the Child I Used to Be: Bernanos and the Spirit of Childhood," *Chesterton Review* 15–16 (1989–90): 465–85.

26. I am citing from an unpublished copy of *Oeuvres de piété* 58 (M. 233, National Archives, Paris), as cited in Guillén Preckler, *Bérulle aujourd'hui*, 95. See Aquinas, *Summa theologiae* 2–2, 87, 4, for the school theology.

27. See Guillén Preckler, *Bérulle aujourd'hui*, 95–96, whose interpretation I am following throughout.

28. *Oeuvres de piété* 59, 3, col. 1034; M. 233 (National Archives, Paris,

Carton 233), 59 B (following Jean Orcibal's classification in "Les 'Oeuvres de piété' du cardinal de Bérulle: essai de classement des inédits et conjectures chronologiques," *Revue d'histoire ecclésiastique* 57 [1962]: 813–62), as cited in Guillén Preckler, *"État" chez le cardinal de Bérulle*, 190; cf. 190–91.

29. *Oeuvres de piété* 66D (Oratory Archives, Houssaye Papers, n. 2, 93–94 Orcibal's classification), as cited in Guillén Preckler, *Bérulle aujourd'hui*, 98.

30. See Guillén Preckler, *"État" chez le cardinal de Bérulle*, 191; *Oeuvres de piété* 117, col. 1141; *Grandeurs* 5, 9, 135–37; *Oeuvres de piété* 31, 3, col. 964; *Oeuvres de piété* 64, 2, col. 1041. On the theme of *pati divina* see Dionysius the Areopagite, *The Divine Names* 2, 9 (any edition), and Andrew Louth, "Denys the Areopagite," in Jones, Wainwright, and Arnold, *The Study of Spirituality*, 189. Balthasar, *Mysterium Paschale*, 11–147, offers a very stimulating rehabilitation of the theme of Jesus' life as "ordered" to the cross from its very trinitarian foundations, as in the French School. Balthasar dialogues with the French School approvingly, but seems to miss its trinitarian dimensions (see 35, 93ff., 205–6, 271 n. 71).

31. *Oeuvres de piété* 63C (Michel Dupuy, "De nouveaux inédits de Bérulle," *Revue d'histoire de la spiritualité* 53 [1977]: 276; cf. 63E, 280–82, and 68D, 283–88); *Grandeurs* 10, 6 (*Oeuvres complètes*, 331; cf. *Grandeurs* 2, 8 [*Oeuvres complètes*, 180]). Cf. Aquinas, *Summa theologiae* 48, 6. Enduring suffering "from the Father" brings us into the theological trajectory of Balthasar, in which Jesus somehow undergoes the misery of sin on the cross — in order from the inside to transform it — but without being a sinner and without being disunited with the Father in a yet deeper sense. This is also a view with links to Karl Barth and the Protestant *patres*. See Balthasar, *Mysterium Paschale*, 49–188; and Barth, *Church Dogmatics*, 4:1, 157–357. See *Oeuvres de piété* 135C (Dupuy, "De nouveaux inédits de Bérulle," *Revue des études augustiniennes* 26 [1980]: 268), where, alluding to 2 Corinthians 5:21 in an elevation for Lent's first week, Bérulle daringly says that "Jesus carries the mark of the sinner and of exile" [but without sin]. Olier (H.-J. Icard, *Doctrine de M. Olier*, 2d ed. [Paris: Victor Lecoffre, 1891], 162–89, for texts) will say that Christ suffers abandonment in the soul's "lower part," like John of the Cross (*The Ascent of Mount Carmel* 2, 7, 11, in *The Collected Works of St. John of the Cross*, trans. Kieran Kavanaugh and Otilio Rodriguez [Washington, DC: Institute of Carmelite Studies, 1973], 124). (Special thanks to Raymond Deville and Michel Dupuy for their assistance here with Bérulle and Olier.)

See John Calvin: "But how does it happen . . . that a beloved Son is cursed by His Father? I reply, there are two things to be considered, not only in the person of Christ, but even in His human nature. The one is that He was the unspotted Lamb of God, full of blessing and grace. The other is that He took our place and thus became a sinner and subject to the curse, not in Himself indeed, but in us. . . . For how could He reconcile Him to us if He regarded the Father as an enemy and was hated by Him? Therefore the will of the Father always reposed in Him. Again, how could He have freed us from the wrath of God if He had not transferred it from us to Himself?" (Comm. Gal 3:13, in *Calvin's Commentaries: The Epistles of Paul the Apostle to the Galatians,*

Ephesians, Philippians and Colossians, ed. David S. Torrance and Thomas F. Torrance, trans. T. H. L. Parker [Grand Rapids: William B. Eerdmans, 1965], 55). Martin Luther's view is similar in his *Lectures on Galatians 3:12–13: Luther's Works*, vol. 26, ed. and trans. Jaroslav Pelikan (St. Louis: Concordia Publishing House, 1963), 273–91.

32. *Oeuvres de piété* 109, col. 1126. Cf. *Oeuvres de piété* 102 B (Orcibal classification): "... the virtue and dignity of the body of Jesus does not come from the soul, but from the Word which is hypostatically united to the soul and body, and is not separated even by death" (Oratory Archives, n. 10, 173–74). See Aquinas, *Summa theologiae* 3, 50, 2–3.

33. *Oeuvres de piété* 102, col. 1148; Olier, *Divers écrits*, as cited in H.-J. Icard, *Doctrine de M. Olier*, 186, and *Catéchisme*, 49.

34. *Oeuvres de piété* 15E (Dupuy, "De nouveaux inédits de Bérulle," *Revue d'histoire de la spiritualité* 48 [1972]: 451); *Oeuvres de piété* 12, col. 927 (referring to Ps 22:16 and Jn 14:31). Similarities between the French School and Balthasar: the trinitarian foundations, the tomb as a mystically passive state and one of corruption or "deadness," the saving nature of the descent, its creation of purgatory or a purgative way out of separation from the Father, the full solidarity with the suffering and damned, and even the graces that some have of especially sharing in this state. One could perhaps say of Bérulle, following Balthasar, that the descent creates purgatory, heaven, and the possibility of hell for humans; before the descent, only Sheol or Hades existed, but not really the Christian "states" of eternity. See *Mysterium Paschale*, 148–88, and Saward, *The Mysteries of March*, 105–33. See John Calvin, *Institutes of the Christian Religion*, 2 vols. Library of Christian Classics 20, ed. John T. McNeil, trans. Ford Lewis Battles (Philadelphia: Westminster, 1960), 2:16:3–12.

35. *Oeuvres de piété* 77, 2, col. 1053; 69, col. 1046; 206D (M. 233, National Archives, Orcibal's classification). See Preckler, *Bérulle aujourd'hui*, 100.

36. *Oeuvres de piété* 73A (M. 233, National Archives, Orcibal's classification), cited by Guillén Preckler, *Bérulle aujourd'hui*, 100.

37. *Grandeurs* 8, 8 (*Oeuvres complètes*, 293). See Barth, *Church Dogmatics*, 4:1, 304, for comments on the analogy between Jesus' resurrection by the Father and the Son's obediential receptivity to the Father in the immanent Trinity.

38. *Grandeurs* 12, 2, 154–57; *Oeuvres de piété* 74, col. 1049. An illustration of the fuzziness between ascension and resurrection is the fact that both are the source of "life" for us in the cardinal's thought. See, for the resurrection, *Oeuvres de piété* 73A (M. 233, National Archives, Orcibal's classification), and Guillén Preckler, *"État chez le cardinal de Bérulle*, 204. See Icard, 2.2–38, for Spirit and Pentecost in Olier.

39. *Catechism of an Interior Life*, 142. For Bérulle on joy and impassibility, see *Oeuvres de piété* 73A (M. 233, National Archives, Orcibal's classification), and cited in Guillén Preckler, *Bérulle aujourd'hui*, 102.

40. Guillén Preckler, *"État" chez le cardinal de Bérulle*, 218; *Elevation to Jesus Christ Our Lord Concerning the Conduct of His Spirit and His Grace toward Saint Magdalene*, in Thompson, *Bérulle and the French School*, 172–82 (selections; references will be to this unless otherwise noted).

41. *Elevation* 7, 4, 178–79.

42. Ibid., 7, 4, 178. Bérulle accepts the traditional tendency to conflate Mary of Bethany (Jn 12:3), the Magdalene, and the penitential woman (Lk 7:37). But he quickly "jumps" over the sinful aspect in the tradition, and is somewhat new in this: "Also, you [i.e., Jesus] do not at all mention her sins. You only speak of her love" (1, 5, 174).

43. *Elevation* 15, 181, and 12, 180. As always, there is a strong "mystical" note in Bérulle's treatment of sharing in Jesus' mysteries, and so one senses his view of the Magdalene as someone enjoying the heights of the mystical life, as well as its dark nights. Cf. Guillén Preckler, *"État" chez le cardinal de Bérulle*, 213–20, who is quite good on this. Joseph Beaude's introduction in his recent edition of the work, *Élévation sur sainte Madeleine*, Foi vivante 224 (Paris: Cerf, 1987), 7–29, is also helpful.

44. *Grandeurs* 6, 1, 140; 7, 9, 143; cf. 142.

45. *Oeuvres de piété* 80, 3, col. 1057.

46. See, for Bérulle, *Oeuvres de piété* 80, 1, col. 1056; for Olier, *Catechism of an Interior Life*, 125 (on the theme of the "eternal sacrifice"), and *Journée*, 193, on the priesthood; and Charles de Condren, *The Eternal Sacrifice*, trans. H. J. Monteith (London: Thomas Baker, 1906).

47. *Journée*, 123. These "Acts for the Divine Office" are that portion of the *Journée* which so moved Bremond, his copying them out, keeping them in his breviary, and constantly reading-praying them. See Bremond, *The Triumph of Mysticism*, 393–97. For the theme of the church as suffering, militant, and triumphant, see 119–20 of the *Journée*. At this point, let me mention Olier's *Catechism of an Interior Life*, Lessons 20–25, 119–47, and *The Life and Kingdom of Jesus in Christian Souls*, trans. A Trappist from Gethsemani (New York: P. J. Kenedy & Sons, 1946) by another great Bérullian and disciple of both Bérulle and Condren, St. John Eudes, 193–210, 251–70, as helpful sources in English of examples of contemplations in the mode of the French School, in addition to Thompson, *Bérulle and the French School*. A helpful collection in French, from Bérulle, is *Les mystères de la vie du Christ*, Foi vivante 233, intro. François Monfort (Paris: Cerf, 1988). We still need a good study of the liturgy in the French School, but a helpful start is M. Dupuy, "Bérulle et la Liturgie," *Oratoriana* 11 (1965): 11–33.

48. *Grandeurs* 9, 1, 148; see Thompson, *Bérulle and the French School*, 6–11, for the historical background of the French School.

49. See Hügel, *The Mystical Element*, vol. 1, 25–26.

50. *Grandeurs* 7, 9, 141.

51. Letter 147, 205.

52. *Grandeurs* 1, 6, 111.

53. Ibid., 6, 1, 139.

54. Ibid., 1, 6, 113.

55. Tracy, *Plurality and Ambiguity*, 9.

56. Ibid., 10. "Praxis" means "practice which has been reflected upon," as distinct from aimless and unanalyzed activity. See below, chapter 9.

57. See Bertaud, "Élévations spirituelles," and Bremond, *The Triumph of Mysticism*, 93–132, 393, 536–45, for helpful insights of a literary kind.

Michael J. Buckley, "Seventeenth-Century French Spirituality: Three Figures," in Dupré and Saliers, *Christian Spirituality: Post-Reformation and Modern*, 49–50, helpfully reaches back to Aristotle's genre of epideictic (praise) from the *Rhetoric* 1.3.1358b 16–20. Paul Ricoeur, I believe, might consider the mixed genre of theodoxology a form of "hymnic discourse": *Essays on Biblical Interpretation*, ed. Lewis S. Mudge (Philadelphia: Fortress Press, 1980), 88–90. I have given but a sampling of the genres/forms employed by our principals, and my analysis is at a very rudimentary level, for I have had very little to fall back upon. See my *Bérulle and the French School*, 97–101.

58. See "St. John of the Cross as Pneumopathologist: A Mystic's Hermeneutics of Suspicion," in my *Fire and Light*, 118–42, for one use of the mystics in the way suggested here.

59. For the history of this "formalizing," of the French School and of Loyola, see G. Letourneau, *La méthode d'oraison mentale du séminaire de Saint-Sulpice* (Paris: Victor Lecoffre, 1903) and Cardinal Giacomo Lercaro, *Methods of Mental Prayer*, trans. P. F. Lindsay (Westminster, MD: Newman, 1957).

60. *Grandeurs* 2, 10, 123.

61. *Summa theologiae* 3, 41, 1–4.

62. *Church Dogmatics*, 4:1, 132–35; 4:2, 132–54; cf. 4:2, 248. See John P. Meier, "The Historical Jesus: Rethinking Some Concepts," *Theological Studies* 51 (1990): 3–24, for some helpful observations on the issues involved in the categories of a "historical Jesus" and "Christ of faith."

63. See, of course, Elisabeth Schüssler Fiorenza, *In Memory of Her: A Feminist Theological Reconstruction of Christian Origins* (New York: Crossroad, 1983), especially 105–59.

64. For more on this, see Michel Dupuy, "Intérieur de Jésus," *Dictionnaire de spiritualité* 7/2 (1971), cols. 1870–77.

65. *Introduction to the Christian Life and Virtues*, 221 and 224; a particularly fine formulation by Father Olier of the relation between interior and exterior in the same work (221): "... his exterior mysteries, which were like sacraments of the interior mysteries he was to bring about in souls."

66. Here I would suggest that there is much to be learned on this question of the inner-outer in history from the Blondel-Hügel "conversation": See especially Maurice Blondel, "History and Dogma," *The Letter on Apologetics and History and Dogma*, trans. Alexander Dru and Illtyd Trethowan (New York: Holt, Rinehart and Winston, 1964), 219–87, and Baron Friedrich von Hügel, "Du Christ eternel et de nos christologies successives," *La Quinzaine* 58 (1904): 285–312. Both Blondel and Hügel share a conviction as to the ultimate unity of the "somatic" and the "metaphysical-faith" dimensions, but Blondel emphasizes that unity, while Hügel "pushes" their relative distinction as far as possible. See the helpful study by John A. McGrath, "Fact and Reality: von Hügel's Response," *Heythrop Journal* 30 (1989): 13–31.

67. See, for example, *Oeuvres de piété* 87, cols. 1070–72, which carries the title "On the Solemnity of Jesus."

68. Ibid., col. 1070.

69. *Grandeurs* 5, 9, 137.

70. Ibid., 5, 9, 137–38.

71. *Introduction to the Christian Life and Virtues*, 274; see 273–76, for a nice summary of Olierian principles of discernment, which would be rather representative of the French School.

72. *Grandeurs* 4, 2, 133–34. Besides the works on the Trinity already mentioned, I recommend the following anthology and commentary: Michel Dupuy, ed., *L'Esprit, souffle du Seigneur*, Jésus et Jésus-Christ Resonances 3 (Paris: Desclée de Brouwer, 1988). See below, n. 77 and chapter 8, n. 11, on the theme of Bérulle's view of the "sterility" of the Holy Spirit within the immanent Trinity (*Grandeurs* 4, 2, 131–34), which seems to be a way of pointing out the Spirit's role as one of leading us to the Son (and Father), rather than himself (his "fertility" in the economic Trinity is this leading of us).

73. See Barth, *Church Dogmatics*, 4:1, 320, building upon 2 Corinthians 5:16: "It is quite right that the voice and form of Jesus cannot in practice be distinguished with any finality in the Gospels from the community founded by Him and sharing His life. The historian may find this disconcerting and suspicious (or even provocatively interesting). It is further evidence of that submission to the divine verdict without which the Gospels could never have taken shape as Gospels." This Barthian insight is nicely illustrated, I suggest, by the mystic and saint as understood in this book. Also, Karl Rahner, "Brief Observations on Systematic Christology Today," *Theological Investigations*, vol. 21, trans. Hugh M. Riley (New York: Crossroad, 1988), 237.

74. Denis Amelote, *La vie du père Charles de Condren*, vol. 2 (Paris: Henry Sara, 1643), 80–81.

75. *Grandeurs* 5, 9, 135. Exemplarism — eternal archetypes and their earthly reflections — can be considered an example of the Christianized Neoplatonism of the French School.

76. Ibid., 1, 6, 113.

77. See the very dense *Grandeurs* 4, 2, 131–34, on the role of the Spirit. Bérulle here speaks of the "sterility" of the Spirit within the immanent Trinity, since no person proceeds from the Spirit; yet the overspill of the Trinity in salvation history is the work of the Spirit's fertility. "It is sterile in itself and fertile outside itself. It is the uniqueness of its Person that it is the termination that terminates divinely and brings to a close, in itself, the divine fecundity within the holy Trinity. However, it is the termination that receives, contains and brings to an end within itself the fullness of that fertile nature, so that in receiving, conserving and terminating that fecundity, it may pour it forth powerfully and divinely outside itself" (132).

78. See Brian Hebblethwaite, *The Incarnation: Collected Essays in Christology* (Cambridge: Cambridge University, 1987), especially 11–20. One thinks in this respect of Hans Urs von Balthasar's work, among others.

79. *Grandeurs* 5, 9, 135–36; see Thompson, *Bérulle and the French School*, 68 n. 20, for how Bérulle combines Scotus (God becomes incarnate to communicate with us) and Aquinas (the Incarnation results from God's desire to

repair our sins). Both of these themes run throughout the French School in varying shades.

80. Letter 144, 200. This entire letter, 200–203, is vintage Bérullianism, with an element of Condren's sacrifice mysticism blended in.

81. *Grandeurs* 2, 10, 123.

82. Hebblethwaite, *The Incarnation*, 1; passim.

83. *Grandeurs* 1, 6, 113; 2, 6, 121.

84. See Frank Kermode, "John," in Alter and Kermode, *The Literary Guide to the Bible*, 440–66. In the Prologue "we have three 'becomings' to set against the triple was of eternity." Thus: the eternal "*Was* is thrice repeated: the Word *was*, it *was* with God, it *was* God." To which we can match the triple "becomings" of verse 3: "All things were made by him, and without him was not anything made that was made" (445). And we might add the fourth becoming of the Word made flesh, which is appropriately like and unlike the other becomings.

85. The critiques of this in the literature are legion. The great difficulty seems to be the distinction between "person" and "nature," which to the modern, western ear sounds like the church teaches that Jesus isn't a fully personal human being, but only an abstract nature. But, of course, "person" or "hypostasis" and "nature" mean something basically different from this in the conciliar teaching. The church wants to affirm Jesus' full humanity (= "nature"), yet also to affirm its unique constitution as the final and full personal revelation of God (= "person"/"hypostasis"). Part of the difficulty here is the abstract, hellenistic language of the councils, and the attempt to infuse it with Christian historical personalism. This teaching, called traditionally the *enhypostasia* of the humanity of Jesus in the Logos, is usually associated with the teaching of Constantinople II (553).

86. *Grandeurs* 2, 10, 123. For Bérulle's turn to the christocentric, see Thompson, *Bérulle and the French School*, 3–96. The stress on *anéantissement* and kenosis, and the idea of Jesus' presence through "state" but not necessarily through concept, are examples of the abstract, apophatic element in the French School. On St. Teresa of Avila, see Secundino Castro, *Cristología Teresiana, Redes* 5 (Madrid: Editorial de Espiritualidad, 1978). See, for a primary source, *The Book of Her Life* 22 (*The Collected Works of St. Teresa of Avila*, 1:144–52). Bérulle's christocentrism is particularly pronounced in these passages:

> In truth, the Word spent an eternity without this humanity, but will also spend an eternity with it.
> O divine gaze! O eternal gaze! O gaze full of love and honor! O gaze that should draw our gaze, our love and our homage toward that humanity, which God beholds eternally and unceasingly as his own, and which we should look upon as our own. It is ours through a gift of the Father, through the activity of the Holy Spirit, through the subsistence of the Son, which was given him so that he might accomplish our salvation. Finally it is ours through the power of the cross and his death, which consumed him for us in sacrifice and holocaust (*Grandeurs* 12, 2, 157).

Chapter 4: On "Christologies from Above and from Below"

1. *What Are They Saying about Jesus?* (New York: Paulist Press 1983), 13.

2. English translation by Joseph A. Fitzmyer, with commentary, "The Biblical Commission and Christology," *Theological Studies* 46 (1985), 407–79. See the book edition, *Scripture and Christology: A Statement of the Biblical Commission with a Commentary* (New York: Paulist Press, 1986).

3. Richard A. Norris, Jr., ed. and trans., *The Christological Controversy*, Sources of Early Christian Thought (Philadelphia: Fortress Press, 1980), 156.

4. See most handily his *Love Alone*, trans. and ed. Alexander Dru (New York: Herder and Herder, 1969). This does not mean that one is not profoundly aware of the "from below" alternative. Someone like Balthasar is highly aware of it and judges it the inappropriate way to proceed in christology.

5. Karl Rahner, "Christology Today?," *Theological Investigations*, vol. 17, trans. Margaret Kohl (New York: Crossroad, 1981), 26; cf. 24–38.

6. Ignatius of Antioch, *Letter to the Trallians* 9–10, in H. A. Musurillo, *The Fathers of the Primitive Church* (New York: Mentor-Omega, 1966), 75. Complete but different English translation in *Early Christian Writings*, Penguin Classics, trans. Maxwell Staniforth, intro. and ed. Andrew Louth (Harmondsworth: Penguin Books, 1968), 79–82.

7. *Summa theologiae* 3, 41, 1.

8. Cf. *Summa theologiae* 3, 12, 1–2; 3, 15, 3.

9. Raymond E. Brown, *Biblical Reflections on Crises Facing the Church* (New York: Paulist Press, 1975), 112; see 111–15 for selections from the text and commentary.

10. There is now a growing literature on Anselm's satisfaction theory, indicating that it was not a kind of fideistic appeal to a Father's "decree" of salvation, but rather a view more rooted in medieval corporatism and solidarity; hence, the "mystical body" of Jesus, through which we are linked to Jesus' saving work. It might be argued that Rahner's critiques have stimulated to some extent the modern rehabilitation of Anselm's theory. But Rahner probably has in mind more "popular" versions of Anselm as well, and perhaps mainly these. See my *The Jesus Debate: A Survey and Synthesis* (New York: Paulist Press, 1985), 348–51, 364 n. 13–14, for interpretation and bibliography, and Rahner's "Salvation: IV. Theology," in Karl Rahner, ed., *Sacramentum Mundi: An Encyclopedia of Theology*, vol. 5 (New York: Herder and Herder, 1970), 425–33.

11. See Karl Barth's celebrated grappling with this kenosis in, for example, *Church Dogmatics*, 4:1, paragraph 59 (where he treats of "the way of the Son of God into the Far Country"), 157–357; or Karl Rahner's equally celebrated study, "On the Theology of the Incarnation," *Theological Investigations*, vol. 4, trans. Kevin Smyth (Baltimore: Helicon Press/New York: Crossroad, 1966), 105–20.

12. Walter Kasper, *Jesus the Christ*, trans. V. Green (New York: Paulist Press, 1976), 237; cf. Friedrich Schleiermacher, *The Christian Faith*, vol. 2,

no. 96, ed. H. R. MacKintosh and J. S. Stewart, intro. Richard R. Niebuhr (New York: Harper Torchbooks, 1963), 392–93; and Reginald H. Fuller and Pheme Perkins, *Who Is This Christ?: Gospel Christology and Contemporary Faith* (Philadelphia: Fortress Press, 1983), 121–34.

13. Norris, *The Christological Controversy*, 148.

14. See Hans Schmidt, "Politics and Christology: Historical Background," *Concilium* 36 (1968): 72–84, for some suggestive beginnings. See also my *The Jesus Debate*, 310ff.

15. *Foundations of Christian Faith: An Introduction to the Idea of Christianity*, trans. William V. Dych (New York: Seabury Press/New York: Crossroad, 1978), 298; Wolfhart Pannenberg, *Jesus — God and Man*, 2d ed., trans. Lewis L. Wilkins and Duane A. Priebe (Philadelphia: Westminster Press, 1968), 33–37.

16. Thomas Sheehan, *The First Coming: How the Kingdom of God Became Christianity* (New York: Random House, 1986); Erich Fromm, *The Dogma of Christ and Other Essays on Religion, Psychology and Culture* (Greenwich, CT: Fawcett Books, 1963), 15–93; Milan Machovec, *A Marxist Looks at Jesus*, trans. Peter Hebblethwaite (London: Darton, Longman and Todd, 1976).

17. *On Being a Christian*, trans. Edward Quinn (Garden City, NY: Doubleday & Co., 1976), 448–49.

18. Fitzmyer, "The Biblical Commission and Christology," 426.

19. Ibid., 417.

20. See n. 11. This essay is substantially found in his *Foundations of Christian Faith*, 212–28, and succinctly and beautifully in *Spiritual Exercises*, trans. Kenneth Baker (New York: Herder and Herder, 1965), 97–113, where it is linked with St. Ignatius Loyola's christocentric spirituality.

21. See Karl Rahner, "The Ignatian Mysticism of Joy in the World," *Theological Investigations*, vol. 3, 277–93. His foundational works are, of course, *Spirit in the World*, trans. William Dych (New York: Herder and Herder, 1968), and *Hearers of the Word*, trans. Michael Richards (New York: Herder and Herder, 1969).

22. For some helpful comments on the use of anthropology in christology, I recommend the 1983 statement of the International Theological Commission, *Theology, Christology, Anthropology* (Washington, DC: United States Catholic Conference, 1983).

23. Eduard Schillebeeckx, *Jesus: An Experiment in Christology*, trans. Hubert Hoskins (New York: Seabury Press/Crossroad, 1979), 669.

24. See my *The Jesus Debate*, 45–111, for an overview.

25. *What Are They Saying about Jesus?*, 13.

26. Johannes B. Metz, *Faith in History and Society: Toward a Practical Fundamental Theology*, trans. David Smith (New York: Crossroad, 1980).

27. *Sexism and God-Talk: Toward A Feminist Theology* (Boston: Beacon Press, 1983); see Elizabeth A. Johnson, *Consider Jesus: Waves of Renewal in Christology* (New York: Crossroad, 1990).

28. See my *The Jesus Debate*, 63, and *Jesus, Lord and Savior: A Theopathic Christology and Soteriology* (New York: Paulist Press, 1980), 16–17; Peter C. Hodgson, *Jesus — Word and Presence: An Essay in Christology* (Philadelphia:

Fortress Press, 1971), 68–69; and Nicholas Lash, "Up and Down in Christology," in Stephen Sykes and Derek Holmes, eds., *New Studies in Theology*, vol. 1 (London: Duckworth, 1980), 31–46, among others. Walter Kasper, "Postmodern Dogmatics: Toward a Renewed Discussion of Foundations in North America," *Communio* 17 (1990): 180–91, is helpful on the meaning of "postmodern" meant here.

29. *Theology, Christology, Anthropology*, 12, 9.

30. Karl Barth, "Evangelical Theology in the 19th Century," trans. Thomas Wieser, *The Humanity of God* (Richmond, VA: John Knox Press, 1960), 11; see 24–25: "There is no reason why the attempt of Christian anthropocentrism should not be made, indeed ought not to be made. There is certainly a place for legitimate Christian thinking starting from below and moving up, from man who is taken hold of by God to God who takes hold of man. Let us interpret this attempt by the 19th-century theologians in its best light! Provided that it in no way claims to be exclusive and absolute, one might well understand it as an attempt to formulate a theology of the third article of the Apostles' Creed, the Holy Spirit. If it had succeeded in this, 19th-century theology could have irrevocably stressed once again the fact that we cannot consider God's commerce with man without concurrently considering man's commerce with God. Theology is in reality not only the doctrine of God, but the doctrine of God and man."

31. Dermot A. Lane, *The Reality of Jesus* (New York: Paulist Press, 1975), 18. See Barth, *Church Dogmatics*, 4:2, 110, for a helpful view of how the Incarnation transcends the above-below dualism, relying upon Ephesians 4:9, a view that has influenced me, as the reader will see.

32. *Orations against the Arians* 3, 38 (Norris, *The Christological Controversy*, 97).

33. *Second Letter to Nestorius* (Norris, *The Christological Controversy*, 132).

34. *Foundations of Christian Faith*, 79, among many possible sources.

Chapter 5: Adoration's Centrality in Theology and Christology

1. Citations form Hügel: *The Reality of God and Religion and Agnosticism*, ed. Edmund G. Gardner (London: J. M. Dent & Sons, 1931), 71, and *Letters from Baron Friedrich von Hügel to a Niece*, ed. Gwendolen Greene (Chicago: Henry Regnery, 1955), xxxiv. See also Joseph P. Whelan, *The Spirituality of Friedrich von Hügel* (New York: Newman, 1971), 80–81, basing himself here on Hügel, *Eternal Life: A Study of Its Implications and Applications* (Edinburgh: T. & T. Clark, 1912), 186–88.

2. For the most part I will make use of Hügel's published books; normally his theoretical and so sustained analysis of our theme will be found there. There are important insights in the diaries and letters, and I will use these where appropriate, although these materials would deserve a full treatment by themselves. Important for these latter sources are his letters; see *Selected Letters: 1896–1924*, ed. Bernard Holland (London: J. M. Dent & Sons, 1928);

215

The Letters of Baron Friedrich von Hügel and Professor Norman Kemp Smith, ed. Lawrence F. Barmann (New York: Fordham University Press, 1981); and Michael de la Bedoyère, The Life of Baron von Hügel (London: J. M. Dent & Sons, 1951).

3. For Hügel's appreciation of Kierkegaard, see The Mystical Element, vol. 2, 345, 353. For the Reformers, see Martin Luther, "The Adoration of the Sacrament," Word and Sacrament, vol. 2, ed. and trans. Abdel Ross Wentz (Luther's Works, vol. 36, ed. Helmut T. Lehmann [Philadelphia: Muhlenberg, 1959]), 271–305; John Calvin, Institutes of the Christian Religion, 2 vols., Library of Christian Classics 20, ed. John T. McNeill, trans. Ford Lewis Battles (Philadelphia: Westminster, 1960), 1:5:9, 1:13:24, 1:17:2, 2:8:16, 4:17:35–36. Egan, Ignatius Loyola the Mystic, 29 n. 24, has noted Karl Rahner's increasing stress on adoration, referring to Rahner's statement: "...we are here to adore God...we have to love Him for his own sake and not only for ours..." (Karl Rahner — I Remember, trans. Harvey D. Egan [New York: Crossroad, 1985], 107–8). See, too, Karl Rahner "Christianity's Absolute Claim," Theological Investigations, vol. 21, 179. As regards Hans Urs von Balthasar, an introduction to his sense of adoration is his Prayer, trans. Graham Harrison (San Francisco: Ignatius, 1986). Barth's Church Dogmatics, throughout, are surely adorational. Since mysticism is so crucial here, let me suggest that Barth's views on the issue are much more subtle than often seem thought. He clearly attacks a works-righteous or Jesus-independent form of mysticism, but a careful reading of the Church Dogmatics (s.v. "Mysticism" in the Index Volume) reveals at least a cautious openness to a Jesus-grounded mysticism, I think.

4. Bedoyère, The Life, 330, and James J. Kelly, Baron Friedrich von Hügel's Philosophy of Religion, Bibliotheca Ephemeridum Theologicarum Lovaniensium 62 (Louvain: University Press, 1983), 147.

5. Eternal Life, 160.

6. Ibid., 161. See Hügel, The German Soul (London: J. M. Dent & Sons, 1916), 209: "Philosophies that leave no room for Prayer, Adoration, Sin, Forgiveness, Redemption, may be excellent in many other directions, and also as criticisms and stimulants of religious thought; but, as would-be adequate theories of religion, they cannot fail more or less to misconceive and to explain away facts of inexhaustible vitality."

7. Eternal Life, 159–67.

8. Ibid., 160.

9. Ibid., 164–65.

10. Ibid., 383.

11. Ibid., 64.

12. Ibid., 162. Maurice Nédoncelle's comment that Hügel regards "pure prayer as consisting wholly in adoration, even to the point of forgetting sometimes that prayer must include petition; petition for an increased power of adoration" seems unnuanced (Baron Friedrich von Hügel: A Study of His Life and Thought, trans. Marjorie Vernon [London: Longmans, Green and Co., 1937], 166). Hügel regards adoration as central, not as devouring all prayer.

13. Eternal Life, 162–64; see Whelan, The Spirituality, 260–61, n. 15, and

Bedoyère, *The Life*, 23. Bedoyère, 214–15 attributes the following anecdote to George Tyrrell, which somewhat "mockingly" brings out Hügel's combination of critical religious study and deeply adorational piety: *"The Baron.* There can be no doubt that Our Lady failed to occupy her proper place at the Crucifixion; the evidence of the Synoptic writers makes this clear. *The Friend.* Yes? But it is a long way from this to the *Salve Regina. The Baron.* There can be no doubt that Our Lord's faith broke down on Calvary. *The Friend.* Yes? But it is a long way from this to the Nicene Creed. *The Baron.* There can be no doubt that St. Paul's teaching on the Eucharist is based upon certain forms of Syrian Nature-worship. *The Friend.* Yes? But it is a long way from this to the *Tantum Ergo. The Baron.* I hear the Angelus; I must go and make my evening visit to the Blessed Sacrament!"

14. Hügel, *Essays and Addresses on the Philosophy of Religion*, Second Series (hereafter in this chapter *Essays and Addresses* 2) (London: J. M. Dent & Sons, 1926), 224. For Lateran IV: Henricus Denzinger and Adolfus Schönmetzer, eds., *Enchiridion Symbolorum* (Freiburg: Herder, 1965), no. 806: "... inter creatorem et creaturam non potest similitudo notari, quin inter eos maior sit dissimilitudo notanda." Part of God's "greater dissimilarity" may be the divine ability to draw radically near and "similar" to us in incarnation and kenosis, even when we sin; dissimilarity does not necessarily mean distance, but may go along with a certain form of similarity too. And I think Hügel's ability to bring out the link between Incarnation and adoration illustrates this, as this chapter tries to show. But see, among others, the discussion in O'Donnell, *The Mystery of the Trinity*, 116.

15. *Essays and Addresses* 2:224; for the element of joy in Catherine, see *Essays and Addresses on the Philosophy of Religion*, First Series (hereafter in this chapter *Essays and Addresses* 1) (London: J. M. Dent & Sons, 1921), 291: "... Catherine Fiesca Adorna, that unhappily married, immensely sensitive, naturally melancholy and self-absorbed woman, who ended, as the Saint of Genoa, on the note of joy and of overwhelming joy; ... "

16. *Essays and Addresses* 1:295; *Essays and Addresses* 2:152–53; cf. *Essays and Addresses* 2:210.

17. For the types of mysticism, see *Mystical Element* 2:290–91. References to adoration, explicitly or as the theme, I have found: 1:69, 347, 423; 2:24, 81, 261, 340, 371.

18. *Mystical Element* 1:xv–xvi.

19. Nédoncelle, *Baron Friedrich von Hügel*, 160.

20. *Mystical Element* 2:133; cf. 133–34, and Nédoncelle, *Baron Friedrich von Hügel*, 153–62. For the quietist issue, see Louis Cognet, *Post-Reformation Spirituality*, Twentieth Century Encyclopedia of Catholicism, vol. 41, trans. P. Hepburne Scott (New York: Hawthorn Books, 1959), 126–38.

21. See *Eternal Life*, 376, for references to Condren and Olier. For a reference by Hügel to Bérulle, see "The Spiritual Writings of Father Grou, S.J.," in John Nicholas Grou, S.J., *Spiritual Maxims*, ed. and trans. A Monk of Parkminster (London: Burns & Oates, 1961), 265–93 (appendix) at 277. *Mystical Element* 1:63 refers to the French Oratory, and 1:88, 317 refer to Bérulle. Huvelin is a special conduit of the French School to Hügel. For this see

Abbé Huvelin, *Some Spiritual Guides of the Seventeenth Century*, intro. and trans. Joseph Leonard (New York: Benziger, 1927, especially 63–108 on Olier; James J. Kelly, "The Abbé Huvelin's Counsel to Baron Friedrich von Hügel," *Bijdragen* 39 (1978): 59–69. Huvelin's book is cited by Hügel in *Eternal Life*, 377 n. 1.

22. Amelote, *Vie du père Charles de Condren*, vol. 2, 80–81.

23. St. Thomas Aquinas, *Summa theologiae* 1–2, 7, 2; St. Maximus Confessor, *The Four Hundred Chapters on Love* 3, 46 and 1, 81 in *Selected Writings*, Classics of Western Spirituality, trans. George C. Berthold (New York: Paulist Press, 1985), 67, 44.

24. Balthasar's works are a good contemporary example of the combination of adoration and love in theology and spirituality.

25. Bérulle, *Oeuvres de piété* 156, col. 1199, and 164, col. 1210; Madeleine de Saint-Joseph, "Letter 144," 200, 203. Cf. Louis Cognet, *La spiritualité moderne* (*Histoire de spiritualité* 3/1) (Paris: Desclée de Brouwer, 1966), 362–67.

26. In *Mystical Element* 1:3, Hügel issues the opening question of the book (What integrates the personality?), and only answers it on 367–70. This question illustrates the anthropocentric, love-emphasis of the book.

27. *Letters... to a Niece*, 138–39; *Mystical Element* 1:234. For the notion of *attrait*, see *Essays and Addresses* 2:231.

28. *Mystical Element* 1:234; 2:272–75 at 274; 2:260, for the interesting comment that Catherine of Genoa's last "part" of life, a quite sickly part, would have been considered worthless on the grounds of a Kantian ethic, according to Hügel; Kelly, *Baron Friedrich*, 175. It would be quite worthwhile to compare Hügel's teaching here with that of Newman on conscience. For Newman, conscience seems to embrace both the ethical and the religious (in Hügel's sense), with the religious being the more fundamental. This would seem to cohere with Hügel. See J.-H. Walgrave, *Newman the Theologian*, trans. A. V. Littledale (New York: Sheed & Ward, 1960), especially 203–19, and Ian Ker, *The Achievement of John Henry Newman* (Notre Dame: University of Notre Dame Press, 1990), 141–44.

29. *Mystical Element* 2:395; *Letters... to a Niece*, 77.

30. *Mystical Element* 2:309–40, 246–58.

31. John Henry Cardinal Newman, "Preface to the Third Edition," *The Via Media of the Anglican Church*, vol. 1 (London: Longmans, Green, and Co., 1895), xv–xciv. A helpful analysis, showing the preface's influence on Hügel, is provided by John Coulson, "Newman on the Church — His Final View, Its Origins and Influence," in John Coulson and A. M. Allchin, eds., *The Rediscovery of Newman: An Oxford Symposium* (London: Sheed & Ward, SPCK, 1967), 123–43; cf. Ker, *The Achievement*, 144–51.

32. *Mystical Element* 1:xvi; *The Reality of God*, 72–73; cf. Kelly, *Baron Friedrich*, 136–43. The etymology of *adorare* seems arguable. One early study derives it from *ad* ("to") and *os* ("mouth"), suggesting that it has to do with "kissing" someone/something by the hand that has touched one's mouth (A. Molien, "Adoration," *Dictionnaire de spiritualité*, vol. 1 [1937], col. 210). Another, later study simply rejects this and relates it to a root word meaning

"prayer" (Ernest Klein, "Adoration," "Adore," and "Oration," *Etymological Dictionary of the English Language* [Amsterdam: Elsevier, 1966–67], vol. 1, 27 and vol. 2, 1091).

33. *Mystical Element* 1:xxi.

34. *Essays and Addresses* 2:92; Hügel, "The Case of the Abbé Loisy," *The Pilot* 9 (January 9, 1904): 31. Cf. Kelly, "The Abbé Huvelin's Counsel..."; and Lawrence Barmann, "Friedrich von Hügel as Modernist and as More than Modernist," *The Catholic Historical Review* 75 (1989): 211–32.

35. *The Reality of God*, 72–73; letter cited in Whelan, *The Spirituality*, 226; *Essays and Addresses* 1:275. Hügel's interrelating of the cultic-institutional with adoration would cohere with an interpretation of John 4:23 (adoring in spirit and truth) that avoids a totally spiritualized, gnostic interpretation. Heinrich Greeven gives such an interpretation: John 4:20–24 can give a first impression of a totally spiritualistic adoration, but "the reference in the statement and answer is to the place of worship." And "in the background" we find the "technical use of the word for the pilgrimage of Jews to Jerusalem, so also John 12:20; Acts 8:27; 24:11." Thus, for Jesus "Undiluted 'proskunein,' the act of worship which is concrete in place and gesture, is lifted up to a new dimension; 'spirit and truth.'...There is no longer to be any exclusive place of worship, but prayer is still to take place at specific places and with specific gestures" (in Gerhard Friedrich, ed., "proskuneo, proskunetes," *Theological Dictionary of the New Testament*, trans. Geoffrey W. Bromiley [Grand Rapids: William B. Eerdmans, 1968], vol. 6, 764).

36. *Mystical Element* 1:57.

37. Ibid., 2:290. For the prayer of quiet, see *Essays and Addresses* 2:233.

38. *Mystical Element* 1:66. A text that explicitly links adoration with the Trinity: *Essays and Addresses* 2:151–54.

39. *Essays and Addresses* 2:233. God is always adorable, but can be adored only if somehow "present" to us; this is what I mean by adoration tending in the direction of incarnationalism.

40. Ibid., 220, 218. Cf. Whelan, *The Spirituality*, 33–75, for an ample treatment of Hügel's christology. Walter Kasper's linking of adoration with divine personhood (naming God a person implies an adorational posture of not manipulating God) can be found in *The God of Jesus Christ*, 156.

41. Recall how Bérulle links adoration and Incarnation: *Grandeurs* 2, 13, 126. Note the similar teaching of Olier; "What an adorable mystery of a God adored and a God adoring in [his] son!" (*Catéchisme chrétien pour la vie intérieure et la Journée chrétienne*, 156, the citation being from *La Journée chrétienne*). I would suggest that the French School stresses the transcendent dimension of adoration: our adoration participates in the incarnate Jesus' own expressing forth of the trinitarian Son's homage of the Father. The French School tends to think of the incarnational side of God as expressed in Jesus' "servitude" or "kenosis." Still, for the French School, God's adorable being is revealed to us in the incarnate Jesus, in his servitude and kenosis. In that sense it brings out the incarnational aspect of adoration. For it implies God's condescension to us in history through Jesus' kenosis, which itself mirrors forth the Son's kenotic surrender to the Father in the Spirit. Balthasar,

for example in his *Mysterium Paschale*, and throughout his works, particularly links the revelation of God's "glory" (the divine adorability) with the kenosis of the Incarnation, its dramatic living out on the cross and in the descent into hell, and with the Son's trinitarian kenosis in relation to the Father.

Chapter 6: Saints and Mystics As Christological Sources

1. Paul Imhof and Hubert Biallowons, eds., Harvey D. Egan, trans. ed., *Karl Rahner in Dialogue: Conversations and Interviews, 1965–1982* (New York: Crossroad, 1986), 191. The trilogy of Balthasar refers to his theological aesthetics, dramatics, and logic.

2. *Préface, Oeuvres complètes*, vol. 1, vii. See my *Fire and Light: The Saints and Theology* (New York: Paulist Press, 1987), 1–75, on the history of theology's relation to spirituality.

3. See Patricia Wilson-Kastner, "Macrina: Virgin and Teacher," *Andrews University Seminary Studies* 17 (1979): 105–17. Cf. Gregory Palamas, *The Triads*, Classics of Western Spirituality, trans. John Meyendorff (New York: Paulist Press, 1983); Steven E. Ozment, *Homo Spiritualis: A Comparative Study of the Anthropology of Johannes Tauler, Jean Gerson and Martin Luther (1509–16) in the Context of Their Theological Thought*, Studies in Medieval and Reformation Thought 6 (Leiden: E. J. Brill, 1969); and *John and Charles Wesley*, Classics of Western Spirituality, intro. Frank Whaling (New York: Paulist Press, 1981).

4. St. Teresa of Avila, *The Book of Her Life* 22, 3 (*The Collected Works of St. Teresa of Avila*, vol. 1, 145); Jean-Jacques Olier, *Catéchisme chrétien pour la vie intérieure*, 58, using the Knight translation, *Catechism of an Interior Life*, 160; St. François de Sales, *Lettre* 5 October 1604 (Ed. D'Annecy, t. 12, 306), a reference I owe to Raymond Deville, *L'école française de spiritualité*, Bibliothèque d'histoire du christianisme 11 (Paris: Desclée, 1987), 162.

5. Balthasar, *First Glance at Adrienne von Speyr*, trans. Antje Lawry and Sr. Sergia England (San Francisco: Ignatius, 1981), 85–90.

6. Some of Abbé Huvelin's advice to Hügel (in 1882):"...Scolastiques ...ne s'apperçoivent point que la *vie*, toute vie, échappe à l'analyse. C'est un cadavre mort qu'ils dissèquent; c'est bien peu de chose. Passez-les avec un doux, un bien doux sourire...les expériences ont fait beaucoup de chemin, depuis que la théologie s'est arrêtée" (Kelly, "The Abbé Huvelin's Counsel to Baron Friedrich von Hügel," 63–64).

7. Here I gladly adapt categories from Tracy, *The Analogical Imagination*, 237–41. For Newman on "real" assent, see *An Essay in Aid of a Grammar of Assent* (Notre Dame: University of Notre Dame Press, 1979), 76–92. Newman's commitment to the "real" is perhaps the key theme in Ker, *The Achievement*. See above, chapters 1 and 2, for the linguistic and narrative dimensions of experience.

8. See Balthasar, *Thérèse of Lisieux: The Story of a Mission*, trans. Donald Nicholl (New York: Sheed and Ward, 1954), 280, referring to the strange,

psychosomatic "paralysis" Thérèse suffered just before adolescence. For Balthasar's views on kenosis as God's glory, see besides *Mysterium Paschale* also *The Glory of the Lord*, vol. 7, *Theology: The New Covenant*, trans. Brian McNeil, 239ff.

9. See Patricia O'Connor, *In Search of Thérèse*, The Way of the Christian Mystics 3 (Wilmington, DE: Michael Glazier, 1987), passim, but especially 118–39, for background on Thérèse, in addition to the Balthasar reference in no. 8, and John Sullivan, ed., *Experiencing Saint Thérèse Today*, Carmelite Studies 5 (Washington, DC: Institute of Carmelite Studies, 1990). Citations from Thérèse are, in order, from *Her Last Conversations*, trans. John Clarke (Washington, DC: Institute of Carmelite Studies, 1977), 159 (on the Holy Family); *Story of a Soul*, trans. John Clarke (Washington, DC: Institute of Carmelite Studies, 1975), 198 (cf. 200), 194, 277 (on the furnace, church, and martyrdom of love themes); and *Collected Letters of Saint Thérèse of Lisieux*, ed. André Combes, trans. F. J. Sheed (New York: Sheed and Ward, 1949), 333–34 (for the "little zero" theme; 329–34, for the entire letter). This letter is also in the more recent *General Correspondence*, vol. 2, trans. John Clarke (Washington, DC: Institute of Carmelite Studies, 1988), 1092–96.

10. *Story of a Soul*, 136. A full appreciation of the linguistic and genre dimensions of Thérèse would need to study her letters, last conversations, and especially her poetry and plays. See, besides the references in no. 9, her *Poésies*, 2 vols. (Paris: Cerf/Desclée de Brouwer, 1988, 1979), and *Théâtre au Carmel* (Paris: Cerf/Desclée de Brouwer, 1985).

11. *Story of a Soul*, 168.

12. Ibid., 200; cf. 191.

13. Ibid., 211, 210, 212, 226–27, 206–7; cf. 121–22, 140, 263. Important here is Guy Gaucher, *The Passion of Thérèse of Lisieux: 4 April–30 September 1897*, trans. Anne Marie Brennan (New York: Crossroad, 1989).

14. Balthasar, *Thérèse of Lisieux*, 163, whose view here has impressed me greatly: "Her secret intercourse with the Holy Face should not be seen as separate from the devotion which inspired her first title of the Child Jesus. If the depth of her childishness is only revealed to those who also take into account her adoration of the Head covered with blood, the boldness of this later devotion needs to be seen in terms of her childishness if it is to be properly understood."

15. *Story of a Soul*, 193.

16. Olier, *La journée chrétienne*, 122–23.

17. See the intriguing suggestions on the role of repetitiveness in salvation history in René Laurentin, *The Apparitions at Medjugorje Prolonged*, trans. Judith Lohre (Milford, OH: Stiens, 1987), xiv.

18. Egan is especially helpful in showing how the mystics might apply the *purgatio* to the church in his *Christian Mysticism*, 73–79, 106–9, 150–52, 170–73.

Chapter 7: The Virgin Mary
As a Christological Source

1. "Cyril's Letter to John of Antioch," in Richard A. Norris, Jr., ed. and trans., *The Christological Controversy*, Sources of Early Christian Thought (Philadelphia: Fortress Press, 1980), 142.

2. *True Devotion to the Blessed Virgin* 75, in *God Alone: The Collected Writings of St. Louis Mary de Montfort* (Bay Shore, NY: Montfort Publications, 1987), 313.

3. Note John Henry Newman's comment on Luke 2:19: "Thus St. Mary is our pattern of Faith, both in the reception and in the study of Divine Truth. She does not think it enough to accept, she dwells upon it; not enough to possess, she uses it; not enough to assent, she develops it; not enough to submit the Reason, she reasons upon it; not indeed reasoning first, and believing afterwards, with Zacharias, yet first believing without reasoning, next from love and reverence, reasoning after believing. And thus she symbolizes to us, not only the faith of the unlearned, but of the doctors of the Church also, who have to investigate, and weigh, and define, as well as to profess the Gospel..." ("Sermon XV: The Theory of Developments in Religious Doctrine," *Fifteen Sermons Preached before the University of Oxford* [London: Longmans, Green, and Co., 1896], 313).

4. Austin Flannery, ed., *Dogmatic Constitution on the Church* 60, in *Vatican Council II: The Conciliar and Post Conciliar Documents*, vol. 1, rev. ed. (Collegeville, MN: Liturgical Press, 1984), 418.

5. Ibid., 53 and 54 (414).

6. Raymond E. Brown refers, for example to Jubilees 2:2–3 and 11QPsesa: see *The Birth of the Messiah* (Garden City, NY: Doubleday, 1977), 426 n. 60.

7. *The Birth of the Messiah*, 429.

8. Ibid., 427.

9. *The Truth of Christmas: Beyond the Myths*, trans. Michael J. Wrenn et al. (Petersham, MA: St. Bede's Publications, 1986), 179; see 242–46.

10. Brown, *The Birth of the Messiah*, 429. For this entire section, see 174, 179–88 (on Matthew), and 403–5, 425–31 (Luke), a presentation which has been most helpful to me. Laurentin's *The Truth of Christmas* has also been suggestive. John P. Meier's suggestion, that "the infancy narrative becomes a proleptic passion narrative," has also stimulated some of my observations above: *The Vision of Matthew*, Theological Inquiries (New York: Paulist Press, 1979), 53; see 52–57. Most important, too, have been the biblical studies on adoration by Heinrich Greeven, "proskuneo, proskunetes," *Theological Dictionary of the New Testament*, vol. 6, 758–66, and by Heinrich Zimmermann, "Adoration: B. New Testament," *Sacramentum Verbi*, vol. 1, ed. Johannes B. Bauer (New York: Herder and Herder, 1970), 10–15.

11. Let me recommend Raymond E. Brown et al., eds., *Mary in the New Testament* (New York: Paulist Press, 1978), 137–43, for a good summary of biblical criticism concerning the "Magnificat"; Brown's *The Birth of the Messiah*, 330–66, is also important.

12. Hügel, *Essays and Addresses*, vol. 2, 218.

13. Hügel, *The Reality of God and Religion and Agnosticism*, 66.

14. Staniloae, *Theology and the Church*, 89.

15. Ibid.; the reference to Gregory of Nyssa: *Contra Eunomium* 2, PG 45, 493B, in Werner Jaeger, ed., *Gregorii Nysseni Opera*, vol. 2 (Leiden: E. J. Brill, 1960), 337.

16. Lactantius, *The Divine Institutes*, 4, 25, in The Fathers of the Church, vol. 49, trans. Sister Mary Francis McDonald (Washington, DC: Catholic University of America Press, 1964), 308.

17. *Adversus Marcionem*, 4, 10, 6, in *Corpus Christianorum: Series Latina*, vol. 1 (Turnhout: Typographi Brepols Editores Pontificii, 1954), 563, my translation.

18. "Mysteries of the Life of Jesus (1): Conceived by the Holy Spirit, Born of the Virgin Mary," Medard Kehl and Werner Löser, eds., *The Von Balthasar Reader*, trans. Robert J. Daly and Fred Lawrence (New York: Crossroad, 1982), 142.

19. See the deservedly praised section on God's glory and beauty in *Church Dogmatics* 2:1, paragraph 31, 608–77.

20. *Church Dogmatics* 1:2, 199 (see the entire section, "The Miracle of Christmas," 172–202). For Barth's reservations about mariology, see his "A Letter about Mariology," in *Ad Limina Apostolorum: An Appraisal of Vatican II*, trans. Keith R. Crim (Richmond: John Knox Press, 1968), 59–62.

21. *Jesus — God and Man*, 2d ed., trans. Lewis L. Wilkins and Duane A. Priebe (Philadelphia: Westminster, 1968), 143; cf. 141–50.

22. Walter Kasper, *Jesus the Christ*, 251–52, 272 n. 70, in his comments on how the virgin birth and the divine sonship of Jesus are connected, makes a similar appeal, interestingly referring to the works of Balthasar. "It is in the Spirit that Jesus is the Son of God. Luke expresses this with unusual precision: Because Jesus is in a unique way created by the power of the Spirit, 'therefore (*dio*) the child to be born will be called...the Son of God' (Lk 1.35). Jesus' conception by the Holy Spirit (virgin birth) and his divine sonship, are therefore much more closely connected than is usually assumed." And, appealing to the kind of adorational logic I have in mind, he argues: "The freedom of love in the Holy Spirit has its own plausibility, power to convince, radiance, light and beauty, and by this it impresses man without coercing him." And in the note he says: "I owe this point of view also to H. U. von Balthasar" (i.e., *The Glory of the Lord*, vol. 1).

23. *Jesus — God and Man*, 144.

24. See *Dogmatic Constitution on the Church*, 63; Anthony J. Tambasco, *What Are They Saying about Mary?* (New York: Paulist Press, 1984), 45; and Michael O'Carroll, *Theotokos: A Theological Encyclopedia of the Blessed Virgin Mary* (Wilmington, DE: Michael Glazier, 1986), "Vatican II," 351–57, "Mother of the Church," 251–53. Also see Pope Paul VI, "Devotion to the Blessed Virgin Mary," *The Pope Speaks* 19 (1974): 49–87 (translation of *Marialis Cultus*).

25. See, for an overview, O'Carroll, *Theotokos*, "Eve and Mary," 139–41. One can find elements of this "breakthrough of the *novum*" variously in Barth's "The Mystery of Christmas," in René Laurentin, *A Year of Grace with Mary: Rediscovering the Significance of Her Role in the Christian Life*,

trans. Michael J. Wrenn (Dublin: Veritas, 1987), 82, and in Brown's *The Birth of the Messiah*, 531. Karl Rahner's "Virginitas in Partu," *Theological Investigations*, vol. 4, 134–62, is a most complex and subtle piece of writing establishing Rahner's view of how Mary shares in the Incarnation totally, bodily and spiritually, and how this has its reverberating effects on her being and life. He reads the virgin birth here as a sign of the new age in which concupiscence is overcome, Mary's own child-bearing being free from the "alien and restrictive" forces in the world (159).

26. Newman would be hard to surpass on this theme in his *Certain Difficulties Felt by Anglicans in Catholic Teaching*, vol. 2 (London: Longmans, Green, and Co., 1896), 31–44 (a portion of his letter to Pusey on the latter's *Eirenicon* concerning Roman Marian teachings).

27. Epistle 101, in Edward Rochie Hardy and Cyril C. Richardson, eds., *Christology of the Later Fathers*, Library of Christian Classics (Philadelphia: Westminster Press, 1964), 218.

28. *Communio* 15 (1988): 266. Here I would only add that there does seem to be a trajectory of antibodiliness in part of the tradition, which does seem to "contaminate" the understanding of the virgin birth as well as the celibate charism. The docetic/gnostic tendency seems to creep in in ways at times difficult to unravel. But this is controversial, and it's not entirely clear what the sources are asserting: a simple rejection of the body and sexuality, or its distortion through sinful misuse? Perhaps the sources themselves are not sure? For a helpful introduction, see Peter Brown, *The Body and Society: Men, Women and Sexual Renunciation in Early Christianity* (New York: Columbia University Press, 1988), especially 350–52, 407, 444.

29. On the notion of the unique call, I recommend Karl Rahner, "On the Significance in Redemptive History of the Individual Member of the Church," *Mission and Grace: Essays in Pastoral Theology*, vol. 1, trans. Cecily Hastings (London: Sheed and Ward, 1963), 114–71, and Hans Urs von Balthasar, *The Christian State of Life*, trans. Mary Frances McCarthy (San Francisco: Ignatius, 1983), for suggestive beginnings and approaches.

30. See Susan A. Muto, "Singlehood: A State of Life to Celebrate," *Spiritual Life* 35 (1989): 148–51, and her more ample *Commitment: Key to Christian Maturity* (New York: Paulist Press, 1989), for solid and suggestive insights into the single state.

31. I am using the term "virginity" in its traditional sense of being called by God to forgo the use of sexuality throughout one's entire life. One can be called to "celibacy" while or after one has been married and enjoyed sexual relations.

32. For the history of the perpetual virginity of Mary, see Brown et al., *Mary in the New Testament*, index: "Virginity *post partum*," 323. I have been aided greatly here by my colleague Peter F. Chirico, in our discussion "Mary, Virgin and Wife: A Dialogue," *Chicago Studies* 28 (1989): 137–59.

33. 3, 29, 2; 3, 29, 1, in *Summa Theologica*, vol. 2, trans. Fathers of the English Dominican Province (New York: Benziger, 1947), 2178 and 2176.

34. To be sure, the teaching of Matthew 22:30 about heaven not being a "place" for marriage, but rather a place to live like the heavenly angels, needs

some attention here. I would suggest that perhaps this is looking at the pro-creative aspect of marriage; that, surely, in its physical sense, ceases in eternity (not in its "spiritual" sense). But marriage in its agapaic sense, according to the teaching of Jesus, seems a genuine aspect of the heavenly kingdom. Also, as this chapter suggests, views that reflect an inadequate estimation of marriage might be said to reflect an insufficiently incarnational/personal and trinitarian perspective of God.

35. "The Mystery of Christmas," 188: "The virginity of Mary in the birth of the Lord is the denial, not of man in the presence of God, but of any power, attribute or capacity in him for God. If he has this power — and Mary clearly has it — it means strictly and exclusively that he acquires it, that it is laid upon him.... Only with her *Ecce ancilla Domini* can he understand himself as what, in a way inconceivable to himself, he has actually become in the sight of God and by His agency."

36. Ibid., 177.

37. Here I would agree with those who keep the analogy of faith primary; the analogy of being/experience in general is always in relation to the former; arguments from experience in general must cohere with the faith tradition and, finally, "exist" only because we live in a graced world. This is a view that, according to Balthasar, Karl Barth came to accept, even if Barth seemed to prefer not to draw all the epistemological consequences from it: Hans Urs von Balthasar, *The Theology of Karl Barth*, trans. John Drury (New York: Holt, Rinehart and Winston, 1971), especially 100–150.

38. "The Saving Force and Healing Power of Faith," *Theological Investigations*, vol. 5, trans. Karl-H. Kruger (Baltimore: Helicon/New York: Crossroad, 1966), 460–467 at 467. For a rethinking of the miraculous from a Rahner-ian perspective, see my "The Enlightenment, Miracles, and Karl Rahner's Thought: A Study of the Miracle-Question in Current Theological Discussion in the Light of Karl Rahner's Thought" (Ph.D. diss., University of St. Michael's College, 1973).

39. In place of the *ex nihilo*, we have the *ex Maria:* the order of grace "presupposes" the order of nature (as intended for grace); see Barth, "The Mystery of Christmas," 186.

40. See the English translation in *Origins* 16/43 (1987): 745–66; see, for example, pgs. 45 and 46. See, too, Hans Urs von Balthasar, *Christian Meditation*, trans. Mary Theresilde Skerry (San Francisco: Ignatius Press, 1989), 57–73 ("The Marian Way"); *Mary for Today*, trans. Robert Nowell, illus. Virginia Broderick (San Francisco: Ignatius Press, 1987), and James Heft, "Marian Themes in the Writings of Hans Urs von Balthasar," *Communio* 7 (1980): 127–39.

41. I prefer to speak of the "referential" rather than the "feminine" as the first Marian dimension because I want to avoid accepting uncritically a number of assumptions that can contaminate mariology and christology at this point. For example, I don't want to associate simple passivity with Mary, as if there were not a great amount of free response on her part to the miracle of grace. Sometimes the notion of the feminine gets associated with passivity. Secondly, I am not persuaded that it's helpful to use notions

like the "feminine," which seem to foster simplistic stereotyping of the sexes into women as only or mainly passive, receptive, etc., and men as only or mainly active, initiating, etc. These dualisms get transcended in both Jesus and Mary. See Elizabeth A. Johnson, "Mary and the Female Face of God," *Theological Studies* 50 (1989): 500–526.

42. Bérulle, *The Life of Jesus*, 29, 2, 169.

43. In the strong sense, like the sacraments: "effects what it signifies."

44. In M. Olier's rendering, probably somewhat influenced by Charles de Condren: "O Jesus living in Mary, come and live in your servants, in your Spirit of holiness, in the fullness of your power, in the perfection of your ways, in the truth of your virtues, in the communion of your mysteries; overcome every hostile power, in your Spirit, to the glory of the Father" (from the Latin rendering of the prayer popularly handed on in Sulpician seminaries). Another form of this prayer, an autograph of Father Olier's, is especially beautiful, and more explicitly Marian and ecclesial: "Jesus, you who are living in Mary, in the beauty of your virtues, in the eminence of your powers, in the splendor of your eternal and divine riches, give us a share in this holiness which unites her uniquely to God; communicate to us the zeal which she has for his Church; finally, enable all of us to be nothing in ourselves, so that we will live only in your Spirit, like her, to the glory of your Father." See Deville, *L'école française de spiritualité*, 68.

45. See Raymond E. Brown's helpful commentary, *Biblical Exegesis and the Church* (New York: Paulist Press, 1985), 94–96. Also see, on the notion of how ecclesial and Marian intercession is a corollary of christology, the very helpful study of Elizabeth A. Johnson, "May We Invoke the Saints?," *Theology Today* 54 (1987): 32–52.

46. *The Life of Jesus*, 6, 1, 159. Here I recommend, in the spirit of this "theo-meditation," that the reader take some time to find and "ponder" a copy of the icon of the "Virgin of Vladimir," an icon that powerfully expresses, and even "sacramentally" helps one enter into, this threefold reality of grace expressed in Mary. Henri J. M. Nouwen's book, *Behold the Beauty of the Lord: Praying with Icons* (Notre Dame: Ave Maria Press, 1987), contains a color copy as well as a moving meditation that has been stimulating to me, 31–42. See also Leonid Ouspensky and Vladimir Lossky, *The Meaning of Icons*, trans. G. E. H. Palmer and E. Kadloubovsky (Boston: Boston Book and Art Shop, 1952), 94. Some brief comments on this Byzantine icon (eleventh/twelfth century): *Grace as offer:* Note how Mary's head and arms point to Jesus, suggesting that her being is a "reference" to the Incarnation; note, too, the mysterious eyes, which don't look to Jesus, but mysteriously above him, out into the distance of the (trinitarian?) Mystery in which is grounded the Incarnation; and note the razor-sharp attentiveness of the child Jesus to Mary, as if he is all there for her, and yet gently so, with his cheek caressing hers. *Grace as received:* Note how Mary holds Jesus, gently as if virginally not clinging, yet caringly like a mother; note, too, the stars on her veil and shoulders, indicating the illuminating transformation overtaking her in the Incarnation; but again note these mysterious eyes, with that tone of sorrow, indicating that she has "seen" the kenosis she and her Son will undergo.

Grace as uniquely personal: Jesus is "all eyes" for Mary, indicating the deeply personal and intimate nature of grace; Mary does not cling with her hands: she holds him as though not holding him; he has his unique destiny, in other words, and so does she; and the hands invite us to follow Jesus, but they invite and don't coerce, as if our own unique charisms must come along; and again those mysterious eyes of the Virgin: directing us off into the mystery, not so much staring at us, as if we have to be mirror reflections of her (as she does not stare at Jesus, like a simple mirror reflection of him), but we must move into the mystery ourselves with our partly unique charisms.

Chapter 8: Jesus' Uniqueness and the Dialogue between the Religions

1. Here I am "correcting" what I consider an inadequate presentation of Jesus' uniqueness in my *The Jesus Debate: A Survey and Synthesis* (New York: Paulist Press, 1985), 385–94, and in my "Jesus' Uniqueness: A Kenotic Approach," in Mary Jo Leddy and Mary Ann Hinsdale, eds., *Faith That Transforms: Essays in Honor of Gregory Baum* (New York: Paulist Press, 1987), 16–30. In those studies I inadequately thought through the definitive nature of the Incarnation and the mainly revelatory nature of the Christian and Jewish traditions, in contrast with the Hindu, Buddhist, and Chinese orbits, which appear to me to be more noetic.

2. See my *Fire and Light;* Deville, *L'école française de spiritualité;* Thompson, *Bérulle and the French School;* Paul Coulon, Paul Brasseur et al., *Libermann 1802–1852: Une pensée et une mystique missionnaires* (Paris: Cerf, 1988); and Henri Lebon, "Chaminade (Guillaume-Joseph)," *Dictionnaire de spiritualité*, vol. 2/1 (1953), cols. 454–59. Of course these mystics cannot be separated from their religious communities: French Oratorians (Bérulle, Condren), Discalced Carmelites (Madeleine), Sulpicians (Olier), Eudists and Sisters of the Good Shepherd (Eudes), the Company of Mary, Daughters of Wisdom, and Brothers of St. Gabriel (Montfort), Christian Brothers (La Salle), Spiritans (Libermann), Marianists (Chaminade), confining ourselves only to these, which are but representative of many male and female communities and the laity reached by them.

3. The letter is found in Peter J. Opitz and Gregor Sebba, eds., *The Philosophy of Order* (Stuttgart: Klett-Cotta, 1981), 449–57 at 454.

4. *On First Principles* 2, 6, 6 in Norris, *The Christological Controversy*, 79. I am presupposing a "non-subordinationist" interpretation of this text.

5. *Orations against the Arians* 3, 30 in Norris, *The Christological Controversy*, 88. The writings of Athanasius, especially these orations attributed to him (at least the first three), seem to me crucial for our topic. Cardinal Newman, who made a fine translation of these orations, knew this well. See Philip Schaff and Henry Wace, eds., *The Nicene and Post-Nicene Fathers*, Second Series, vol. 4 (Grand Rapids: William B. Eerdmans, 1980), 306–447, for Newman's translation. On Newman's christology, and the strong Athanasian cast of it, see Roderick Strange, *Newman and the Gospel of Christ* (Oxford: Oxford University Press, 1981).

6. See, for example, Balthasar, *The Glory of the Lord*, vol. 7, *Theology: The New Covenant*, 228–35.

7. See her *Story of a Soul*, especially *Mss. B and C*.

8. See Kehl and Löser, *The von Balthasar Reader*, 111–204; Kasper, *The God of Jesus Christ*; Hebblethwaite, *The Incarnation*, especially 11–20.

9. *The Trinity* 8, 10, 14, in Fathers of the Church, trans. Stephen McKenna (Washington, DC: Catholic University of America Press, 1963), 266.

10. John Henry Newman, "Christ, the Son of God Made Man" (vol. 6, Sermon 5), in *Parochial and Plain Sermons* (San Francisco: Ignatius Press, 1987), 1213. See also his "The Incarnation" (vol. 2, Sermon 3), 242–50, for a fascinating exploration of the difference between the God-man unity in Jesus and the unity between God and other creatures.

11. See Congar, *I Believe in the Holy Spirit*, vol. 2, *'He Is Lord and Giver of Life,'* 24–38, 79–111, 119–41, for helpful comments on the Spirit as the principle of catholicity, of guiding us to Jesus, and yet also of unique charisms. Bérulle's theme of the "sterility" of the Holy Spirit within the immanent Trinity (no "person" comes from the Spirit) is perhaps a way of saying that the Spirit *is* by pointing back to Father and Son, and so the Spirit is "normed" by both. Of course, Bérulle held that the Spirit is "fertile" in the "economic" Trinity by leading us into the life of the Trinity: *Grandeurs* 4, 2, 131–34. Barth is also very helpful on showing how the Spirit is normed by the Son. "Where the Holy Spirit is sundered from Christ, sooner or later He is always transmuted into quite a different spirit, the spirit of the religious man, and finally the human spirit in general," Barth suggested: *Church Dogmatics*, 1:2, 251; cf. 1:2, 203–79. Suggestive on these issues is Hans Urs von Balthasar, "Der Unbekannte Jenseits des Wortes," in *Spiritus Creator* (Einsiedeln: Johannes, 1967), 95–105.

12. Kasper, *The God of Jesus Christ*, 155–56.

13. Refer to the citations from Bérulle and his colleagues in our previous chapters.

14. Henri de Lubac, *Aspects of Buddhism*, trans. George Lamb (New York: Sheed and Ward, 1953), 38, 51, 38. This work seems to me to be superbly subtle in its analysis, especially the first chapter, "Buddhist Charity."

15. I am using *The Bhagavad Gita*, Penguin Classics, trans. Juan Mascaró (New York: Penguin, 1962), 95. One can conveniently consult, for the Chinese orbit, *The Analects of Confucius* 4, 3–4 (on love); 7, 22 (on heaven); trans. Arthur Waley (New York: Vintage, 1938), 102, 127; and Lao Uzu, *Tao Te Ching*, Penguin Classics, trans. D. C. Lau (New York: Penguin, 1963).

16. Voegelin, *The Ecumenic Age*, 332. Cf. Placher, *Unapologetic Theology*, 123, for some comments helpful for the thoughts in this section.

17. Voegelin, "On Christianity," in Opitz and Sebba, *The Philosophy of Order*, 455. Voegelin seems to be referring to the notion of a co-redeemer who might claim equality with Jesus.

18. See n. 13 above; see Guillén Preckler, *Bérulle aujourd'hui*, 64–65 n. 39, for this transposition of Bérullian "servitude" into our contemporary "service."

19. Hebblethwaite, *The Incarnation*, 51–52, 23. See Bérulle *Grandeurs* 2,

2, 116–77, for a classical expression of the same sentiment: "An excellent mind of this age [Copernicus] claimed that the sun and not the earth is at the center of the world.... This new opinion, which has little following in the science of the stars, is useful and should be followed in the science of salvation.... For Jesus is the sun that is immovable in his greatness and that moves all other things."

20. Thomas Merton, *Zen and the Birds of Appetite* (New York: New Directions, 1968), 47, 76, 75.

21. See John Carmody and Denise Lardner Carmody, *Interpreting the Religious Experience: A Worldview* (Englewood Cliffs, NJ: Prentice-Hall, 1987), especially 49, and all of chaps. 4, 5, and 6. The crucial Voegelin works here are *Order and History*, vol. 2, *The World of the Polis* (1957), as well as *Plato and Aristotle* and *The Ecumenic Age*.

22. See especially his *Plato and Aristotle* and *The Ecumenic Age*

23. Abraham Heschel is suggestive here: *The Prophets*, 2 vols. (New York: Harper Torchbooks, 1971).

24. Carmody and Carmody, *Interpreting*, 15–48.

25. "Questions Not Tending to Edification," in E. A. Burtt, ed., *The Teachings of the Compassionate Buddha* (New York: New American Mentor, 1982), 32–36 at 34–35; "It is as if...a man has been wounded by an arrow thickly smeared with poison, and his friends and companions, his relatives and kinsfolk, were to procure for him a physician or surgeon; and the sick man were to say, 'I will not have this arrow taken out until I have learnt whether the man who wounded me belonged to the warrior caste, or to the Brahmin caste.' " Note that it is the sick man, not the surgeon, who is lost in these dogmas. Gautama continues: "Whether the dogma obtain...there still remain birth, old age, death, sorrow...for the extinction of which in the present life I am prescribing."

26. Voegelin's *Order and History* is especially fine on this. Hebblethwaite, *The Incarnation*, especially 5–6, is stimulating on how the Incarnation promotes a strong notion of God's therapeutic involvement in our suffering and sin, an involvement not identically seen in non-Christian traditions.

27. I lean heavily on the differentiation of the world-transcendent God as the necessary presupposition for the Incarnation. But this differentiation appears to have been ambiguous for women, transcendence being more rightly identified with males, and immanence with females. That is the weight of Judith Ochshorn, *The Female Experience and the Nature of the Divine* (Bloomington: Indiana University Press, 1981). To the extent that this happened, it certainly calls for a hermeneutics of suspicion. I would be inclined to view it as one of those disastrous "cultural mortgages" (to use a Voegelinian phrase) that punctuate our ambiguous historical process. Perhaps we could view the Incarnation as a divine "cleanup operation," a critique of any denigration of immanence, as well as of any simple stereotypical identification of women with immanence.

28. These comments on analogy have been inspired by Ricoeur's discussion of the *Sophist* 254b–259d in *Time and Narrative*, vol. 3, 142–56. See as well, Tracy, *The Analogical Imagination*, 405–21; his understanding of plu-

ralism, which he correlates with the analogical imagination, seems to me just right: 446–56. On Barth in this regard, see *Church Dogmatics*, 4:2, 58–60; on Balthasar, see *Mysterium Paschale*, 95, 228–29.

Chapter 9: The "Contemplation and Action" Question in Christology

1. For a rehabilitation of the notion of "common sense," informed by the Scottish School of philosophy, especially Thomas Reid, see Eric Voegelin, *Anamnesis*, trans. and ed. Gerhart Niemeyer (Notre Dame: University of Notre Dame Press, 1978), 211–13.

2. Gregory Baum, the *"pater"* of my doctoral dissertation, has always been a "critical voice" somewhere in my conscience, for which I am very grateful. If I can't always share what he considers his more "radical" views on some of these socio-political issues, that does not mean that I am not always attentively listening to what he has to say. See Gregory Baum and Duncan Cameron, *Ethics and Economics*, Canadian Issues Series (Toronto: James Lorimer & Company, 1984).

3. For an introduction to the theological debate, I recommend reading, in any order, one after the other, Dermot A. Lane, *Foundations for a Social Theology* (New York: Paulist Press, 1984), Michael Novak, *Will It Liberate?: Questions about Liberation Theology* (New York: Paulist Press, 1986), and George Weigel, *Catholicism and the Renewal of American Democracy* (New York: Paulist Press, 1989). For the application to christology, see Elizabeth A. Johnson, *Consider Jesus*, 83–113, and Michael Novak's theo-political reading of the Incarnation in his *The Spirit of Democratic Capitalism* (New York: American Enterprise Institute/Simon & Schuster, 1982), especially 340–44, and more fully in his *Confession of a Catholic* (San Francisco: Harper & Row, 1983), especially 42–70. For the issue of postmodernity, see, again, *Communio* 17/2 (1990), for a variety of views.

4. I am clearly drawing from, in my own way, a very complicated philosophical tradition stretching back especially to Plato and Aristotle. See Lane, *Foundations for a Social Theology*, 32–55. My impression is that Plato keeps activity, practice, and theory in a more compact state, while Aristotle differentiates and perhaps contributes toward a separating. Greek drama is a wonderful example of the passage from "activity" to "practice." See Voegelin, *The World of the Polis*, 243–66 (Voegelin speaks of "action" and "drama,"in a way equivalent to my "practice"), and *Plato and Aristotle*. Michel Despland, *The Education of Desire: Plato and the Philosophy of Religion* (Toronto: University of Toronto Press, 1985), has some very careful and insightful comments on the theory-practice relationship in Plato throughout his book: see the "Index of Themes," s.vv. "action" and "practice," and especially 217–23.

5. For suggestive possibilities in this regard, see Don S. Browning, ed., *Practical Theology: The Emerging Field in Theology, Church, and World* (San Francisco: Harper & Row, 1983). An excellent example of theory reflecting on practice in spiritual theology is Joann Wolski Conn, *Spirituality and Personal Maturity*, Integration Books (New York: Paulist Press, 1989).

6. On conceptualism, see Bernard J.F. Lonergan, *Method in Theology* (New York: Herder and Herder, 1972), 336; on doctrinization, see Voegelin, *The Ecumenic Age*, 56: "The language symbols belong, as to their meanings, to the Metaxy [In-Between] of the experiences from which they arise as their truth. As long as the process of experience and symbolization is not deformed by doctrinal reflection, there is no doubt about the metaleptic [participatory] status of the symbols.... The In-Between of experience has a dead point from which the symbols emerge as the exegesis of its truth, but which cannot become itself an object of propositional knowledge. If the metaleptic symbol... is hypostatized into a doctrinal Word of God, the device can protect the insight gained against distintegration in society, but it can also impair the sensitivity for the source of truth in the flux of divine presence in time which constitutes history. Unless precautions of meditative practice are taken, the doctrinization of symbols is liable to interrupt the process of experiential reactivation and linguistic renewal. When the symbol separates from its source in the experiential Metaxy, the Word of God can degenerate into a word of man that one can believe or not." This is a controversial view, of course, but the key point seems to be to take precautions to see to it that doctrine doesn't derail into doctrinization. One of the reasons why Voegelin has a high regard for the mystics is precisely because of their attempt to keep the experiential roots of doctrine secure (see *Anamnesis*, ed. Niemeyer, 192–99). Cardinal Newman's great *Grammar of Assent* is surely within the same trajectory.

7. See Tracy, *Plurality and Ambiguity*, 111, and my "The Dark Night: A Theological Consultation," and "St. John of the Cross as Pneumopathologist: A Mystic's Hermeneutics of Suspicion," in *Fire and Light*, 76–142.

8. Imhof and Biallowons, *Karl Rahner in Dialogue*, 191–95. Perhaps the most helpful illustration of this contemplative thrust in his theology is his *The Practice of Faith: A Handbook of Contemporary Spirituality*, ed. Karl Lehmann and Albert Raffelt (New York: Crossroad, 1984).

9. A good example: Christos Yannaras, *The Freedom of Morality*, trans. Elizabeth Briere (Crestwood, NY: St. Vladimir's Seminary Press, 1984).

10. Karl Barth, *Evangelical Theology: An Introduction*, trans. Grover Foley (Garden City, NY: Doubleday Anchor, 1964), 141.

11. Here I am following Karl Rahner's interpretation in *Spiritual Exercises*, trans. Kenneth Baker (New York: Herder and Herder, 1965), 24 (cf. the "Principle and Foundation of the First Week" of Ignatius's *Spiritual Exercises*).

12. I have been inspired here by a number of sources: the Cappadocians, Augustine, Staniloae, Barth, Rahner, Balthasar, Jüngel. See the remarks of O'Donnell, *The Mystery of the Trinity*, 147. Note that the Greek for "revealed" in John 1:18 is *exegesato*.

13. Basil, *Peri Tou Agiou Pneumatos* [*On the Holy Spirit*] 18, 45, in *Sources chrétiennes* 17, intro. and trans. B. Pruche (Paris: Cerf, 1968), 409, my translation.

14. In hermeneutical terms, through the graced doxological orientation of

our existence, "understanding" does not shrink to "explanation," or faith in its noetic aspect does not shrink to analytic reason, etc.

15. See the comments of Moltmann on "The Doxological Trinity" in *The Trinity and the Kingdom*, 151–61. It is significant to me that a leading *practical* theologian like Moltmann gives this primacy to doxology. "Only doxology releases the experience of salvation for a full experience of that salvation. In...adoring perception, the triune God is not made man's object; he is not appropriated and taken possession of. It is rather that the perceiving person participates in what he perceives, being transformed into the thing perceived through his wondering perception. Here we know only in so far as we love" (152).

16. Voegelin, *Israel and Revelation*, ix.

17. Wolfhart Pannenberg, *Human Nature, Election, and History* (Philadelphia: Westminster Press, 1977), 100; see 100–116, in which he draws upon Voegelin extensively, but also adds his own helpful glosses, from which I have also benefited. Readers should consult the volumes of Voegelin's *Order and History*, his *The New Science of Politics*, and most handily his *Autobiographical Reflections*, for many of the notions in this section of the chapter.

18. *Human Nature, Election, and History*, 101.

19. Ibid., 101–2. Pannenberg appears to be articulating the eventual view of the matter arrived at through Augustine, Pope Gelasius, and Thomas Aquinas. See William C. Placher, *Readings in the History of Christian Theology*, vol. 1 (Philadelphia: Westminster Press, 1988), 119–20, 123–24, as well as Thomas Aquinas, *2 Sent.*, d. 44, q. 2, aa. 3–4.

20. Pannenberg, *Human Nature, Election, and History*, 103. I have been very stimulated by Pannenberg's meditation on the history of church-state tensions (102–5), but I have not always followed him.

Postlude

1. I have been stimulated by Karl Barth's distinction between the "primary" and "secondary conversation" as sketched in his *Evangelical Theology*, 154–63, although I've adapted it in my own way.

2. This "certitude" is the ground of a meaningful human and Christian life, without which the very ability to converse, and so question and learn, would be replaced by an *indocta ignorantia*. See Newman's *A Grammar of Assent*, especially 234, 239, 274–75.

3. Recall Voegelin, *Plato and Aristotle*, 12.

4. I am theologically adapting Eric Voegelin, "The Eclipse of Reality," in Maurice Natanson, ed., *Phenomenology and Social Reality* (The Hague: Martinus Nijhoff, 1970), 185–94; see *In Search of Order*, 46–47: "I frequently use the term 'Second Reality,' created by Robert Musil and Heimito von Doderer, to denote the imaginative constructs of ideological thinkers who want to eclipse the reality of existential consciousness."

5. See above, 102.

6. See R. P. C. Hanson, *The Search for the Christian Doctrine of God: The Arian Controversy 318–381* (Edinburgh: T. & T. Clark, 1988). See William M. Thompson, "Gnosticism as a Diagnostic Tool in Contemporary Theology," in George Kilcourse, ed., *The Linguistic Turn and Contemporary Theology*, Current Issues in Theology 2 (Macon, GA: Mercer University Press for the Catholic Theological Society of America, 1987), 101–16, for my own views on gnosticism, especially as understood by Voegelin.

7. *Church Dogmatics*, 2:1, 219. On Barth's own application of these ideas to christology, see John Thompson, *Christ in Perspective*, and Charles T. Waldrop, *Karl Barth's Christology: Its Basic Alexandrian Character*, Religion and Reason 21 (Berlin: Monton Publishers, 1984).

Index

Plato, 21–22, 31, 169
Plenitude of personality, 117–18, 140
Pluralism, 185
of saints/mystics, 131
Pneumatology. *See* Spirit, Holy
Poetry, 9
Political theory, 182–85
Popular suspicion, 172–73
Postmodernism, 10, 29, 97
Practice, 69–70
in christology, 173–75
theory and, 178, 181
Prayer, 8, 12, 177–78
Hügel on, 115
Prejudgments, 68–69
Presence, divine, 104
Prevenience, divine, 103–4, 112
Priesthood, 63, 126
Privatism, 184–85
Proskynesis, 137
Purgation, 125, 132–33

Quietist controversy, 108–9

Rahner, Karl, 88–95, 177
on saints, 122
Rapture, 2
Rationalistic universalism, 28
Reappropriation, 9
Reason, 187–88
Recognition, 31
Redemption, 59
Relativism, 28
Religion, 101–5
elements of, 108, 113–20
non-Christian, 18, 156–71
Revelation, 27
divine ground and, 33
non-Christian religions and, 167–68
saints/mystics and, 123–26
Reverence, 46, 48–50
Reversal of expectations, 137–38

Sacrality, intraworldly, 158, 162–64
Sacrifice, 53, 63

Saints, 8–11, 16–17, 190
as christological sources, 121–33
contemplation and, 181
conversation and, 35
narrative and, 43
Salvation, 60, 81–83, 90
Mary and, 154–55
non-Christian religions and, 169
Science of the saints, 46, 65
Scriptures, 8–9, 42
Incarnation and, 34
non-Christian religions and, 168–69
tradition and, 24
Senses, 103
Sensus misticus, 76–77
Servitude, 73, 79–84
French School and, 67–68
Incarnation and, 50–54
Jesus', 54–60
Jesus' uniqueness and, 166
Sexism, 174
Sexuality, 146–49
Silence, 37
Sin, 58
Sociopolitical theology, 174–75
Son-christologies, 40–41
Soteriology, 81–83, 145–47
Mary and, 154–55
non-Christian religions and, 169
Spirit-christologies, 41
Spirit, Holy, 33, 116, 187
christomonism and, 161–62
contemplation and, 178–79
saints/mystics and, 131–32
unleashing of, 61
virgin birth and, 142–43
Spirituality
definition of, 4–6
turn to, 6–14, 187–90
waves of, 1–3
State, political, 183–85
States, 46–47
contemplative, 180–82
Stigmata, 12, 190
Strengthening, 25
Subjectivism, 114